Sketches and Recollections
of
Lynchburg (Virginia)

by the Oldest Inhabitant

Margaret Couch Cabell

HERITAGE BOOKS
2008

HERITAGE BOOKS
AN IMPRINT OF HERITAGE BOOKS, INC.

Books, CDs, and more—Worldwide

For our listing of thousands of titles see our website
at
www.HeritageBooks.com

Published 2008 by
HERITAGE BOOKS, INC.
Publishing Division
100 Railroad Ave. #104
Westminster, Maryland 21157

Copyright © 1858,1990 Margaret Couch Cabell

All rights reserved. No part of this book may be reproduced or transmitted in any form or by any means, electronic or mechanical, including photocopying, recording or by any information storage and retrieval system without written permission from the author, except for the inclusion of brief quotations in a review.

International Standard Book Numbers
Paperbound: 978-1-55613-312-1
Clothbound: 978-0-7884-7616-7

TO THE

Oldest Inhabitants of Lynchburg,

AND TO

THE DESCENDANTS

OF THOSE WHOSE NAMES

ARE IN THESE SKETCHES RECORDED,

NOW RESIDENT IN THAT PLACE,

AS WELL AS

THOSE SCATTERED OVER THE UNITED STATES,

THIS LITTLE VOLUME

IS MOST AFFECTIONATELY

Inscribed.

INTRODUCTION.

"The following sketches are cherished memories of the past, penned during the winter of 1857, to interest and amuse a young household," and thereby bring them acquainted with the just and good of former times. Whilst to render morality and religion attractive, we must introduce them in a fiction, how prone are we to pass by the holy, exemplary lives of those in our midst, many of whom have passed away, leaving no monuments, save those tenderly engraven on warm, loving hearts; and now, like old Mortality, we would, with the few survivors mentioned, wander awhile amidst the grave yards of Memory, drawing aside the long grass, obscuring these records, and brightening those hidden inscriptions of the heart, over which the mouldering hand of Time has partially spread the moss of forgetfulness.

In the course of the succeeding pages, should inaccuracies in dates, or any mis-statements, occur, the writer desires to be exonerated from any intention to state what is not strictly true, as, excepting in a few instances, her own memory has been solely relied on for dates; and many of the impressions having been imbibed in the earliest stages of childhood, even if literally true, may naturally be somewhat vague and shadowy. Nor is it expected that those whose names are here recorded were the only good persons living in Lynchburg: we doubt not but that there were more than enough to fill another volume; but with nearly all mentioned in the sketches, a personal acquaintance, and in many instances a warm friendship, existed. In the year 1819, the matrons of Lynchburg, were, many of them, peculiarly lovely in their walk and conversation. Those who had attained middle age, having passed their childhood immediately succeeding the years of our Revolutionary war, of course had early acquired habits of self-denial and simplicity, now worthy of imitation. The slow modes of travel did not, as now, facilitate the ever-changing novelties of costume and furniture; so that, in those fruitful sources of disquiet, there existed, at this time, no rivalry.

Considering that Lynchburg is as justly entitled to a memorial as "Belford Regis, and Our Village," of Miss MITFORD, yet, as we pass by the old familiar places, now inhabited by strangers, we would fain, like

INTRODUCTION.

Trevillian, in the "Pilgrims of the Rhine" weave a romantic story of requited love, long life, and happiness; but, alas! the history of the past is too painfully written in broken households, and lonely burying-grounds, and it is hither we must come to learn that the death, as well as the life of the good, is fraught with Heavenly teachings.

"For who to dumb Forgetfulness a prey,
   This pleasing anxious being e'er resigned,
Left the warm precincts of the cheerful day,
   Nor cast one longing, lingering look behind.

On some fond breast the parting soul relies,
   Some pious drops, the closing eye requires;
Even from the tomb the voice of Nature cries,
   Even in our ashes, live our wonted fires."

Sketches and Recollections of Lynchburg.

THE LYNCH FAMILY.

"The family of John Lynch, Col. Charles Lynch, and all the other Lynches of that family, took up a tract of land on James River, within view of the celebrated Peaks of Otter, and the mountainous scenery. After his decease the tract of land, now the site of Lynchburg, became the property of his son John Lynch, who established the ferry over James river. It was his brother, Charles Lynch, who originated and enacted, practically, the celebrated code called 'Lynch Law.' Col. Charles Lynch was an officer in the army of the American Revolution. His residence was on Staunton River, a branch of the old Roanoke, that ran through 'my plantation,' as John Randolph was in the habit of speechifying. It is now owned by his grandson. During the Revolutionary war, the country on James river and on the Roanoke, about the Blue Ridge and mountain passes, was harassed by a lawless band of Tories and desperadoes, and their depredations at one time extended into the regions round about Lynchburg. The case required a species of operation adapted to cure the evil. Col. Lynch was a resolute, determined man, of elevated patriotic principles and a staunch Whig, as was all the Lynch family. He organized and took the lead of a strong body of determined patriots—men of moral character and commanding influence, and scoured the country night and day. They took many of the desperadoes, gave them a summary trial, at which Col. Lynch sat as judge; empanneled a jury, and, on conviction, executed the punishment in a prompt manner. The villains were permitted to defend themselves, and to show mitigating circumstances, and when punished to clear out. Many well-meaning persons are frightened at the name of Lynch law, without knowing its history, code or appliance. It is a better term, and has a more orderly and civilized aspect, than Squatter Sovereignty. It requires proof positive and circumstantial, such as would produce conviction of guilt in a candid and honest mind. Col. Lynch raised a regiment of riflemen, after he had officiated as judge, in relieving the country from Tories, thieves and murderers. He was present at the battle of Guilford Courthouse, where he behaved with great gallantry. He died soon after the war. Charles Lynch, Esq., afterwards Governor of Mississippi, was his son."—*St. Louis Republican.*

CHARLES LYNCH, the ancestor of the Lynch family of America, left the north of Ireland*

---

* Honorable mention is made by Shiel, in his "Sketches of the Irish Bar," of one of the Lynch family, who was a member of that bar.

when a boy, and came to the Colony of Virginia in the early part of the last century. The immediate cause which actuated him, is said to have been a punishment which he received at school. Meeting soon thereafter with the captain of a ship, which was on the eve of sailing for North America, young Lynch was easily persuaded to avail himself of an opportunity of embarking on the broad wave of the Atlantic, in quest of a far distant home in the western world. The ship in which he took passage was but a short distance from port, when young Lynch, relenting, actually plunged into the sea, and made for the land; he was, however, taken up, and the vessel resumed her course. It has been stated in the extract from the St. Louis Republican, that Mr. Lynch took up a large body of land on James river, in sight of the Peaks of Otter. He made his home and residence at Chesnut Hill, just below Lynchburg; which place was afterwards owned by Judge Edmond Winston. Mr. Lynch was said to possess, naturally, pleasing and graceful manners. He married, when young, a Miss Clark,* a young

---

*It may not be altogether uninteresting to some to relate a little incident in connection with this lady, and three other sisters, married about the same time. Each of these sisters received, on their marriage, half dozen silver spoons. As may be imagined, silver spoons were rare articles in the British Colonies. One of these spoons has descended, and is now in the possession of one of the family, who keeps it as a precious relic of the past.

lady belonging to a wealthy and influential family. Mr. Lynch represented the counties of Campbell and Bedford in the House of Burgesses, which then sat at Williamsburg, and he was elected to this honorable office without his knowledge. Soon after his death, on the division of his property, his son John became heir to the spot on which stands Lynchburg, and by him it was vested in the hands of trustees, to be laid off in lots for the erection of a town.

JOHN LYNCH, founder of the city of Lynchburg, was a member of the Society of Friends, whose peculiar doctrines and tenets were beautifully exemplified in his life. Naturally ardent and impetuous in his temperament, by constant spiritual communion with God, and by placing always before him as a model the high and holy character of Christ, he had succeeded in conquering every disposition save what was in perfect harmony with the character of a Christian.

By those who knew him, John Lynch was loved and reverenced for his exemplary life, but he rigidly scanned and judged himself—depreciating those very actions for which he was commended by others. So conscientious was he, that in matters of controversy he was prone to look upon himself as the aggressor. It is related by one who knew him well, that once upon an occasion, drawn unexpectedly into a controversy, and encountering from his adversary exceedingly irritating and provoking remarks, Mr. Lynch was led on to say more than he intended, expressing himself with a considerable degree of warmth. After his return home, he felt unhappy and dissatisfied with himself, so that even secret communion with the High and Holy One could not restore his peace and tranquility. The following morning, continuing dejected, he retired to read and meditate, but he was interrupted by a member of his family, who came to tell him that Mr. —— was in the parlor desiring to see him. This gentleman had on the day previous been the antagonist of Mr. Lynch, and he now came to ask pardon for the language he had used towards him. Mr. Lynch cordially tendered him his hand, ingenuously telling him he considered himself the aggressor. This venerable man lived to see the town which he had founded flourish and increase in size and population. He died at an advanced age, on the 31st October, 1821. His widow survived him, and continued to reside for many years in the old family mansion, now occupied by Alexander Liggatt, Esq. The following obituary appeared in "The Press," then edited by John Hampden Pleasants, and was written by his friend and relative, the late Christopher Anthony, Esq., and is so appropriate that we insert it entire:

" Departed this life, after a lingering illness, which he bore with unexampled fortitude, JOHN LYNCH, Sen'r, the patentee and former proprietor of the lands upon which the city of Lynchburg was built. It is very much the custom of the living to bestow praises upon the dead. This error, if it be one, has its origin in christian charity, and is therefore entitled to much indulgence. The writer of this does not design it as a panegyric on the character of Mr. Lynch; it is a feeble effort to do justice to his memory. He was a zealous and pious member of the Society of Friends, and, although laboring for the last fifty years of his life under a pulmonary complaint, which rendered him extremely weak and feeble in body, he was nevertheless active and prompt in the discharge of the various duties of husband, father and friend. He possessed a mind of the first order—a mind unimpaired by disease or old age, until a very short time before his death; and a fortitude and firmness of character seldom equalled. He lived to see those lands which he acquired for little more than the fees and expenses of location, advance in value, so as to constitute immense fortunes for all his descendants. He witnessed the rise and progress of the town of Lynchburg, from laying the first corner-stone—in fact, from the period when the site was a howling wilderness—to its present size and grandeur; and such was the veneration which the inhabitants of the town entertained for him, that he might be regarded as standing amongst them very much in the light of one of the patriarchs of old. Few measures of a general nature were set on foot without consulting him, and he was always found a zealous promoter of whatever tended to advance the general good. Amongst other traits of character in this excellent man, those of charity and benevolence were very conspicuous. To the poor, his doors were ever open. 'Large was his bounty and his soul sincere.' But, alas! 'the places that have known him shall know him no more.' He has 'fought the good fight, he has kept the faith,' and hath, no doubt, ascended into another and a better world, where is laid up for him a crown of immortal glory. 'Oft he fought and oft obtained fresh triumphs over himself; and never-withering wreaths, compared with which the laurels that a Cæsar reaps are weeds.'"

With the name of Lynch are associated recollections of the most grateful and pleasing interest, and to give complete memoirs of many of this most excellent family would be a task in every way gratifying. What a host of recollections move before us! filling the heart with vivid scenes of the past; and, as if touched by some mighty unseen power, the burial places of memory give up the dead, and loved and venerated forms surround us, in the back-ground appearing the aristocratic form and contemplative face of Anselm Lynch, of Staunton river, and by him the stalwart form of Staunton John Lynch, his brother, with mighty stature and brave heart, united to a nature as tender and gentle as that of a loving woman. These two last were sons of Charles Lynch, of Staunton, who was the originator of Lynch law. Anselm Lynch married Miss Miller, of Lynchburg, a daughter of one of the oldest and most worthy of the first settlers. Of the members of his family who survive him, are Mrs. M. A. Dearing, of Campbell county, and Charles Henry Lynch, Esq., an esteemed citizen of Lynchburg. Susan Lynch, the second daughter, died many years since, at the country seat of her brother, on Staunton river. She was a young lady of great worth and excellence, and a few lines extracted from a notice which appeared at the time of her decease, will show the estimation in which she was held:

"To a close and vigorous intellect the deceased added an imagination sprightly and chaste. Her heart was benevolent, kind, generous and pure. Her frank and engaging manners, and great goodness of heart, warmed acquaintances into friends and made her an acknowledged favorite with all who knew her. She was a bright and happy illustration of most that is attractive, interesting or useful in the female character. Her family have sustained in her death, a loss most deeply irreparable. It was in her intercourse with them, that her cheerfulness, good temper, tenderness, thoughtful kindness and affection, gave touching sweetness to her character, and created for her a love which few can inspire, and none who has felt it can forget."

JOHN LYNCH, of Staunton River, was married in early life to Miss Terrel, and when past middle life they emigrated to West Tennessee, where they both died some years since. Their descendants surviving them continue to reside in the vicinity of Jackson, Tennessee.

Capt. John Lynch died in 1840, in the seventy-third year of his age. The following notice of this most excellent man, appeared at the time of his decease in a Tennessee paper, and it does him no more than justice:

"Died, at his residence in this county, Capt. JOHN LYNCH, in the 73rd year of his age. Capt. Lynch was a native of Virginia; for many years a citizen of Lynchburg, and his old friends in that place would scarcely recognise this as a notice of a man they once knew, were we to omit a passing tribute to his sterling integrity, his warm philanthropy, and the primitive simplicity of his manners and deportment. His early associations were with the Society of Friends, which doubtless served to mould the character so much admired and respected wherever he has lived. Capt. Lynch's father was a worthy Quaker, and soldier of the Revolution,— having commanded the cavalry at the battle of Guilford; was dismissed from his peace-abiding congregation because a strong sense of duty to his suffering and struggling country impelled him to bear arms in her defence. Such a sentiment, transmitted to his son, may have restrained him from connection with that worthy sect of Christians to whom he was strongly assimilated by the purity of his life, the sobriety of his manners, moderation of his desires, and the marked kindness of his deportment to every human being who came within the range of his benevolence. To the members of his family, who have so long profited by his excellent precepts and enjoyed the benignant smiles of this venerable patriarch, we would offer our sincere condolence; and to his whole circle of acquaintances, we would offer the life and character of Capt. John Lynch, as the best model for their imitation."

EDWARD LYNCH, eldest son of the founder of Lynchburg, was also a member of the Society of Friends. Possessing a strong and vigorous mind, fine personal appearance, combined with manners most winning, he acquired in society an influence not easily lost. In person he bore a striking resemblance to the late judge William H. Cabell, of the Court of Appeals, displaying, too, like this eminent jurist, all those genuine, kindly feelings of the heart, which so aid in forming those high-toned manners of the Virginia gentleman. Edward Lynch was blessed with a hopeful, cheerful disposition; passing through various alternations of fortune, he has manifested through life these traits, preserving, in the midst of adverse storms, a tranquil heart and serene countenance. In early youth he was united in marriage to Mary Terrel, an elegant and queenly personage, and, without exception, the most beautiful woman ever seen in Lynchburg. In her youth, she was surpassingly lovely; in her middle age, she was beautiful; and it is told, that, even after death, the exquisite loveliness of her youth remained. She was the mother of eight children,*

---

* Mrs. Charles Withers and Mrs. Dr. Pretlow, of Covington, Kentucky; Mrs. Winston, Charles E. Lynch, and the Misses

seven of whom still survive her, and several of her daughters, inheriting the beauty of their mother.

About thirty-eight years since, ZALINDA, the oldest, was married, by Friends' ceremony, to Nathaniel Winston. The family had just the day before moved into their new residence, the house now occupied by Col. Maurice Langhorne; and the writer, though not five years old, distinctly remembers the appearance of the beautiful young bride, and the large procession formed from her father's house to the Quaker meeting-house. This day is memorable in Lynchburg, on account of the most terrific storm ever witnessed. The tempest prevailed for some hours with unabated fury, and so suddenly was the atmosphere darkened, that, at two o'clock, candles were lighted throughout those spacious apartments, in which were assembled the bridal party; and, if memory does not deceive me, it was on the afternoon of this day, that the young son of Mrs. Mary Brown met with a tragic death. He was crossing the street to his mother's residence, when a violent whirlwind of dust prevented him seeing a loaded wagon which drove over him, causing his instant death.

The family of Edward Lynch emigrated about twenty-three years since to Ohio, where Mrs. Mary

---

Lynch, of Waynesville, Ohio; and Dr. Micajah T. Lynch, of Richmond, Virginia, are the members of the family of Edward B. Lynch.

Lynch died in 1855. Her venerable husband survives her, happily surrounded by the greater part of his family, who reside near him, in Ohio and Kentucky.

Of all this large family,* Mrs. Alexander Liggat is, with the exception of Edward Lynch, the only surviving member. What a mournful retrospection, to look back on the bright, hopeful faces which encircled the family hearth, and to find their places vacant!—the lovely Hannah, fading in early womanhood; the frank, cheerful Micajah, just embarked on life's voyage; the amiable Anselm, the young son John,† the inheritor of his father's venerated name; but on none of this family does more tender, romantic and mournful interest linger, than on William and Jane Lynch.

WILLIAM LYNCH was one of the younger sons‡ of the founder of the city. In early life, he had sought and married the lovely Jane Humphreys,

---

* Of John Lynch, the founder of Lynchburg.

† His tragic death is mournfully remembered by the oldest inhabitants.

‡ Micajah Lynch served his country in the late war, being stationed at Norfolk. He married Ann, the daughter of Jas. C. Moorman, and they survived their marriage only a few years. William Lynch was a colonel in the late war, and was stationed at Camp Holly. His regiment was remarkable for its perfect drill. The life-like portraits of these two brothers are to be seen at the country residence of Miss S. L. Davis, near Lynchburg.

second daughter of Dr. Humphreys of that place. To gratify the taste of her husband, she adopted the Quaker garb in all its beautiful simplicity, and a more captivating personage than Jane Lynch could not be found in our town. The young husband and wife together trod smoothly the path of life, blest with a lovely boy, their only child; gifted with wealth and happy in mutual affection, where could be a brighter prospect or more unclouded future? Preferring retirement and the quiet of domestic life, they built a modest dwelling just overhanging our ivy cliff, where they passed their lives in innocent and rational pursuits; Jane busied with her maidens in domestic manufactures, while William was occupied with his farming pursuits. But, alas! a dark cloud appearing, dissipated in a short time their tranquil happiness. William Lynch was seized with the incipient symptoms of consumption, and although the disease did not then, as now, carry off its victim in the course of a few months, yet from year to year his life was prolonged as by a miracle; and to add to the gloom already surrounding them, the health of Jane began to decline, the bright spot on her cheek too surely evincing that she, too, was marked out for an early grave. The skill of medicine, the tenderness of friends and relatives availed nought; and finding death for them both inevitable and near at hand, their only remaining desire was that they might depart at the same time, and together pass through the dark valley of the shadow of Death; but this being denied them, the grief of the survivor was stilled by the hope of a speedy re-union in Heaven.

In a brief time their habitation was left desolate, and their orphan boy was removed to the home of his father's kindred. He was a bright, happy child; rejoicing in life, unconscious of the loss sustained by himself, caring nought, as yet, for the abundant wealth lavished on him, and ignorant that, along with it, he inherited a fearful legacy. As he grew up, he became aware that his parents had died of consumption, and this knowledge caused him much unhappiness. Convinced that he, too, would become a victim of that disease, he determined to grapple with the destroyer, and if possible avert the fate overhanging him. Being placed as a student at the University of Virginia, he left that place, his friends remaining ignorant of his plans and intentions. For a long time, his fate was involved in doubt; his friends fearing that with all of the ship's crew he had gone down to a watery grave. But an American vessel touching at one of the South Sea Islands, young Lynch was seen and recognized by one of the officers, who brought tidings of him to his friends in America. He was a captive in the Islands, condemned by his master to strike in a blacksmith's shop. But this very circumstance wrought for him the blessing for which he would have exchanged all his wealth. The constant exercise of the muscles of the chest, brought about a healthy action of the lungs, and he believed himself entirely free from any predisposition to consumption. In a few years he returned to his native land.* Buoyant with health and cheerfulness, he mingled in society, admired for the graces of his mind and person and invested with romance from the circumstances attending his voyage. Becoming deeply attached to one of the loveliest girls in Lynchburg, he met with a severe disappointment in failing to secure in return her affections. In a very short time afterwards, this sweet girl was suddenly removed, and during the great depression of spirits after this sorrow, the symptoms of consumption revealed themselves. He hastened to a warmer climate; but the disease advanced with great rapidity, and he only returned to Lynchburg to breathe his last, and to be laid quietly to rest in the old Quaker burying ground.

---

* This gifted and generous young man inherited, from his mother, more than twenty valuable servants. On Christmas morning after his return, they all went to him to ask for a Christmas gift; he told them, he gave them themselves; and he not only liberated them, but provided the means for sending them to Liberia.

QUAKERISM IN LYNCHBURG.

"True Quakerism (which is true Christianity) stands distinguished from every other religion in this particular—that it is altogether spiritual, and only aims at accomplishing effects by means of their causes. Thus, it never aims at making the creature affectionate, but by means of love; nor merciful, but by means of mercy; nor good, but by means of goodness. And herein it demonstrates its origin to be from the fountain of Divine wisdom; for, through all nature and creatures, this is the method of God's proceeding."

EDWARD STABLER.

Thirty-eight years since, Lynchburg was the abode of many of the disciples of Fox and Penn. Passing along the streets, you would not unfrequently meet reverend looking gentlemen in curved coats and broad-brimmed hats; gentle matrons in sad colored dresses and coal-scuttle bonnets, and occasionally the sweet face of a young Quakeress, rendered still more lovely from the severity of the dress and bonnet. The Society worshiped every Sunday and Thursday at the ancient stone meeting-house, a few miles from Lynchburg, and the carriages then used exclusively by Friends were precisely like the fashionable ones of the present day, hung low, with the driver's seat somewhat under the roof of the carriage. At their solitary place of worship everything tended to promote solemnity; the remoteness from the habitations of man, the burying-ground attached, the profound stillness, uninterrupted, save by the song of the wild bird in Spring, and the fall of the eddying leaf in Autumn, the grave faces of the silent worshipers—all these impressed with awe even the most worldly, and with hearts softened and a'tuned to the praise of God, even the hum of bees, the sound of the mosquito, and the distant whoop of the whippoor-will, heard even in the day from these deep shady valleys, were like a dirge or requiem calling their thoughts from earth.

It was here, in solemn communion with God, that these silent worshipers obtained grace and strength to aid in time of need. When on again returning to the active duties of life, the worldling might express wonder to see the Quaker pass calmly on, regardless of the stormy, boisterous battle of life around him, finding all things bearable, if not pleasant, and carrying about him a defence more available than one of Colt's revolvers. Whence was it that no one raised his hand or voice against a Quaker? It was that they followed the golden rule, and pursued in its broadest sense our Saviour's precept, "Love your enemies." They were stout-hearted, brave men, yet they discountenanced war; they governed well themselves, avoiding angry disputes and contentions; they wronged no man; they gave no offence in any way, and as a natural consequence, peace and tranquillity were the result.

Quakerism exists now in Lynchburg only in name; the meeting-house is deserted, and no longer within its sacred walls assemble the Lynches, the Davises, the Johnsons, the Powells, the Cadwalladers, the Douglasses of former times; and rarely is met one now wearing the Quaker garb, or speaking the plain language, so sweet and beautiful, from the lips of those we love. The entire absence of form and ceremonial has doubtless been the cause of the decay of a system embodying so much that is pure and holy in the religion of Christ.

The most venerable member of their Society, at this time, was WILLIAM DAVIS, Sr. He was a man of great worth and purity, and, together with his family, was a constant worshiper at the Quakers' meeting-house. He lived to a great age, and at the time of his death he was considered the patriarch of the town. His remains are interred in the burying ground attached to the church. His venerable wife survived him many years, her lonely pilgrimage cheered by the attentions of a devoted family.

Amongst those who worshiped in this forest sanctuary was Mrs. RICHARD TYREE. Her maiden name was Douglas, and she was a niece of Mrs. Edward Lynch, whom she resembled in personal appearance. She had been united in marriage when very young to Richard Tyree, Esq., of Lynchburg, whom she still survives, and resides in Lynchburg amongst her devoted children.* For some years she has been afflicted with blindness, and

"With wisdom at one entrance quite shut out,"

she must feel the advantage of that self-discipline which was taught her in her youth, and doubtless the inner spiritual light now illumines her soul, gilding with its rays the evening of her well-spent life.

About the year 1819, CHARLES FISHER, an English Friend, was the beloved instructor of all the children belonging to Quaker families in Lynchburg and its vicinity. Of most prepossessing appearance, and gifted in an extraordinary degree with the ornament of a meek and quiet spirit, Charles Fisher passed through all the trying scenes incident to school-keeping, without once losing his temper, though exceedingly delicate in his physical organi-

---

* This excellent lady died during the past summer, since the above was written.

zation, and highly nervous in his temperament. Happy was the little band of Quaker children under his mild reign. A sudden close occurred to his labors in Lynchburg, and we were forever deprived of the services of our faithful teacher.

On Friday evening, Charles called on William Rohr to recite his lesson. Rohr was one of the largest boys in school, and being very refractory and insolent about his recitation, he was mildly reprimanded by Friend Fisher. William Rohr replying very passionately, Fisher took hold of his arm, upon which the broad-shouldered pupil returned the compliment, carrying the school-master round and round the room, and performing a series of evolutions that would have astonished a dancing-master, inflicting at the same time a series of thumps and blows on the beautiful white forehead of Charles Fisher. Campbell, the poet, witnessed the battle of Hohenlinden, and has thrillingly embodied his feelings in the animated poem of Hohenlinden; yet I doubt whether that fearfully sublime scene inspired the poet with half the awe, terror, and emotion felt by the alarmed and agitated band of children who cowered around the room. Friend Fisher took his seat much exhausted after the contest, and to the surprise and sorrow of the pupils, he stated that it was necessary for him to abandon his school, but that he had provided a successor whom he hoped we should esteem. That successor was K. B.

Townley, who continued to occupy his post as teacher for many years in Lynchburg. In those days traveling Friends were appointed by the Society to make tours of the States, calling as they passed along on all Quaker families, and on all connected with the denomination. Strange as may appear the idea of a French Quaker preacher, it is true that an eminent one of that nation traveled through Virginia in company with two female friends. His name was Stephen Grillet, and one of the ladies was called Margaret Judge, a very beautiful and pious woman. On the occasion of a visit to our residence, the younger members of the family were permitted to be present with the older ones. When the Spirit moved him, Stephen Grillet spoke feelingly and appropriately, with only a slight foreign accent. He was followed by Margaret Judge, who addressed us in a strain so fervid and eloquent, so true, simple and solemn, that many of her words still remain deeply engraven on the memory of those who listened.

WILLIAM DAVIS, junior, with his noble face and manly form, is now present to memory. How many in Lynchburg can remember with admiration his fine, clear, brown complexion and honest benevolent face—a true specimen of a refined Quaker. He was a native of Bedford county, and, amongst all the male members of the society, none were so attractive as William Davis, Jr.; a worthy follower of Ellwood and Barclay, without the obstinate opinionativeness of the former, and exempt from the superstition of the latter, he adorned the doctrine of God his Saviour, pursuing through life that calm, quiet course, so conducive to the happiness of those with him associated, and, doubtless, bringing to himself peace at the solemn hour of death.

He had married, in early life, Zalinda, the daughter of John Lynch, and, surviving her many years, he had the additional calamity of becoming totally blind. A small profile likeness of him, taken by his grandson, depicts beautifully his perfect cast of face and feature. His only son, John Davis, a young man of fine promise, died many years since; and of his two excellent daughters, Sarah, the oldest, alone survives; and to her was accorded the dear privilege of soothing and comforting the declining years of her venerable father. She can only now look back, with sweet, though mournful recollection, to those quiet, happy days, passed at the dear old homestead, whose floors are no longer trodden by familiar feet.*

---

* Since this was penned, this lady has returned to live at the old country residence.

"There was an air of peace about her which was irresistible, in seducing all with whom she conversed, under her gentle influence. This was the effect upon strangers, and in no degree was it abated by the closest intimacy." (*Sir Thomas Fowel Buxton's description of his sister-in-law, Priscilla Gurney.*)

Who is there among us that can ever forget MARY ANNIS, the lovely Quakeress—the "bonny gem" in the Society of Friends. Highly endowed, both personally and mentally, she was tenderly beloved in a large circle of friends and relatives. Reared in the doctrines of Quakerism, which are opposed to every kind of music, her voice was so sweet that, even in conversation, it was melody, and sweetly she sang the simple, beautiful songs of Burns, because music was natural to her.

It was said that Mary Annis had refused the hand of every young Quaker in Virginia; and it was known that she had rejected many suitors, unconnected with that society, so that it was surmised that she had determined never to marry; and calmly and happily, as yet, passed her life in the cultivation of her mind and in the peaceful performance of all those sweet duties which pertain to the sister and daughter.

It was the custom of William Davis to attend, with his family, the yearly meeting of Friends, then held in Alexandria; and during one of these visits, they sojourned at the house of Edward Stabler, an eminent member of the Society of Friends, and one of the most eloquent preachers * of that denomination. He was a man of the highest order of intellect, possessing all those lovely traits which adorn the Christian Minister. Greatly beloved in the family circle, and revered by a large acquaintance and connection, his household was often the scene of a large concourse of young and old, who would assemble to hear him speak on religious subjects, and discourse eloquently on Scripture passages.

It was during this visit that an acquaintance was formed between Mary Annis and Robinson, a son of Edward Stabler. After their return to Lynchburg, the acquaintance was renewed, and frequent visits from the young member of Friends' Society resulted, early in the month of November, 1828, in a marriage, by Friends' ceremony, at the Quaker meeting-house. Besides the invited guests, a large concourse went out from town to witness the ceremony — so touching from its simplicity, and so deeply interesting from the romance with which the principal actors were invested. Widely different was the scene in this secluded spot, from a

---

* See deeply interesting Life of E. Stabler, by his son, William Stabler.

fashionable Quaker marriage, the description of which has recently appeared in the public prints; and, amongst the large concourse then assembled, there was probably not one who did not feel, mingled with curiosity, a thrill of tender emotion, on witnessing that beloved Quakeress take on her the sacred vows of a wife. A bunch of Autumn's latest, fairest flowers rested on the folds of crape, which beautifully encircled her neck—the quick beating of her gentle heart alone displayed by the motion of these flowers, and by a slight tremor in the tones of her silvery voice, as she pronounced these vows.

A few brief, happy years passed, and many who then went with this bridal party were again assembled and sat within the walls of the old church. The friends, sister and parents were there. The young husband was there, but he sat alone; his head bowed; his countenance no longer wearing the joyous, happy expression of the former time. The bridal robes of the wife had been exchanged for the vesture of the grave, and friends and relatives now accompanied her remains, to lay them in the old church-yard by the side of her kindred.

MRS. HENRY DAVIS.

> "Her parents held the Quaker rule,
> Which doth the human feeling cool,
> But she was trained in Nature's school,
> Nature had blest her."
>
> CHARLES LAMB.

Mrs. SALLY DAVIS, wife of Henry Davis, Esq., was a native of Bedford county, and a sister to the late Christopher Anthony, whom she greatly resembled in those shining qualities for which he was so eminent. Reared and educated, like her brother, in the pure, lovely, spiritual doctrines of Quakerism, she carried with her, through life, all those beautiful traits so naturally fostered in a well ordered mind, by habits of self-discipline, early acquired from the example of those around her, as well as by constant intercourse with a large circle of friends and relatives, worshiping in the Society of Friends.

In the beauty of early womanhood, she was married to Henry Davis of Lynchburg. Removing to that place, and residing on Bank square, she brought with her to the town many simple primitive habits of the country, carrying on domestic manufactures for amusement and employment, taking great delight in such pursuits; so that, on entering her more retired apartments, a visitor might almost imagine herself in the country, instead of being in the midst of a noisy, busy town.

Mrs. Davis possessed a peculiar talent for rendering domestic life happy, as well as for acquiring a great influence over the young. This was not effected by blind indulgence, but by interesting and occupying them in useful pursuits. She pursued this plan, not only with her own family, but with the children of relatives, temporarily under her care. The good and pious Bishop White attributes his success and eminence in after life to his mother, from the circumstance of her keeping him, whilst young, interested and occupied in useful pursuits, producing thereby a tranquilizing and sedative effect on his mind, and keeping thus at bay wandering idle thoughts. To the same circumstance may probably be traced the capacity of the family of Mrs. Davis for concentrating their minds and energies on any given point, and thus arriving at success in their undertakings.

Though unable to worship in the sanctuary of her beloved people, Mrs. Davis adhered to their peculiar dress and language. Her mild blue eyes and blooming face will long be remembered in Lynchburg by those who knew her, nor will her gentle loving words ever be forgotten by those to whom they were spoken. She wisely mingled with other Christian sects, preferring the old Methodist Church, which then, as now, was the scene of the most ardent and zealous pastoral labors. Regarding with peculiar reverence the indwelling Spirit, and considering her soul as God's temple, Mrs. Davis, attending closely to the voice within, was thus naturally led to observe strong impulses, and when once convinced that she was called on to perform a duty, she arose at any hour, night or day, attending to it instantly; and several times, during her residence on Bank square, she was thus the means of preserving life. On one occasion she awoke after the hour of midnight, firmly possessed with the idea that some great danger attended two female servants, who occupied an attic as a sleeping room. The doors between were all closed, and she had no means by sound or otherwise to cause such a belief; but arising immediately, she ascended the stair-cases that led to the third story, and on opening the door of the servants apartment, she found the two girls in a profound slumber, with their bed and coverlids in a bright blaze of fire, which in a very few moments must have caused their death. Several instances of this sort are well known in the family of Mrs. Davis, and a member of her own houshold was, in the same manner, rescued by her, when placed in circumstances of great peril.

A dutiful, affectionate wife—a devoted mother, Mrs. Davis gratefully pursued her life journey, though called on to give up several lovely children in infancy. Her eldest son, Samuel Davis, was greatly beloved in the community in which he lived. Of splendid stature, handsome face, fine sense, and gifted with all those amiable traits for which his mother was so remarkable, Mrs. Davis could not but look on such a son with joy and pride, anticipating the time when, in the natural course of events, he should soothe and comfort her declining years. But, alas! for the instability of human hopes! Samuel Davis, whilst on a visit to Botetourt, was seized with the incipient symptoms of a malignant fever, called at that time "the big lick fever." He hurried home to Lynchburg, where, after lingering some days, he breathed his last. From that hour, the health of his mother declined. She endeavored to submit patiently to the affliction, and even at times appeared to have recovered her wonted cheerfulness; but the stroke had fallen heavily on her devoted heart, and ere long she was herself laid on a bed of languishing, from which she was destined never more to rise. Those who witnessed the triumphs of her last hours, can never forget that chamber of death; her prayers at that solemn hour have been answered; her children have mostly chosen the better part, and one beloved daughter has long since joined her mother in Heaven.

CHRISTOPHER ANTHONY.

"Of them who wrapt in death are cold,
   No more the smiling day shall view;
Should many a tender tale be told,
   For many a tender thought is due.

Why else the o'ergrown paths of time,
   Would thus the letter'd sage explore;
With pain these crumbling ruins climb,
   And on the doubtful sculpture pour?"
LANGHORNE.

CHRISTOPHER ANTHONY was born in the county of Bedford, at the close of the year 1776. His parents were in easy, prosperous circumstances; but, on uniting themselves with the Society of Friends, they liberated a large number of slaves. Reared under the gentle, quiet influence of Quakerism, Christopher Anthony early learned those habits of self-government, which in after life so materially contributed towards forming his perfect exemplary character. Passing his boyhood amid the trying scenes of the Revolution, and the times immediately succeeding, the means of education were not abundant, yet Mr. Anthony profited by every opportunity, early acquiring a thorough knowledge of the English language in all its purity and beauty. Remarkable, when a boy, for the ease and elegance of his language, he was peculiarly sensitive even at that time to any coarseness and defective idiom. He used to relate, for the amusement of his children, an anecdote of his going, when very young, to attend a rural festival in his father's neighborhood, in all the pride of a new suit of homespun. On his arrival at the place of rendezvous, a momentary feeling of dissatisfaction was produced, by seeing an elegant looking gentleman from town, in all the magnificence of broadcloth, ruffled-shirt and showy brooch; but the young Quaker was immediately set at his ease, by hearing this fine gentleman remark to a by-stander, "I always in generally, when I rides, wears boots!" Becoming early acquainted with the standard English authors, Mr. Anthony carried with him through life the impressions then derived, retaining his literary taste, and continuing constantly to improve and cultivate his mind by diligent reading. Placed at an early age, as a clerk in his father's store in Bedford county, he there acquired that knowledge of mankind and of human nature, which, in after years, so contributed to his success as a lawyer.

The years immediately succeeding the Revolutionary war were necessarily attended with difficulty and hardship. The habits of the most wealthy were those of primitive simplicity; their dress, the product of their own loom: and, in the execution of these homely employments, the females of our country manifested a noble pride. The young men were often called to assist on the farm, and to take part in all the rural occupations then going forward. Christopher Anthony, doubtless, found amid these scenes, fruitful sources of self-culture; and, in free converse with nature, in the forests of Bedford, he could call to mind the contents of books he had been reading, and, whilst pursuing these avocations, his mind and heart could soar far above them, to the Eternal Source of all. To him, all things in nature were fraught with instruction: even the silent furrows, appearing, one by one, as the plough passed over them, were suggestive of the cultivation of that patient perseverance for which he was so remarkable in later years; and to his early familiarity with rural scenes, may be traced the unalloyed pleasure which, in more mature life, he derived from the poetical works of Robert Burns.

Shortly after he attained the age of twenty-one, he removed to the city of Richmond, and entered into business with Joseph Anthony, his half-brother. Visiting Philadelphia, at this time, he found the city in commotion; the piracies on the high seas, the threatened war with France, and anticipated troubles with England, had so excited the public mind, that every apprehension was felt that our country would soon be again involved in war, both by land and sea. Public amusements were discontinued, the theatre was nightly opened to vacant boxes; the benefit night of a favorite young actor approaching, Judge Hopkinson was induced by his persuasions to write something patriotic, to be sung on that occasion, as nothing short of an absolute novelty could procure an audience. Accordingly the song of "Hail Columbia!" was written, and its announcement drew a crowded house. The scruples of the young Quaker being removed, he attended the theatre on that night, and he often spoke with gratification of the impression produced by hearing this song sung for the first time. The enthusiasm of the audience knew no bounds, and the song was called for again and again. During this visit, Mr. Anthony was seized with a tedious intermittent fever, and, being attended by Dr. Rush, he nearly fell a victim to the disease, or to the remedy, which was a preparation of arsenic, then recently introduced into the medical world, and administered for ague and fever. Dr. Rush entrusted to the landlady a phial containing this medicine, but she, misunderstanding his prescription, instead of administering it in small portions, gave him the greater part of it at once; and, in consequence of this mistake, Mr. Anthony received for some weeks the personal attention of Dr. Rush, deriving from his friendship and acquaintance pleasant impressions which remained with him through life.

He returned to Richmond, where he continued to carry on business as a merchant, and just as he was on the eve of marriage, an unexpected reverse rendered it necessary to defer for a short time his union with Anna Couch; but this event taking place on the 6th of August, 1803, Mr. Anthony removed to the county of Goochland, where, for several years, he was occupied as a merchant. Retaining the Quaker garb and language, he adhered to the religion of his parents, conscientiously practising its precepts. The members of Friends' Society, not being allowed to take an oath, Mr. Anthony, on accepting the office of magistrate, found himself obliged to leave that sect, though throughout life he cherished the beautiful doctrines by them inculcated.

At the time of Burr's trial, Mr. Anthony was in Richmond, and having of Burr a very bad opinion, he expressed such publicly, hoping thereby to avoid being put on the jury. Being asked by a friend what had brought him to Richmond, he remarked: "I have come to Richmond to hang Burr." Notwithstanding this remark was reported to this wretched man, yet he chose Mr. Anthony as one of his jurors. Copious notes were made by Mr. Anthony of the trial, as well as many incidents connected with it, but the circumstances of Burr's acquittal, as well as of the incarceration of the ill-fated Blænnerhasset, are too well known to render any detail here of these events at all desirable.

Continuing for several years a magistrate, Mr. Anthony's friends perceived in him such talents for the bar, that they began to persuade him to study for that profession. The late Wm. Pope, and the numerous members of the talented families of Pleasants and Bates, were amongst his warmest friends, and his own inclinations prompting him to follow their advice, he accordingly, at the age of thirty, commenced his legal studies: obtaining in a brief period a license to practice law, he removed to Lynchburg, where at once he rose in his profession, his practice soon becoming so large that he could attend to it but with difficulty. Placed thus for a period of eight or nine years in opulent circumstances, Mr. Anthony considered himself a wealthy man; but about the year 1819, a sudden reverse plunging him into poverty, it was at this time that the cheerful hopefulness of his disposition shone brightly; for over this stormy sea serenely he passed, feeling thankful that amid the wreck he had his own energy and strength remaining. With an unshaken trust in Providence, the day succeeding his failure, he walked forth from his happy home with the knowledge that everything owned by him must be given up. But only for a short time was the reverse felt. On that very day he was met by a wealthy client, who engaged his services in a new case, and insisted on his receiving compensation beforehand: from that period the tide of business was so great, that even the energy and industry of Mr. Anthony were scarce sufficient to attend to the numerous demands made on his time by his very extensive practice. During many years, Mr. Anthony nobly sustaining himself, exemplified in his character all that forms the upright man and the Christian, when death suddenly cut short his useful career, in his fifty-eighth year, in the month of September, 1835.

It would be impossible to enumerate the many charities of this excellent man during the course of his practice in Lynchburg. Many widows were by him befriended, and their business matters attended to without charge; many orphans, to his exertions owed the possession of their property; and the last professional visit he ever made was to a widow lady in the country, in order to aid and advise her in conducting her affairs.

Many interesting legal anecdotes of him might be recorded, but in this place only one simple one shall be introduced. In the early period of Mr. A.'s practice, he was often opposed to the late Christopher Clark, at that time an eminent lawyer of the upper country. It had often been necessary for Mr. Clark to call on one particular witness, whose name was Enoch Hogan. Hogan was a busy, prying man, generally more occupied about the affairs of others than his own, and Mr. Anthony and the members of the bar had been in the habit of jesting with Mr. Clark about his standing witness, and saying to him whenever he got into a hard place, "Clark, call up Enoch Hogan." At one time Mr. Anthony was engaged in a lawsuit in which it was necessary to prove the hand-writing of an obscure woman residing in Kentucky. From time to time he had urged his client to take the deposition of this person, without which he would inevitably lose his cause. The case was brought to trial—they were unable to prove this hand-writing. Much discomfited and brought to bay, Mr. Anthony was about to surrender, when Mr. Clark whispered, "Anthony, call Enoch Hogan." Though aware that his advice was given in derision, Mr. Anthony calmly desired the sheriff to summon Enoch Hogan. Enoch was called, and came in amidst a roar of laughter from the whole court room; he was sworn and interrogated by Mr. Anthony as to his knowledge of the hand-writing of the surviving witness. "Do you know that hand-writing?" Hogan took the paper, giving a quick, sulky glance at it, and handing it back with this remark, "I reckon I ought to know it; it is the signature of my own sister:" and so it was. She lived in Kentucky, and he had many letters from her in possession, and the similarity of the hand-writing and other circumstances put the matter beyond dispute. "This," said Mr. Anthony, "taught me one lesson, which in my after practice I never forgot: that was, never to give up a cause until I had lost it."

A brief sketch of CHRISTOPHER ANTHONY, *by the late* JOHN HAMPDEN PLEASANTS.

"Died at his residence in Lynchburg, on Thursday, the first of October, CHRISTOPHER ANTHONY, Esq., in the 59th year of his age. Mr. Anthony's illness was congestive fever, and from confidence in the uniform firmness of his health, and excellence of his constitution, he unfortunately neglected remedies in the incipient stages of the disease. But who shall say that mortal skill could have availed to save him, or who shall decide the problem, destined to be hidden in everlasting obscurity, that the appointed hour is fixed for all, by an unalterable fate? The calamities which Death visits on surviving friends are sufficient without their being aggravated by the painful, perhaps in every case, false supposition, that the stroke of his scythe might have been averted. We can never know the truth, and the mode of faith is the happiest and wisest, which refers all to the wisdom and providence of God.

Few men have lived in this community more useful in their sphere than Christopher Anthony, or died more inopportunely for the usefulness they were capable of exerting. An active and patriotic citizen, a most devoted husband and tender parent, there was no relation of life which he did not sustain with zeal and fidelity. Subjected at two periods of his life to severe pecuniary reverses, his unflinching spirit and indomitable energy refused to succumb to misfortune an instant, but rather with that admirable elasticity which belongs to the consciousness of capacity, derived renewed energy from the necessity which required it. He was for a third time reaping that fortune so well due to his talents and vigor, when Providence, in its inscrutable wisdom, closed his active and useful career.

"Mr. Anthony was a native of Bedford county, and was born in the Society of Friends, to whose benevolent principles he firmly adhered, while he relinquished outward conformity to their manners. He was bred a merchant, in which capacity he, at one time, conducted business in Richmond. Failing in this he adopted the profession of the law, and speedily attained the highest eminence at the bar, which he maintained for a long series of years, and enjoyed to the end of his life. A seat on the bench was repeatedly in his power, but he declined it as being less lucrative than his practice. His native capacity was of the highest order, and had he possessed the advantages of early instruction in elementary knowledge, he had been amongst the most shining men of his generation. As it was, he had few superiors; in intuitive knowledge of men, that best of knowledge, none. May his ashes repose in peace until the great day, when all the dead will come forth to meet their Judge."

MRS. ANNA W. ANTHONY.

"What are the trophies gained
  By power alone, with all its noise and strife,
To that meek wreath, unstained,
  Won by the charities that gladden life!"
                                BERNARD BARTON.

ANNA WOOLSTON ANTHONY was the eldest daughter of Samuel and Anna Couch. Her father was by birth a Philadelphian, and her mother was a native of Mount Holly, New Jersey. Emigrating soon after their marriage to Virginia, they estabished themselves in the city of Richmond, where Anna was born in the month of January, 1786. Shortly after this event, Mr. Couch purchasing the estate of Little Creek, in Goochland, he removed there with his family, and he continued to reside there till his death. Being a man of large property, Mr. Couch was exceedingly liberal and generous, esteeming the privilege of bestowing on others, as one of the most refined pleasures. Possessing a fine mind, highly cultivated, his tastes were literary, his temperament highly poetic, and many of his compositions, both in prose and verse, are preserved in the family, evincing a high order of talent. His daughter received her education under his immediate superintendence, and becoming early acquainted with all the standard literature of the English language, her retentive mind preserved these impressions, which were in after life deepened by still further cultivation. When at the age of six years, her parents left the established Church, and united themselves to the Society of Friends, liberating at this time a large number of slaves. At the age of 10 years, owing to the infirm state of her mother's health, an infant sister was confided to the charge of Anna, and assuming the entire care of the child, she reared it as tenderly as though it had been her own. About four years after this time, her father was seized with a severe illness, from which he never recovered, and Mrs. Couch, with all the tenderness of a devoted wife, gave herself up entirely to administer to the comfort of her husband, confiding the whole care of a large establishment to her daughter Anna, who not only administered wisely the domestic affairs, but materially aided her mother in nursing her sick father. On the death of Mr. Couch, obeying one of his last requests, they gave up their residence in the country, and removed again to the city of Richmond. In the course of a few years, Anna was united in marriage to Christopher Anthony, of Bedford county, also a member of the

Society of Friends. Removing with her husband to Goochland, Mrs. Anthony there found herself surrounded by the beloved friends of her childhood, and most happily sped away the few years of her residence in that county. In the year 1811, they made their home in the town of Lynchburg, where, very soon, Mrs. Anthony took a prominent station in society, forming these ties of friendship which remained unbroken through life, and are now considered by her children a sacred inheritance.

For some years she resided in the house at present occupied by Henry Dunnington, Esq., leading there a useful, happy life, active in her duties to her family, and dispensing good to all within her sphere. Large and abundant were her charities, many poor persons being entirely supplied by her with comforts. A woman in indigent circumstances, named Meredy, lived in a house immediately in rear of the old Methodist Church: her husband having made his arrangements to move with his family to Richmond, they packed up all their small amount of goods, and just as they were tying on their bonnets to start, the new tenants who were to take the house appeared on the steps with their parcels and bundles. Mrs. Meredy shook hands with the new comers, regretting that it was not in her power to aid them; but, said she, "in leaving Lynchburg I bequeath to you Mrs. Anthony, and I consider that I leave you a rich legacy."

Being endowed with great firmness and presence of mind in times of sickness and danger, she was once sent for at midnight, to come to the house of a relative, whose little son was said to be dying. On her arrival there, she found the family all sitting around in profound grief, and it was told her that the little child was dead. The dreary array of grave clothes was spread out, and one of the friends of the family was just about to prepare his little form for burial. Mrs. Anthony suggested that life might possibly not be extinct; but the family assured her that the child was dead, and that no breath for some moments had been apparent. "I will at least try to restore him," said Mrs. Anthony. She accordingly proceeded to administer restoratives, and very soon the little sufferer began to show symptoms of returning animation, and ere long a feeble cry issuing from the babe, showed that Mrs. Anthony's efforts had been entirely successful. The child recovered and is now residing in one of the Western cities, a vigorous man in the prime of life.

Shortly after the return of Mr. Anthony from the Legislature of 1817, he was seized with a severe attack of inflamatory rheumatism, which, for a time, baffled the skill of even the eminent medical men then residing in Lynchburg, and threatened him with loss of life. His sufferings were so great, that it was with difficulty a moment's ease could be procured. The use of opiates was much more rare than at present, and chloroform, happily for mankind, unknown at that time; the only thing which composed Mr. Anthony was the voice of his beloved wife, whilst occupied in reading aloud to him; it appeared to possess a mesmeric effect, and, whilst she was reading, he would seem to sleep, but the moment her voice was silent, he would awake to a sense of his sufferings. During this trying period, Mrs. Anthony read aloud to her husband all the volumes of the British Essayists; nor was his recovery complete, till he had made a long sojourn at the Warm and Hot Springs. When the unexpected reverse occurred in 1819, Mrs. Anthony bore it all with cheerful serenity. Not a murmur escaped her, not a cloud appeared on her countenance; possessing her soul in patience, she calmly rested all her cares on Him who had borne earth's trials. Her ways were committed to God, who speedily brought her out of adversity, establishing her in even greater comfort and prosperity than she had before enjoyed.

The house now occupied by Samuel McCorkle, Esq., was planned and built by the late Christopher Anthony. The dwelling was completed in 1831, and the family took possession of it during the summer of that year. Mrs. Anthony, though, could not but regret leaving her old home, on Courthouse Hill, where she had enjoyed so much happiness, and mingled with her regret a feeling that her domestic circle was soon to be broken up; yet, repressing these sad thoughts, she cheerfully engaged in all of her duties, and entered with zeal and ardor into the work of improving her new residence.

In the year 1829, Mrs. Anthony communed in the Episcopal Church, but it was not till the spring of 1836, that she became a member of that denomination. During the second Episcopal Convention, held in Lynchburg, she was baptized and admitted into the church, of which she continued a zealous and devoted member till the time of her death, like the pious and good Susan Allibone,* of Philadelphia; showing forth, in her life, the beauty of holiness, and proving that Episcopacy, based on Quakerism, can produce a Christian character, so formed after the model of our great Exemplar, so meek and lovely, that even the most worldly, on meeting with such, must own the power of the religion of Christ to exalt and purify the character.

---

* See "Life of Susan Allibone," written by Bishop Lee. The writer considers it a privilege to have been in the same house with this lovely woman, for more than a week, in Philadelphia.

About three years after being settled in their new home, Mr. Anthony was, in the month of September, suddenly called hence ; and very soon after this mournful event, Mrs. Anthony, leaving Lynchburg, went to reside with her daughters in the counties of Nelson and Buckingham. She survived her beloved husband more than twenty-one years: during that solitary pilgrimage, cheered by the hope of a joyful re-union in Heaven. It would be impossible to record here, the numerous ways of doing good which were found out by Mrs. Anthony during her residence in the country. A course of the most active industry was by her pursued, taking for her watch-word, "Occupy till I come!" She was strength, energy and comfort to her immediate household; and, when she could think of nothing else to be done, she subscribed liberally to different religious newspapers, which she would send throughout the country, thus supplying many poor families with religious knowledge, and lightening their trials by the hopes thereby inspired. A long course of usefulness was closed when she breathed her last, in the month of December, 1854, in the sixty-ninth year of her age. It is not the intention, at present, to portray the touching and beautiful scene of her death, so in accordance with her life, though aware that a record of this sort would be beneficial to the Christian community, by affording strong proof of the power of religion to comfort and sustain the believer at the close of life; and we can only close this brief tribute, by a clause from our beloved Service: "We give Thee hearty thanks, O Lord! for the good examples of all these Thy servants, who, having finished their course in faith, do now rest from their labors."

REMINISCENCES OF THE

COURT AND BAR OF LYNCHBURG.

> "Each pedant sage unlocks his store
> Of mystic, dark, discordant lore,
> And points with tottering hand the ways
> That lead me to the thorny maze;
> There, in a winding, close retreat,
> Is Justice doomed to fix her seat;
> There, fenced by bulwarks of the law,
> She keeps the wondering world in awe,
> And there, from vulgar sight retired,
> Like Eastern queen, is more admired."
>
>   SIR WILLIAM BLACKSTONE.

The old courthouse of Lynchburg was associated with many pleasing memories of the past, in those good old days of 1819, when Chancellor TAYLOR held there his courts in the months of May and October. The members of the bar from all the surrounding counties then convened in Lynchburg, and when relieved from the cares of business, they formed a most brilliant and refined social circle.

Judge CREED TAYLOR was truly a gentleman of the old school, with a most aristocratic manner and bearing. His dress even, in those days, was singular, consisting of short breeches, long stockings fastened at the knee with large buckles, and his silvery hair was combed from his forehead and confined in a queue at the back of his head. His legal abilities and reputation are too well established to need here eulogy, even were the ability possessed of so doing; but a more elegant gentleman in society, or at a dinner table, could not be found, his courtesy extending from his hostess to her youngest boy, whose health he would insist on drinking, as the little fellow ran through the dining-room—and there was a peculiar grace in all his actions, even in the simple one of manufacturing the impromptu olive, from the bread-basket and salt-cellar, previous to taking his wine, between the time of dinner and dessert. His manners at this time were bland and courteous, with all the formality of Sir Charles Grandison. In after years his health declined; he suffered from chronic gastritis; his eye lost its brightness, his form its roundness; and becoming exceedingly irritable and fretful, it was only by laying a powerful restraint on himself, and feigning politeness, that he could be brought to conduct himself with common civility towards the members of the bar.

During his last visit to Lynchburg, on adjourning his court for the day, he appointed the hour of twelve on the following day, as the time for again assembling. Becoming restless though, before the hour of eleven, he caused the courthouse bell to be rung long and loudly. In great haste the lawyers came pouring in from all directions to meet his ireful glance. He first accosted the late Peachy Gilmer, reproaching him in an angry voice for being so dilatory, whereupon Mr. Gilmer remarking to him that it yet wanted three quarters of an hour to the appointed time, the Chancellor losing all command of himself, exclaimed in a passionate voice, " Gentlemen, I will have you in future to know that when *I* take *my* seat on the bench, it is 12 o'clock." This reply, so worthy to have been made by a native of the Emerald Isle, instead of a Virginian, naturally leads us to think of the Irish bar during the time of Curran, Grattan, and Barrington; and it is doubtful whether the bar of that country surpassed in talent and brilliancy that of upper Virginia at the time of which we write.

The honorable Judge William Daniel, Sr. of the Campbell and Cumberland district, Daniel Sheffey, Colonel Townes, of Pittsylvania, Judge William Leigh, of Halifax, Peachy Gilmer, Christopher Anthony, Callowhill Minniss, and a host* of others,

---

* CHISWELL DABNEY, JOHN BLAIR DABNEY, though much the juniors of those mentioned above; Judge ALLAN TAYLOR, of Botetourt, in his manly stature and pure eloquence, reminding us of the great Burrowes; and in connection with these distin-

each one deserving more than a passing tribute. Of this large circle only four or five survive, and amongst them an interesting volume might be made up from reminiscences of that period.

PEACHY GILMER was a son of Dr. Gilmer, of Albemarle; he was born about the time of the breaking out of the Revolutionary war, and his boyhood was spent amid the mountains of his native county. He received an excellent education, and graduating with distinction, he studied for the bar, and soon after obtaining a license, he was united in marriage to MARY HOUSE, of Connecticut, a most estimable and highly gifted young lady. They settled in the county of Henry, then a wilderness, and doubtless the cheerful hopefulness of his wife's disposition, contributed largely to his extensive popularity and unbounded success in his profession. After residing there for a few years, Mr. Gilmer removed to the town of Liberty, in Bedford county, where, by a long course of diligence, he secured an independence. His house was ever

---

guished men, JOHN W. WILLS, at that time clerk of the county, but afterwards an eminent lawyer; and just before the abolishing of the chancery court system, (which, in spite of the evils disclosed by "Jarndyce v. Jarndyce," we still like,) the beloved and lamented Judge THOMAS T. BOULDIN, of Charlotte, might have been called a member of the Lynchburg bar, as he was a constant attendant of the courts there held.

the abode of the most unbounded hospitality, apart from ostentatious display; and in the exercise of his profession, Mr. Gilmer displayed the most cheerful assiduity, the very necessity for exertion being esteemed by him as a blessing, calling healthfully into action his mental and physical powers. Gratefully and affectionately does the retrospective thought carry us back to those happy days of childhood, when, under his hospitable roof, the privilege was enjoyed of witnessing his hourly manifestations of tender interest to those around him, and of listening to his witty, brilliant, intellectual conversation, carried on with other gifted spirits, who, too, have long since passed away;* nor will many of their words, then spoken, be ever effaced from memory, though they were heard years since, far in the past of long ago.

On the death of a relative in 1829, Mr. Gilmer became heir to a large property in Albemarle. He was now no longer obliged to practice his profes-

---

* In the Summer of 1828, a convention was held in Charlottesville for internal improvement, at which ex-Presidents Madison and Monroe, Chief Justice Marshall, B. W. Leigh, Chapman Johnson, and other distinguished men were delegates. Peachy Gilmer, William Radford, Esq., James W. Pegram, and Christopher Anthony were delegates from Bedford and Campbell, and the pleasant remembrance of that occasion is clouded by the thought, that of those good men, William Radford, Esq., of Bedford, is the only survivor.

sion, and as it was desirable for him to live on his estate, he removed with his family from the county of Bedford.

After being settled in his new abode, he missed the pleasant social circle he had for years been accustomed to meet in Liberty, and a letter written by him shortly after this period warmly expresses these feelings—indeed, he found his associations so linked with the past, that the new scenes in which he now moved failed to impart the happiness expected. His experience was like that of Charles Lamb, who, when emancipated from the India house, with his time completely at his own disposal, expressed himself as having no holidays. The health of Mr. Gilmer, about this time, became impaired, and he continued gradually to decline till about the year 1836, when this exemplary man and eminent lawyer breathed his last, at Leigh, his country seat, in the county of Albemarle.

GEORGE W. NELSON, at that time of the bar of Lynchburg, was a native of the county of Hanover, and a member of the old Virginia family of that name. A qualified lawyer, endowed with fine talents, and possessing a refined literary taste, a gentleman of most kindly feelings, yet was Mr. Nelson so deficient in suavity of manner, that he failed to make himself popular. He could not follow the precept of St. Paul, and "be all things to all men," and, consequently, to strangers he appeared reserved and even haughty. Those who knew well, and associated with him in a private circle, could form a more just estimate of his fine qualities, than others could who met him only in the courthouse.

During the summer of 1826, whilst on a visit to his relatives in the lower country, Mr. Nelson becoming deeply interested on the subject of religion, connected himself with the Episcopal Church, abandoning the profession of law and studying for the ministry, which he afterwards adorned by his zeal, piety and eloquence. His first visit to Lynchburg, after his change of profession, was in the spring of 1835, during the second Episcopal Convention, held in that place. An appointment having been made for him to preach at the old Baptist Church, and a crowd assembling to hear him, Mr. Nelson, ascending the pulpit after evening service, surveyed the congregation with some natural trepidation, and feeling somewhat nervous concerning this, his first sermon in Lynchburg. Immediately after taking his place in the pulpit, he felt himself blinded by a shining body, and turning hastily aside, in some agitation, he upset and broke a glass of water, nearly losing his presence of mind. Many of our inhabitants doubtless remember old Mr. Norvell, a member of the Baptist congregation, who being very deaf was accommodated with an elevated seat on a line with the pulpit, and who used an enormous bright tin ear trumpet. Rev. Mr. Lee, pastor of that Church, having been long accustomed to the vicinity of that tin body, had not recollected to prepare Mr. Nelson for its appearance.—Mr. Nelson married an excellent young lady of Georgetown, and he was for some years the beloved pastor of the Episcopal Church of Clarke county, where he died in the year 1840, his triumphant death bearing ample testimony to the power of religion to sustain, in that solemn hour, the steadfast believer.

JAMES W. PEGRAM, a native of Petersburg, settling in Lynchburg in 1826, was a brilliant addition to the bar of that place. Bright and pleasing memories of the past are so closely linked with James W. Pegram, that one solely dependant on memory can scarce define his character, or seize on any one prominent trait. Elegant in manners and personal appearance, brilliant in conversation, and of a disposition most affectionate, one would not long be in his society without a feeling of regret at not having sooner formed his acquaintance. In striking contrast to the talented Nelson, Pegram possessed that nice, ready tact, that blest capacity of adapting himself to others, and causing them to shine in discourse, by leading them to speak on subjects with which they were well acquainted.

Whether in his gallant military uniform, or in citizen's dress, his manly form was graceful and elegant. He was very successful in the practice of his profession; but on his marriage with Miss Johnston, in 1828, he removed to Petersburg, continuing to increase his reputation as a lawyer. Being appointed President of the Bank of Virginia in Richmond, he removed to that city, and whilst in the bloom of manhood and arrived at the zenith of prosperity and domestic happiness, he was called from home to the Western States on business connected with the banking institution to which he was attached.

After a prosperous journey, he was returning home, buoyant with health and glad expectation of again meeting his beloved circle at home, taking passage on the ill-fated steamboat, the "Lucy Walker" which was blown up on the Ohio river, with nearly every passenger on board. One saved from the wreck, told that to the last James Pegram was endeavoring to save the lives of others, and that when last seen he was making efforts to save the lives of ladies and children. As he had lived, so died this noble-hearted, chivalrous man, ever mindful to the last of others, thus sacrificing his valuable life in unavailing efforts to rescue his fellow-passengers.

Major JAMES B. RISQUE, also a member of the bar at this time, was a remarkable man. Both in personal character and professional career, a striking parallel exists between himself and James

Philips of Dublin, who was called to the Irish bar in 1812. The reputation of Major Risque as a criminal lawyer in the first outset of his career, and his undisputed bravery, concur in placing him along side of this remarkable Irish barrister. It is said that in his youth Major Risque was a rival and competitor at the bar, with Mr. Wickham and other distinguished lawyers. It is a well established fact that he was a very brave man, not at all afraid of pistols, which, at the present day, would be saying a great deal for any man. During his residence in Fincastle he fought several duels, in one of which he was shot entirely through the body, a silk handkerchief being drawn entirely through him.

He married a beautiful woman, a Miss Kennedy, who was a sister of Mrs. General Clarke. Being left a widower whilst quite a young man, he devoted himself most affectionately to the rearing and educating his three children. For many years he resided in the large house now occupied by the Misses Gordon as a seminary. He died about 17 years since, at an advanced age. His family survive him; his daughters, Mrs. Ward and Mrs. Hutter, residing in the vicinity of Lynchburg, and his son Ferdinand Risque, Esq., being a citizen of Georgetown, D. C.

SAMUEL BRANSFORD.—In connection with the court and bar of Lynchburg, may properly be mentioned SAMUEL BRANSFORD, for many years the able and efficient Sergeant of the corporation of that place. This excellent man being by nature peculiarly adapted to his office, adhered with unshrinking fidelity to its duties, regardless alike of their difficulty or painfulness. Though not of large stature, his presence had a magical effect in dispelling a mob; and there was something in the very expression of his eye, which caused even the most rebellious to submit. On one occasion, a desperate man, well armed, was holding at bay the sheriff and several police officers. Information of this state of affairs being conveyed to Samuel Bransford, he immedietely walked up to the offender, glancing fiercely at him, and saying, "You audacious rascal, how dare you rebel against the laws of your country?" The man instantly ceased resistance, and delivered himself up quietly to the officer.

Once only, in the recollection of the Oldest Inhabitant, was this energetic man baffled. It was told him that a party of gentlemen were convened in the ball-room of the hotel, engaged in card-playing. Accordingly, Mr. Bransford stationed himself at the door, which was locked and barred. He had several attendant officers with him, and a posse stationed in the street under the end window, to prevent the escape of the delinquents by that outlet. For many hours Mr. Bransford waited, and watched most patiently: to his surprise, no one even attempting to come out. At length, the hum of suppressed voices in the room entirely subsided, and all was silent. Unable to account for this, the door was now forced, and there stood the chairs, tables and glasses, just as they had been left, and the party had made their escape by cutting their way through the ceiling, making there a passage through to an upper room; and, one by one, they had quietly descended the stair-case, passing Mr. Bransford at the door of the ball-room, and, descending the steps leading to the first floor, they went forth to their several homes.

His ability and firmness commanded the greatest respect, even from the evil-doers who viewed with terror his approach. Regarding him with almost a superstitious reverence, they actually believed that Mr. Bransford could control the elements, and reduce them to proper order, when out of the course of nature. There are many now in Lynchburg, who well remember that memorable night in November, 1833, when the inhabitants of Lynchburg were so much terrified at what was called the "falling stars." Many enlightened persons were not a little afraid, whilst multitudes of the poor and ignorant fled to the residence of Mr. Bransford for protection, thinking that the day of judgment was at hand, and that he alone, of all living persons, could protect them.

Nor was it only in his civil and public capacity, that this good and honest man was eminent. In his family, most kind and affectionate; in the Methodist Church, of which he was a devoted member, most prompt in good works; and, by his zeal and energy, greatly aiding in the formation and growth of the Church in Lynchburg, where he lived beloved and respected till his death.

Mr. Bransford married a Miss Walton, of Buckingham, a lady of great worth and usefelness. She survived her husband some years, and died in the city of Lynchburg. Of the family of Samuel Bransford, three members survive:—Alfred Bransford, Esq., of Lynchburg, and Mrs. John H. Tyree, of its vicinity, and John William Bransford, Esq., of Richmond. Mrs. Charles Hudson, the second daughter, was a very lovely woman, with a cast of features and expression of countenance strongly resembling the portraits of Letitia Landon. Her sweet grave face, the bright intellectual expression of her large black eyes, the refined simplicity of her dress, and her graceful movements, will ever be remembered with pleasure and interest in her native town. She died in the city of New York, far from friends and home; but her remains repose in the Presbyterian graveyard of Lynchburg, where a splendid monument marks the spot.

SAMUEL BRANSFORD, Jr., was a young man of great promise, graduating at West Point, with high honors. After his graduation, he was honored with the position of Assistant Professor of Mathematics, at West Point, and met his death, while exercising a fiery horse on the parade ground. He is buried at West Point. His memory is kindly cherished by friends and classmates in Lynchburg.

"Revenge, my friends! revenge and the natural hatred of scoundrels, and the ineradicable tendency to *revancher* one's self upon them, and pay them what they have merited: This is forever more a correct and a divine feeling in the mind of every man."

THOMAS CARLYLE.

Immediately in rear of the old courthouse, stood the whipping post, pillory and wretched old jail, any one of these three objects being sufficient to disgrace the town. The jail was built of hewn logs and consisted of two rooms, one above the other, without fire-places, and appeared to have been planned and erected after Mr. Carlyle's own ideas. Now, a medium is desirable between that philanthrophy, which causes the imprisoned offender to be better lodged, clothed and fed, than the hard working, industrious day-laborer, and that excessive severity in prison discipline, advocated by Thomas

Carlyle. Doubtless the prison discipline of the present day has arrived at this happy medium, and it is not here the intention to discuss that matter.

The old jail must have been very insecure, and it is a matter of wonder, that prisoners did not more frequently make their escape. The lower room being used for criminals of the worst description, the upper apartment was kept for disorderly persons, and was, also, used as a temporary place of safety for maniacs. An unfortunate free colored man named Archie Cooper, being subject to periodical attacks of insanity, was often placed there, and crowds frequently assembled outside the jail, to listen to his eloquent prayers and exhortations—for when to his mental vision all else was dim and clouded, the glorious light of the gospel shone into his soul, enlightening with a ray of hope, his dark and gloomy pathway.

Not unfrequently might be seen, on the sidewalks, persons in a state of intoxication. This class found, also, at the jail an asylum, being escorted to that edifice by their polite and faithful friend Mr. Mason, who perambulated the streets of the town with a most expressive stick, his movements being a counter-part of those of Mr. Inspector Bucket, the detective agent. Very often a large group of school children would repair to the jail after the hours of recitation, and they would make a signal to the prisoners, who would send down a telegraph twine, to which the children below would attach a basket containing biscuit, confectionery, pastry and various other little comforts.

Lynchburg has enjoyed a very unenviable reputation abroad, having been called a wicked, dissipated place; but those charges can scarcely be just; for during a residence of 19 years in that place, the writer only recollects two persons there imprisoned for murder. A person named Joseph Cohen killed a man, and being found guilty of manslaughter, he was for a term of years sent to the penitentiary. On being released from confinement, he returned to Lynchburg, establishing himself on the Richmond road, at a little place called since that time by the name of "Cohensville." The circumstances attending the murder of Hamilton by John M. Jones, are too well known and remembered in Lynchburg, to be here discussed. Jones was imprisoned in the new stone jail for 15 months, and before the close of this period many inhabitants signed a petition to the Governor requesting his pardon, but to no avail. Jones was an exceedingly handsome man, rivalling in beauty the famous Gilderoy, and like him meeting the fate of

"Hanging high above the rest."

He met his doom with great firmness, saying that he sorely repented his past sins, trusting alone for pardon to Jesus Christ. After he was suspended in the air, the rope broke, giving him a tremendous fall. The unfortunate man, rising to his feet, called for water, saying, "for God's sake tie the rope tight this time." Sympathy now inclines us to think that he ought to have been pardoned, and that, having been hung *once*, was quite sufficient. Had his life only been spared one hour after his fall, a few moments conversation with him would greatly have enlightened the medical and scientific world, and relieved mankind in general of that intense curiosity felt respecting the sensations of a man who had been hung. He might have been permitted to make his home on some far distant shore, where he was unknown, untaunted and free from all those persecutions experienced by the man who had been hung, and whose wretched condition is so quaintly and even humorously described by Charles Lamb.

MRS. MARGARET DANIEL.

"The world is filled with the voices of the dead. Sweet and solemn voices are they, speaking with unearthly authority, coming back to us as the messages of angels. And when the business of daily life is for a while suspended, and its cares are put to rest, nay, often in the midst of the world's tumult, their voices float down clearly and distinctly from heaven, and say to their own, 'Come up hither.'"

ISABEL, OR INFLUENCE.

Mrs. MARGARET DANIEL, wife of the late Honorable Judge William Daniel, and daughter of Dr. Baldwin, was born in Winchester, Frederick county, about the year 1786. Her father was a gentleman of high standing, eminent alike for his domestic virtues and his skill in medicine. From early childhood, she was the friend and companion of her father, imbibing his feelings on most subjects, and learning from him to take prompt and decisive measures in all emergencies. Her education being carefully attended to by her father, and every advantage given her that could at that time be obtained, it is no matter of surprise, that as she grew up, her mind was remarkable for its brilliancy and cultivation. Endowed likewise with personal beauty* and elegance, it is but seldom that so many gifts have so perfectly harmonized in the character of one individual.

She sympathized so with her beloved parent, in the pursuits incident to his profession, that she would often accompany him to the bed-side of the sick and dying, materially aiding him by her timely suggestions; and in times of prevailing epidemics, she would find books of reference for him, and cases bearing a similitude to those under his care. Applying herself to find out remedies to relieve the sick, ere she had attained womanhood, Miss Margaret Baldwin was a most accomplished nurse, and an efficient and faithful friend to the sick and afflicted. When scarcely seventeen years old, she was married to Judge William Daniel, bringing to her husband a rich dowry in those splendid, shining qualities for which she was so remarkable. Settling in the county of Cumberland, she there made a home alike distinguished for its elegance and hospitality.

To her graces and accomplishments was added a

---

*A portrait of this lovely woman was taken in crayon by Harvey Mitchell, Esq., and a few years since it might have been seen at Union Hill, the residence of Mayo Cabell, Esq.

brave spirit, which enabled her to meet and confront danger with a firm heart and an unfaltering voice. During their residence in Cumberland, Judge Daniel was called unexpectedly from home, leaving only Mrs. Daniel and a family of small children. In the night, being awakened by a noise, Mrs. Daniel perceived by the moon-beams the figure of a man entering the house by one of the windows. Judge Daniel had left a large sum of money in his escritoir, and as it had been received on the previous day at court, it is not improbable that this circumstance was generally known. Presuming that the man had come for the purpose of plunder, Mrs. Daniel instantly arose, and taking down Judge Daniel's gun, walked directly up to the man, saying, "What are you seeking here? Go instantly, sir, and if you prolong your stay one instant, I will shoot you dead!" The cowardly man fled with precipitation, and Mrs. Daniel, after calling up her servants to find whether any one else was lurking about, retired again to rest, deeply thankful to the Giver of all good that her young family and herself had been preserved from the robber and probably the assassin.

About the year 1819 Judge Daniel removed to Lynchburg, his gifted wife rapidly making friends in that place, and acquiring there an influence which will long be felt in the families who enjoyed the privilege of her friendship. After organizing her household, she set out to find ways of doing good and means of benefiting the sick and indigent. Opportunities were not wanting for the exercise of her benevolent feelings, for Lynchburg was at that time the abode of some of the most wretched and destitute white families. It is not surprising that such a woman should have nursed and tended those in the same enlightened sphere in which she moved; but when we reflect that she would leave her own comfortable home, regardless of rain and storm, to visit quietly the lowliest dwellings, and there to watch by the couch of the sick and dying, this indeed excites our warmest admiration. Howard, the philanthropist, visited the prisons of Europe, greatly ameliorating the condition of their inmates, but even his most partial biographers have not been able to deny that he was but an indifferent domestic character, a tyrannical husband, and a father most culpably negligent of his only son. So that it is easy to be perceived, that the traits of great public characters do not always harmonize, in such way as to produce a character we can love and reverence in all of its bearings. But in Mrs. Daniel we behold a woman fulfilling the commands of our Saviour, doing good in the most quiet, unobtrusive way, and constantly seeking out for objects of charity, attending diligently to the ways of her household, whilst tenderly anxious and careful in rearing up her children.

Happy the children of such a parent, happy the husband of such a woman, and thrice blest were the domestics who were guided and governed by her wise, just and mild sway.

During her residence in the house now occupied by Dr. James Saunders, Mrs. Daniel met with a severe domestic affliction in the death of her daughter Margaret, a lovely child of five years old. For a time overwhelmed, she could not feel submissive or resigned, but ere the lapse of many weeks, she aroused herself from the torpor of grief, having been made sensible that its excessive indulgence was sinful, as well as unfavorable for the execution of any plan for the benefit of others; and soon she found comfort in administering to the suffering in her own neighborhood, and not unfrequently was her own grief moderated in alleviating the woes of others.

"Tread softly—bow the head,
  In reverent silence bow,
No passing bell doth toll—
  Yet an immortal soul
    Is passing now.

"Beneath that beggar's roof,
  Lo! Death doth keep his state;
Enter—no cowards attend—
Enter—no guards defend
    This palace gate."

MRS. SOUTHEY.

An indigent family lived in a small tenement by the side of Mrs. Daniel's yard and garden. The wretched wife and mother languished on a bed of sickness. Mrs. Daniel prepared her food, administered her medicines, and did all she could to enlighten the unfortunate woman on the subject of a future state. Death soon liberating the sufferer, Mrs. Daniel, with thoughtful and tender care, provided for her the snowy habiliments of the grave.

About the year 1822, Mrs. Daniel moved to the large brick building then owned by William Lynch, and since used as a temporary college. Soon becoming acquainted with the wants of her present neighborhood, she was ever ready to extend the hand of sympathy.* Having recovered, in a measure, from the death of her daughter, her health now restored, she, for several years, rejoiced in a genial atmosphere of prosperity. The death of her youngest son was another lesson of mortality, coming as a voice to remind her of the vanishing nature of earthly happiness. During the summer of 1825, her household was gladdened by a visit from a beloved sister and her family, and the generous heart of Mrs. Daniel expanded in all the

---

* The interesting invalids, William and Jane Lynch, were her peculiar care.

delights of sisterly intercourse. It was during the absence of Judge Daniel, at his circuit court in Cumberland, on the night of — October, the summons came suddenly at midnight, and the terrified young family were aroused from rest, to behold their beloved mother in the agonies of death. We would fain throw a veil over the scenes of the next few days—the grief of her children, the anguish of the husband's return to his desolate home; but, through the lapse of years, the impression of confused and hurried scenes of woe, is as vivid as is the tender and grateful remembrance of the many virtues of this noble-hearted woman:

" Tell them, it is an awful thing to die,
   ('Twas even so to thee ;) but the dread path once trod,
Heaven lifts her everlasting portals high,
   And bids the pure in heart behold their God!"

A few years after this mournful event, the mansion of Judge Daniel was thrown open for a large assemblage, unshadowed with gloom. On the night of — December, 1827, the young, the old, the grave, the gay and the beautiful, thither hasted, to witness the bridal of Eliza, the lovely and gentle girl, the pride and delight of the circle in which she moved. She had given her young heart to William Lewis Cabell, and, as they stood before the venerable Minister, one was reminded of the delicate clematis in its native grace and beauty clinging to the wild, dark forest oak. His splendid dark eyes, hair and Spanish complexion, afforded a striking contrast to her fair complexion, brown hair, and laughing blue eyes. A smooth, unclouded journey seemed to lay before them; and, to add, if possible, to the tenderness and romance of this attachment, they were to live in a cottage—the stately mansion on his beautiful estate having been leased for a term of years previous to his marriage engagement. They even rejoiced at this; for they felt that there would be less to keep them asunder, in a small, simple abode than in a large dwelling: For them,

"There was no home in halls of pride!"

For more than two years they resided in their cottage; the lease of his mansion having then expired, the building was put into a complete state of repair and newly fitted up, and the young husband and wife, leaving their simple abode, took possession of the mansion-house. But, alas! in a brief space, without any warning, a hereditary predisposition, consumption, claimed William Lewis Cabell for its victim. Medical aid was in vain; hastily they journeyed to the Red Sulphur Springs, but the waters only accelerated the disease, and, early in the summer of 1830, he there breathed his last. Eliza had always said that she could not survive her husband, and truly prophetic were her words; for, from the hour of his death, life was to her a torture;—the persons whom they had met, the scenes which together they had visited, the sound of military music that had been the signal for his appearing in the uniform in which, with girlish pride, she had so admired him,—all these were perfect agony to her, and she entreated that she might be borne away from a place where every object so forcibly reminded her of what she had lost. Her request was complied with, and she was carried to the home of her sister, in the county of Nelson, where, in a short time, the fatal spot appeared on her pale cheek, followed by a cough. Who that saw her at that time, could have recognized the blooming bride and happy wife, so lately at the summit of earthly happiness! Insidiously and rapidly did the disease advance, and, ere the grass had waved, or the wild-flowers had bloomed, over the grave of the husband, his gentle wife had joined him in the world of spirits!

"Departed this life,* on Tuesday, the 26th instant, at Union Hill, the residence of Mayo Cabell, Esq., in the county of Nelson, Mrs. ELIZA B. CABELL, relict of William Lewis Cabell, deceased, late of Lynchburg, in

---

* Since writing the above, the obituary was sent from Lynchburg by one who dearly loved the deceased, and who has preserved the notice carefully, though quite a child at the time of Mrs. W. L. Cabell's death.

the 21st year of her age. When the aged and helpless pilgrim, who, with sorrowing steps, has toiled through life's painful journey, alternately sipping the bitter cup of human misfortune, and culling the few scanty flowerets of enjoyment which are strewed along his path, full of years and full of infirmities, bids adieu to the world's fleeting scenes, and sinks down forever into the last sad receptacle of humanity, we are oppressed with sorrow, and tears of affliction fill our eyes! But our sorrow is mitigated, and our tears are dried up, by the reflection, that such is the inevitable fate of man,—such is the dreadful penalty which he owes to the violated law of his Creator. But when the young, the lovely and beautiful,—when they for whose fruition life seemed to be just unfolding its fairest prospects,—to whose enraptured gaze the spring-time of existence had hardly disclosed its verdant and enchanting beauties,—are suddenly snatched away in the midst of youth and loveliness;—then, indeed, is the cup of anguish presented, from which we recoil with horror—tears fill our eyes, which scald as they fall on our cheeks, and sorrow inexpressible burthens our hearts. The kindly sympathy of friendship is forgotten and disregarded. Time, and time alone, can soften and alleviate our affliction. Such are the feelings inspired by the death of the interesting lady whose memory is designed to be respected by this brief notice. Young, lovely and beautiful—possessed of every charm that graces her sex, and every accomplishment which renders it irresistible;—surrounded by affectionate friends and relatives—furnished with every blessing that can gild the path of life, and smooth its rugged asperities,—she seemed to be formed by Heaven, as its own especial favorite, designed for happiness—happiness here and hereafter. But unsearchable and mysterious are the ways of Providence! The tie which bound her to life, seemed to have been burst asunder by the death of her husband; and, clinging to his memory with a constancy of affection peculiar to herself, she slowly and gradually declined, until, like the tender vine torn from the staff to which it clings, she drooped and sunk to the tomb, a monument of female loveliness and conjugal affection. Such is life. The fair flower which bloomed but yesterday in matchless beauty, to-day is cut down and withered forever. The sylph-like form that lately moved among us, full of grace, full of sweetness, is now encircled in the cold, icy embrace of death! What a commentary on the vanity of all human happiness! How faithfully does it prove the slender tenure by which all earthly enjoyments are held, and speak to us in tones which we cannot disregard, the solemn warning—that, 'In the midst of life, we are in death!'"

THE IRVINE FAMILY.

"A lighted lamp is a very small thing, and it burns calmly and without noise; yet it giveth light to all who are within the house: And so there is a quiet influence, which, like the flame of a scented lamp, fills many a home with light and fragrance."
M'CHEYNE.

CHARLES IRVINE was a native of Ireland, and a member of one of the first families of the Emerald Isle. Emigrating to America, he became the husband of Anne Rose, a daughter of Hugh Rose, Esq., of Amherst. Mr. Irvine was a liberal, high-minded, gentlemanly man, hospitable in the extreme, and fond of cultivating all those arts which embellish life, particularly music, which was necessary to his enjoyment; so that he spared no pains or expense, in giving to his daughters every advantage calculated to perfect them in that science.

MARY IRVINE, the eldest daughter, was a very beautiful and accomplished woman, and for several years she held the pre-eminence over all her contemporaries in the circle in which she moved; and it was said that more than one duel had been fought by rival competitors for her hand. During her girlhood, she was the occasion of an accident which well-nigh resulted in a very tragic manner. Her father was rubbing and polishing some old pistols, which for a long time had laid in his desk. Calling to his daughters, who were standing by, to take them in their hands, he said to them: "With the exception of Mary, I have not a daughter with the least courage or bravery!" Whereupon, Mary seized one of the pistols, laughingly pointing it at her mother, then at Matilda, her sister, when, to the horror of all present, the pistol went off, and Matilda fell to the ground apparently dead. Rushing out of the house, Mary went, she knew not whither, and she had no recollection of anything, till she found herself in the house of a friend on Main street, with the family around her endeavoring to find out the cause of her agonized grief. By almost a miracle, Matilda's life was preserved, by means of a surgical operation. There had been, previous to this accident, a very peculiar attachment subsisting between these two sisters; but after this time the cord seemed strengthened, and, on the part of Mary, this sisterly affection became almost idolatry.

Mary Irvine, in 1814, became the wife of Samuel Anthony, Esq., and her fine traits expanded, adorning the state of wife and mother. Her lot was smooth and unclouded, till the year 1819, when the pecuniary pressure occasioned to them a reverse as great as that experienced by many others in Lynchburg. It was then that her sterling qualities shone conspicuously, whilst her mental resources still further developed themselves. Thus may it not be considered that trials are frequently our best friends; and that they are one of the phases of our mortal existence, designed for our good, by the Author of our salvation, who "was made perfect through suffering"—and frequently do the dark clouds of adversity disperse, leaving behind a rich increase of such dispositions as are "pure, lovely, and of good report." The spirit of Mrs. Mary Anthony rose gently and serenely from the depressing influence of adversity, and for a time she willingly threw aside all those accomplishments with which she had so embellished life; and, retiring to the country with her husband, they took possession of a small cottage, which, with her taste, she adorned, till, from a wilderness, soon arose a cultivated garden, with flowers, vineyards and orchard—her simple dwelling being the abode of the most kindly hospitality. In all the situations of life, this excellent woman faithfully performed her duties; so that, as of Mary of old, she merited the commendation of our Saviour, "She hath done what she could!" And when, in 1820, the first English edition was published of Washington Irving's Sketch Book, all who read his exquisite sketch of "The Wife," were struck with the remarkable resemblance of that lovely woman to Mrs. Mary Anthony.

About the year 1832, Mrs. Anthony removed again to her native place, where she continued to reside till the time of her death. She was a devoted member of the Episcopal Church for some years, having connected herself with it during the time when that church was under the pastoral care of the Rev. F. G. Smith. She died in the summer of 1839, leaving the most satisfactory evidence that she was fully prepared to meet the Judge of all, and rejoicing in the hope of re-union with a beloved daughter who had died the year previous.

Ann Eliza Irvine will long be remembered in Lynchburg. Her perfect beauty and early death, invest her with a tender and mournful interest, which is increased from associating her with the bright gifted spirit to whom she was united a year previous to her death. No portrait of her has been preserved; but a fancy picture of a French girl, much resembling her, is highly valued by the surviving members of the family. Shortly after the death of Ann Eliza, Mrs. Irvine went into the parlor of the late Mrs. Daniel, where hung this picture, and she was so much affected at the resemblance, that Mrs. Daniel immediately had it taken down and carried to the house of Mrs. Irvine.

JOHN HAMPDEN PLEASANTS was the eldest son of James Pleasants, Esq., of Goochland county. The brilliant mind and great genius of this distinguished man, is now the admiration of his native State; and well may Virginians feel a pride in claiming for their own John Hampden Pleasants. As early as 18— he moved to Lynchburg, establishing there a paper called "The Press." When he commenced his editorial career, the Press of Lynchburg was at a low ebb—the type, paper and printing were intolerable, and the articles dull. Hampden Pleasants produced a great revolution in this printing establishment; and, even at that early date, he gave promise of that brilliant editorial career, which, in after years, awaited him. He was a first cousin of Ann Eliza Irvine, on the mother's side; and their intercourse ripening into a devoted attachment, about the year 1819 or '20 they were married. She survived her marriage only one year, her death occurring so suddenly, as to cause her friends for some hours to suppose that she had only fainted. This mournful event threw a gloom over the whole town; and, even now, the old inhabitants lower their voices and drop a tear when they speak of Ann Eliza Pleasants.

MRS. FRANCES PATTERSON, wife of Dr. John

Patterson, was the youngest daughter of Mrs. Ann Irvine. She was a pious, lovely woman. Dying many years since, she left two children, William M. Patterson, Esq., and Mrs. Ann Eliza Boggs, wife of the Rev. F. J. Boggs, of the Methodist Church.

Rev. SAMUEL IRVINE, of the Methodist Church, is a son of Mrs. A. Irvine. This worthy man is an acceptable Minister of the Gospel, highly esteemed in the community, and beloved in the church to which he belongs.

The house at present occupied by Rev. Bishop Early, was, in 1821, the residence of MARCELLUS SMITH, Esq. He was the associate editor with John H. Pleasants of the only paper at that time published in Lynchburg. Of brilliant talents, and refined, cultivated mind, Mr. Smith was worthy to have been joined with that gifted son of Virginia in wielding the mighty engine of social and political life.

Some years previous, Mr. Marcellus Smith had married MARCELLA, the sister of John Hampden Pleasants. She was a lady of fine talents, possessing all those kindly virtues and excellent qualities, for which the family of Pleasants is so remarkable. This excellent and beloved lady survives her husband, making her home with her daughter in the county of Louisa.

"Slight withal may be the things which bring back on the heart," not always, "the woes which it would fling aside forever," but many pleasing and amusing incidents of by-gone days.

Portions of two old newspapers lie on the table; and what a record of the past do they contain! One was printed about thirty-three years since, and, amongst other articles, it contains Chancellor Taylor's high-bred advertisement of his law-school, forcibly bringing before us his old-fashioned manner and polished address; whilst one, printed twenty-seven years since, contains the obituary of one of the loveliest women of Lynchburg; and close by that sad memorial, an advertisement of Claborne Gladman's* house—that yellow edifice, which stood in rear of the old Methodist Church, and which, for some purpose, was afterwards moved on rollers, with unheard-of difficulty, up the hill leading to the residence of Henry Dunnington, Esq.; and, when placed half-way between that house and the dwelling of Mrs. Irvine, the workmen employed, rested from their labors, leaving the house there for several weeks,† to the intense

---

* A well-known free colored man.

† What would our worthy town-authorities of the present day, say in reference to a house placed in the middle of a street, and there left for several weeks? A few years since, an

gratification and delight of the small boys of Lynchburg, who used the building as a play-place, which only wanted a bell at the door to place it on a perfect equality with the "untenanted house" mentioned in " Dickens' Sketches," where "ringing the door-bell was such a resource to the boys of the neighborhood, notwithstanding the numerous wash-hand basins of water thrown from the next house upon the youthful offenders, till the bell was taken off by a humane broker, and placed for sale in his own old establishment."

The paper and type of this ancient newspaper are greatly inferior to that of the present day; but "The Virginian" then, as well as at present, ranked amongst the very highest and best papers in the State. The spirits of Pleasants and of Toler seem yet mysteriously to linger around it; and we are now reminded of the interesting period when that paper was under the able auspices of "Fletcher & Toler."

ELIJAH FLETCHER Esq., was a native of one of the New England States, and, on the father's side, was a near relative of " Grace Fletcher," the first wife of Daniel Webster. Mr. Fletcher

---

old hack was driven up somewhere on Church street, where it remained for some time, eliciting numerous amusing editorial remarks, which greatly entertained the readers of "The Virginian."

emigrated, when a young man, to Virginia, and settled near New Glasgow, Amherst county, where he married Miss Marie Antoinette Crawford, a lady of great intelligence, and a relative of Crawford, whom a few years subsequent was a candidate for the Presidency of the United States. For a time, Mr. Fletcher was Principal of the Female Seminary of New Glasgow; but, on removing to Lynchburg, he took the charge of "The Virginian," assisted by Richard H. Toler. Mr. Fletcher devoted a considerable part of the columns of that paper to articles on agriculture, of which pursuit he was enthusiastically fond. Having amassed a large fortune, this gentleman retired to one of his estates in the county of Amherst, where his farming arrangements and domestic management are said to be the most superior in the State of Virginia.

RICHARD H. TOLER was a native of Richmond. His mother was early left a widow, in straitened circumstances, so that her son had nought to depend on, save his own exertions. He, for a while, lived in the office of one of the newspapers printed in Richmond; but, on removing to Lynchburg, he was found to possess such talents and energy that he speedily rose in his profession of an editor, being second only to his great predecessor, John Hampden Pleasants. Greatly prized and beloved in Lynchburg, the memory of Mr. Toler is one of the brightest recollections of the past; nor is the interest lessened when we think of him in connection with Frances Duval, his devoted and excellent wife, who survived her marriage only a few years. She was second daughter of the good Major William Duval,* of Buckingham, inheriting from her honored parent all those lovely dispositions for which he was so remarkable. Mr. Toler was thrice married; his last wife survives him, and is, we believe, a resident of Lynchburg.

---

* This most excellent man was a perfect exemplification of the Christian character, and he deserves a long memoir, so that the influence of his bright example may still be felt by the rising generation. He was at one time an eminent lawyer of the lower country; and it was during this time that Henry Clay lived in his office. When Mr. Clay visited Lynchburg many years since, he made an especial visit to Buckingham, to pass a few days with the friend and patron of his young days, Major William Duval.

THE HARRISON FAMILY.

"She had a wise, kind word for all. All loved her. All felt that her message was not from herself, nor of man's invention, but that in her Master's name, she invited others to "love and good works."

BIOGRAPHY OF MRS. FRY, *by her Daughter.*

SAMUEL HARRISON was a native of Bedford county, and was, like the late Christopher Anthony, reared in theu sages of the Society of Friends. His mother's maiden name was Jordan, and she was one of that old Virginia family from whom so many of our best citizens trace their descent. She was a sister of the venerable mother* of the late Christopher Anthony, and for many years the families resided happily in the good old neighborhood of Goose Creek, Bedford county. Whilst a young man, Mr. Harrison removing to Lynchburg, soon

---

* This excellent lady survived her son some years, dying in Cincinnati about the summer of 1839; to which place she had, with her husband, emigrated about 1812.

after was united in marriage to Sarah Burton, a young lady of fine disposition, and gifted in a great degree with strength of mind and energy of character. Mr. Harrison possessed a fine order of intellect, united to great sprightliness of mind, so that at all times he was the witty, cheerful and agreeable companion. By his energy and industry he accumulated a fortune, and during the time of his prosperity, he planned and built the Franklin Hotel * of Lynchburg, which, with all the alterations since made, has never been so prosperous, desirable or convenient, as it was in its early days.

The great pressure of 1819 caused Mr. Harrison, like many others in Lynchburg, to experience a reverse of fortune; but submitting cheerfully to circumstances, he was still able, by means of the vigor and industry of his character, to make ample provision for the comfort and education of a large family. He passed through a long life, surviving some years his estimable wife, and blessed in the respect and affection of his devoted children.

Several years previous to his death, he made a public profession of religion, connecting himself with the Episcopal Church. This touching and interesting occasion was rendered still more so, from

---

* Called the "Norvell House" at present.

the circumstance of two of his daughters standing as sponsors for their venerable parent at the baptismal font. During the remainder of his life, he was a meek, consistent Christian, deriving much peace and comfort from the services of the sanctuary.

Mrs. SARAH HARRISON was a lady of great worth and piety. She governed well and wisely at her beautiful home,* her establishment being a perfect model of elegant management and domestic economy.

A zealous and devoted member of the Methodist Church, she was one of that chosen band of females that so materially aided and strengthened the influences of the pastors of that denomination.

Like the good Sir Thomas Fowell Buxton, Mrs. Harrison may be said to have resembled in her walk through life, "one passing through the wards of a hospital, and stooping down on all sides to administer help where it was needed."

A true sister of charity, constant in her visits to the sick and afflicted, a diligent member of the Dorcas Society, Mrs. Harrison thus passed through life, scattering good, and although from the depths of her heart she would say, in the language of the Psalmist, "Oh, my God, *my* goodness extendeth not to *Thee,* but to the *saints* and to the excellent

---

* This home was the house now occupied by Anderson Armistead, Esq.

in whom is my delight;" it was in doing good to others that she in her life thus glorified God, and on her death-bed bearing fullest testimony to the sustaining grace of her Saviour, saying, in his own sacred words, that "her heart was neither troubled nor afraid."

The five daughters of this family all survive, an unbroken sisterhood—Mrs. William Norvell, Mrs. Robert Robinson of Philadelphia, Mrs. Lorenzo Norvell of Lynchburg, Mrs. James Metcalfe of its vicinity, and Miss Mary E. Harrison of Bedford. All of these ladies are well known and esteemed in our community, as well for their superior wit and intelligence as for their admirable traits of character.

JESSE BURTON HARRISON, second son of Samuel Harrison, Esq. was born about the year 1806. His boyhood was passed in his native place, where, in all of his school exercises, he greatly distinguished himself, and during this time the progress he made in his studies was such as to excite the wonder and admiration of his instructors.

To an extraordinary memory and great quickness, he united remarkable perseverance and habits of application, together with a fondness for every branch of literature. Passing with distinction through Hampden Sidney College, he was then sent to Harvard University, where his proficiency was so great in all the branches he undertook, as to cause him to graduate there with high honors, eliciting marks of approbation from all the professors of Harvard, as well as from Thomas Jefferson, a visitor of that institution, who expressed his high appreciation of the young student in a most gratifying and complimentary letter to his father, Samuel Harrison, Esq.

On leaving Cambridge, he studied for the bar, and, soon after obtaining a license, he established himself in his native place as a practising lawyer; and though the bar was ably supplied by many so much older than himself, the success of J. Burton Harrison was much greater than usually attends the young barrister under these circumstances.

A few years subsequent to this time, he determined to make the tour of Europe, and to visit in particular the celebrated German Universities—perhaps with some reference to there obtaining a professorship, or of embarking in some literary enterprise. In the month of ——, he accordingly set sail for the French capital, and, on arriving, he was kindly received by Virginians, resident in the city of Paris, and with them he enjoyed the privilege of visiting the Marquis La Fayette and other distinguished Frenchmen of that time. His letters, written at this period to his friends at home, possessed great interest, and were worthy of publication. He traveled through Germany, and had access to all the distinguished literary institutions, forming the acquaintance of many erudite German professors, the learning of whom he confessed astonished him: for he wrote that it was astonishing to see so many great men, whose names and reputation extended not beyond the walls of their Universities. For some cause or other, he, at this time, abandoned forever any wish or desire to occupy a post in a University, and, shortly afterwards, he returned to his native land, his mind much enlightened by his travels, and his manners having acquired all the ease, elegance and polish of the French nation.

It is much to be regretted that Mr. Harrison did not at least write a description of his tour through Germany. Had he done so, his book might probably have rivalled and excelled the popular work of William Howitt, "The Student Life of Germany,"* and a flood of light and interest might have been thrown around the literature of that country, entirely divesting it of all darkness, obscurity and mysticism, with which Thomas Carlyle has surrounded it. But, though fully capable of writing eloquently, Mr. Harrison, with the exception of his speeches, has left no published writings to

---

* This work was written by a German for William Howitt, and by him it was translated into English, and we believe that Mr. Harrison could have himself written on this subject an able book.

attest his superior intellect and high literary attainments. It is a saying of Thucydides, that "ignorance is bold and knowledge reserved;" and the fact that Jesse Burton Harrison has left behind him no literary work, goes far to prove that this ancient writer was correct in his opinion.

In the year 1832, leaving his native State, he settled in the city of New Orleans, where, in a few years, he was married to a lady residing in that city. His health becoming much impaired, he, in the summer of 1840, returned to Lynchburg, and thence with his father visiting the watering places of Virginia. In the autumn he returned to Louisiana, and he was destined never more to gaze on his beloved native hills, nor feel invigorated by the pure life-giving winds that had gladdened him in boyhood. During the winter of the succeeding year, he breathed his last in New Orleans, and his remains repose in the cemetery near the city. In the hearts of those who knew and esteemed him, his memory is deeply enshrined, and we cherish a pride in claiming for our own beloved native place, Jesse Burton Harrison.

Extract from the Address of JAMES P. HOLCOMBE, *Esq., before the Society of the Alumni of the University of Virginia.*

"No nation can retain its character in the scale of history, without a distinct and original literature. The literature which would express the spirit or supply the wants of a people, must not be filtered through the strata of a foreign society, but drawn fresh from the wells of a native soil. Noble sentiments, beautiful imagery, profound thoughts, lives of heroism or beauty, speak to us from what region or in what tone they may, must always inform, delight and elevate the soul. But when embodied in a foreign language, and tinctured with the colors of a social and political atmosphere remote from our own, they do not possess the power that belongs to a literature which can thrill the heart with the echoes of its mother's tongue. I fully subscribe to the remark made by one of Virginia's most gifted sons, whose taste, learning and genius would have placed him, but for an untimely death, by the side of Legare,* that the practical loss to mankind, if arithmetic was reduced to counting on the fingers, would be less than if the department of fancy was blotted out of our libraries; for practical, to all intents and purposes, must that knowledge be, which raises or keeps alive any feeling touched to fine issues. Yes, far beyond the horizon of a sense-bound existence, in the sacred regions of poetry and philosophy, lie those eternal springs which alone can keep fresh and warm the inner life of a people. A literature which draws its aliment from the materials that surround their daily walk—which embellishes with its forms of grace—and images of beauty their world

---

* The late J. Burton Harrison. It is peculiarly appropriate that this beautiful extract should form the connecting link between the brief memoir of J. B. Harrison, and the Cyclopædia of Lynchburg Literature.

of home which takes up the gross body of popular sentiment and opinion, and, by the transfiguring power of genius, converts its muddy vesture of decay into a luminous mantle of immortality;—such a literature must be fruitful of results upon the character and destiny of a people. It cannot but infuse into their bosoms such a sense of the dignity of human nature, and the true ends of human life, as will either work its way through all difficulties to freedom and civilization, or invest the adverse fortunes of the nation with a glory, which, like the beauty of Juliet, shall make the grave itself " a feasting presence bright with light."

CYCLOPÆDIA OF LYNCHBURG LITERATURE.

"There has been no question so often asked, and so variously answered, of late years, as this: 'Shall the South have a literature of her own?' It is one of vital importance to her social and political interests—a question on which hangs the integrity of her peculiar institutions, and on which is based the preservation of her social and political independence."—*Southern Literary Messenger.*

In this chapter will be given a brief sketch of some of the literary characters of Lynchburg, a few of whom have been eminent for literary progress and mental cultivation; and it is but due that the brothers, HARVEY and STEPHEN MITCHELL, should have the first place, not only as pioneers, but as gentlemen of fine talents and literary taste.

HARVEY MITCHELL, well known and beloved in our community, spent his boyhood and early youth in the town of Lynchburg. His parents resided in the county of Amherst, at a beautiful place, visible from almost every point of Lynchburg; and their vicinity to town enabled the children of the family to attend daily the schools of Lynchburg. When a small boy, Harvey Mitchell manifested a great talent for drawing, painting and taking likenesses; and with this was combined, a genius highly poetic—his knowledge of drawing enabling him to view with a poet's eye the whole page of Nature. He practised his profession of portrait painter, in the town of Lynchburg, for some years, writing manuscript pieces for his friends, as well as articles for periodicals. Endowed with wit, and with a spirit and genius akin to that of Sidney Smith, there is no doubt but that Harvey Mitchell was even superior to that gentleman, who has of late years acquired such celebrity in the world of letters. His sketches were illustrated by his own humorous drawings, and his writings were somewhat in the style of those of Port Crayon, who has contributed in the last two years so agreeably to Harper's Magazine; and had Mr. Mitchell's articles been published also in the North, they would have attracted more notice and would have obtained greater success. Mr. Mitchell also wrote dramas, depicting admirably the foibles of the community in which he lived. In conjunction with Stephen Mitchell, his younger brother, he attempted to publish a periodical, but the undertaking failed for want of sufficient encouragement. Mr. Harvey Mitchell resides, at present, in the city of Washington, where he holds an office under Government.

Stephen Mitchell was a young lawyer of great promise, and of fine literary taste. About twenty-eight years since he made ineffectual efforts to resuscitate the literature of his native State, by publishing a periodical, but meeting with so many discouragements, he was forced to abandon the enterprise. He wrote a play, called "The Maid of Missilonghi," which was, without doubt, a splendid literary production. He carried it to New York, where the managers of the Bowery theatre were so delighted with it, that they offered a very liberal sum for it, which was to be paid immediately after its reception on the stage. Accordingly, splendid scenery and magnificent dresses were provided for the occasion, and the young author already saw plainly before him the path to fame. But, alas! for the uncertainty of human affairs! The very day before the one fixed for the performance, the Bowery theatre taking fire, the scenery and dresses were consumed, and, worse than all, the manuscript of "The Maid of Missilonghi" was burned; and, as no copy had been preserved, the reading public were thus debarred the pleasure of perusing this beautiful production. Under these favorable auspices, had this play been brought out, it would probably have held a rank almost equal to Bulwer's "Lady of Lyons." Shortly after this disastrous overthrow of all his hopes, Stephen Mitchell, returning to Virginia, made Norfolk his temporary home, and, his health declining rapidly, in a brief period he was numbered with the dead.

GEORGE TUCKER, Esq., was a native of the Island of Bermuda, from which place he had emigrated when a very young man. He removed with his family to Lynchburg, about the year 1817, and resided in that town till the opening of the University of Virginia. Being appointed Professor of Moral Philosophy in that institution, he, for some years, filled that post with great ability. During his residence in Lynchburg, he wrote a touching little memoir, called "Recollections of Rosalie," a beloved daughter, who died in the winter of 1818. The work has been printed and published at his own expense, by a man named Boyce, and the binding would do credit to any publishing house of the present day—so neatly and substantially done, that, after a lapse of thirty-eight years, the little volume looks fresh and new. It was during his residence in Lynchburg that Mr. Tucker also wrote "The Valley of Shenandoah." The descriptions, in that novel, of Virginia life, are unsurpassed, and the pictures of slavery in the the Old Dominion are quite inimitable. Since then he has written "The Voyage to the Moon," and "The Life of Jefferson," a voluminous work, which has placed his reputation as a writer on a firm basis in the literary world. This polished and intelligent gentleman now lives in the city of Philadelphia, where he is said to be at present employed on a new work, the appearance of which will be anxiously desired by his friends and admirers.

Mrs. ANN URSULA BYRD was a sister of the late Mr. William Munford, for many years the able and efficient Clerk of the House of Delegates. She was the wife of William Otway Byrd, Esq., of Westover; and subsequently to his death, she took up her residence in the town of Lynchburg, making her home with two married daughters living in that town. Mrs. Bryd was a most excellent woman, with a vigorous mind and poetic fancy. Delighting greatly in reading, her memory was so remarkable that she was able to recall at will the pleasure derived long since from books she had perused. For many years she was engaged in writing a novel, and hopes, at one time, were entertained of its publication; but, for some cause or other, it has never appeared in print. The work was styled "Education, or the Family of Mountflorence;" and it was pronounced exceedingly interesting by those who had the privilege of its perusal. A few years previous to her death, this lady had a violent spell of illness, causing her for a time to lose her memory almost entirely, so that she could only remember a few choice pieces of old English poetry. On regaining her health to a degree, and discovering that she had forgotten how to read, with a strength of mind and perseverance worthy of being imitated, she immediately commenced at the simple rudiments, and actually learned again to spell and read. She was a devout Episcopalian, and was one amongst the few belonging to that church at the time of its establishment in Lynchburg. This amiable woman lived to an advanced age, and died in the city of Lynchburg, where her remains are interred.

BRANSFORD VAWTER was a native of Lynchburg, and was born about the year 1815 or '16. His father was, by profession, a tailor, and he had been one of the oldest and earliest settlers of the place. Mr. Vawter was a man of some eccentricities, but he possessed good sense, combined with great honesty and a most kindly disposition. He was particularly attached to Bransford,* his second

---

* Mr. Vawter was justly proud of this son, whom he always addressed as "Buddy," bestowing on his oldest boy the soubriquet of "Jake." When under the influence of ardent spirits, Mr. Vawter would seat himself in his upper window, carelessly attired, singing out the following recitative: "The world is good, the people are good, and God bless 'Buddy' forever"—adding then, in a sort of undertone,—"and, at the same time, *please don't* forget Jake!"

son, but he gave each of the brothers every advantage of education that could be procured in Lynchburg. At a very early age Bransford was remarkable for his elegant personal appearance and graceful manners; and, as he grew up, his mental gifts so developed themselves, that he was found to possess talents of a superior order. A high-minded, chivalrous young man—honorable in his feelings and distinguished by his winning modesty—Bransford Vawter will ever be remembered with interest and affection by friends and school-mates with whom he was associated in Lynchburg; and had he lived, he would doubtless have ranked high among the poets of his native land. His early death was a great disappointment to his numerous friends in Lynchburg;—the light of a brilliant genius was suddenly quenched, and only a few of his pieces have been preserved to attest his poetic talent. The following song has been set to music, and is sung throughout the United States, whilst few are aware of their authorship, or of the feelings which prompted the lines:

> "I'd offer thee this hand of mine,
>   If I could love thee less,
> But hearts so warm, so fond as thine,
>   Should never know distress.
> My fortune is too hard for thee,
>   'Twould chill thy dearest joy;
> I'd rather weep to see thee free,
>   Than win thee to destroy.

> I leave thee in thy happiness,
>   As one too dear to love—
> As one I think of but to bless,
>   As wretchedly I rove.
> And Oh! when sorrow's cup I drink,
>   All bitter though it be,
> How sweet 'twill be for me to think,
>   It holds no drop for thee.
>
> And now my dreams are sadly o'er,
>   Fate bids them all depart,
> And I must leave my native shore,
>   In brokenness of heart.
> And Oh, dear one! when far from thee,
>   I ne'er know joy again,
> I would not that one thought of me,
>   Should give thy bosom pain."

After the appearance of these lines, a great curiosity was felt to know the name of the author; and, accordingly, an advertisement was inserted in a periodical, desiring him to avow himself, for it was the intention of the proprietors to award him a prize. Bransford Vawter then acknowledged himself to have been the author, and an expensive volume was immediately forwarded to him by the proprietors of the Magazine.

Mrs. MARGARET CABELL BELL, wife of Lieutenant Bell, U. S. N., at present a resident of Newburgh, New-York, was a former resident of Lynchburg. She is the daughter of the late Major Richard Pollard, Chargé-des-Affaires to Chili, and a grand-daughter of the late Robert Rives, Esq., of

Oakridge, Nelson county, Virginia; at which place she was born. This lady possesses a very superior mind and fine talents. Some years since she contributed largely to the Literary Messenger, as well as to several periodicals published in the North. One of her poetical effusions, which, some years since, appeared in the Messenger, attracted, at the time, much notice and commendation, and is still remembered with much pleasure by those who have read it. The piece was called, "Lines on seeing a sprig of laurel from my birth-place"—and, about the time of its appearance, she wrote for the same periodical a novellette, entitled "The Vicissitudes of Life:" it possessed great interest, and was written in a most finished style. This accomplished lady has written many other interesting articles; but, of late, we believe, she has not published any of her writings.

A few years since, Mrs. MARTHA HARRISON ROBINSON, a sister of the late Jesse B. Harrison, translated, from the French, a celebrated work, for which, from the reviews, she received the highest commendation. It was said that the sense of the original was perfectly preserved, and the style unimpaired by the translation, so as for the work to be fully appreciated by the American reader. Works of this sort generally suffer much from their translation; and, it is said that, whilst in this country, the son of Marquis de la Fayette was heard to say, that "Corinne" (Madame de Staël's celebrated work) had been so marred by the English translation, that no one could have a proper perception of its beauties, unless it was read in the French language. The same remarks are also frequently made respecting the beautiful little book called "Picciola."

Mrs. CORNELIA M. JORDAN is a native and resident of Lynchburg, and is on the mother's side a near relative of the Goggin family of Bedford county. Mrs. Jordan is a lady of decided poetic talent, and amongst her pieces, the lines on "Confirmation" deserve a higher place than the corner of a newspaper. Of late she seems to have confined herself to literature for very young children, and we hope that she will persevere in that department, till she makes herself as useful as Mrs. Trimmer or Mrs. Barbauld.

The talented and excellent Mrs. WOODSON* laid our children under great obligations by the publication of "The Southern Home"—and her untimely death is deplored by the rising generation as a real misfortune. It is highly desirable that we should have a juvenile literature of our own: such books as "Queechy" and "Wide, Wide

---

* Of Charlottesville.

World" are not adapted to Southern children; and, until they can procure better books than "My Brother's Keeper," it is high time for the South to arise and furnish literature for the young, which can afford amusement and instruction.

Dr. VALENTINE, the celebrated ventriloquist and entertaining delineator of eccentric characters, was, in the year 1829, a resident of Lynchburg, being employed in the druggist establishment of the late Dr. Howell Davies; and doubtless he was at that very time, like "Count Smorltolk" (Mr. Pickwick's great traveller), laying up materials in his brain for the very amusing book published by him a few years since. Even at that early period Dr. Valentine showed strong talents for the line of life he has since chosen. He was somewhat an *improvisatore*, and performed in private for the amusement of his friends and acquaintances. He was a man of gentlemanly appearance, of good family, well-educated, and a native of one of the Northern States. He made a wise choice in selecting for his profession that of a ventriloquist and delineator of eccentric character. It is much better to take at once to the stage, than to be an amateur-professor of these arts.

[Since the above was penned, an advertisement in the Virginian tells us that Dr. Valentine has recently visited Lynchburg, delighting the good people of the place by his exquisitely humorous exhibitions.]

PUBLIC AMUSEMENTS OF LYNCHBURG.

" 'Tis sweet to view from half-past five to six,
Our long wax-candles, with short cotton-wicks,
Touch'd by the lamp-lighter's Promethean art,
Start into life, and make the lighter start:
To see red Phœbus through the gallery pane,
Tinge with its beams the beams of Drury Lane,
While gradual parties fill our widen'd pit,
And gape and stare and wonder as they sit."
HORACE SMITH'S imitation of Rev. G. Crabbe.

" You've only got to curtesy, whisper, hold your chin up, laugh and lisp,
And then you're sure to take:
I've known the day, when brats not quite
Thirteen, got fifty pounds a-night,
Then why not Nancy Lake?
HORACE SMITH'S imitation of Wordsworth.

The site of the reservoir was a public lot, called "Black's Lot"—and it was there, in 1819, that the Circus companies reared their pavilions, and there nightly did the ring-master and clown delight an admiring audience,—the frequent repetition of their wit and repartee having not the smallest effect to diminish the rapture with which all their sallies were received by the throng which constantly attended their exhibitions. In those days, it was said that equestrian companies came earlier and staid later in the season in Lynchburg, than at any other town of its size in the Union.

Some few years later, the Circus was held on the lot on which now stands the house erected by Captain Jesse Perry; and, for a season, Clown Lewis, Messrs. Hunt and Foster, Master Lipman and Birdsall were the admiration of the town. On one occasion, during their performance, a violent thunder-storm raged, so as to put an end for the night to the exhibition, and the audience had to take shelter in the ring with the performers. On a near approach, how much of their grandeur disappeared, and how paltry looked then their spangles and decorations; and what a great disappointment ensued, on finding the grotesque expression of the clown's face was altogether owing to paint and burned cork.

A few years after this, an equestrian company was established on the vacant lot belonging to Dr. JOHN CABELL, and just above his residence. They were enjoying a brisk popularity; and one night, the audience being particularly brilliant, the performers were so elated that some of them began to play off practical jokes upon those upon whom they thought they might venture with impunity. Dr. John Cabell had come in quietly and taken his seat in a retired part of the pavilion. Having been engaged that day in practice, and feeling much fatigued, Dr. Cabell soon fell asleep. The clown, entirely ignorant of the rank of this distinguished gentleman, walked, or ran up to him in a very comic manner, saying, "Wake up, old gentleman, I say—presently you'll be going home, saying you did not see any of the performance!" But the wrong passenger had certainly been waked up this time. Dr. Cabell, jumping up from his slumbers, seized the astonished and terrified clown, crying out "'Blood and thunder'—pack up and be off from here before day to-morrow!" The performance was stopped, the audience retired, and the grand trampaline, hastily assembling, came into council. It was decided that the most imposing of their number should go immediately, offer an apology, and petition for a little delay in their sentence of departure. After a brief interview this permission was granted, and their bills for the next night's performance were posted up in the morning, exhibiting a more tempting programme than had ever before been presented to the good folks of Lynchburg; and these performers were in future very studious to avoid anything approaching to a practical joke.

It was from Black's lot that Messrs. DUNNIHEW & CHARLES for a series of months sent up their balloons, which, though they were not as now, made of silk and inflated with gas, still they were really pretty exhibitions, delighting a Lynchburg audience; and their failures produced as great excitement amongst this primitive people, as did their success. A lad by the name of Ogilbie, reared in Lynchburg, was so much allured by their mode of life, that, leaving his profession, he appeared before his former acquaintances at the gate or entrance of the lot, to dispose of tickets of admission; and so much were his former associates dazzled at his appearance in all the grandeur of pink cambric, black cotton-velvet and spangles, that for some time he was not recognised.

These balloons were inflated by means of burning brown paper dipped in spirits-of-turpentine, placed in a small wire car. On one occasion, two balloons were sent up—Adams and Crawford; but, on cutting the cords, by reason of some failure, the balloons refused to ascend. Adams went a short distance, landing to the delight and ecstacy of Lynchburg, in the well-lot belonging to Mr. C. Anthony, whilst Crawford rolled pensively over the heads of the alarmed audience, occasionally dropping amongst them coals of fire and burning paper from its conflagration—brothers and sisters, parents and children, husbands and wives* being parted in

---

* A bride and bridegroom attended this exhibition, and the tragico-comico distress of the husband and piercing cries for his bride, were amusing at the time.

the confusion. Sometimes these exhibitions were very successful and went off with great eclat, but to the major part who attended, the conflagration of balloons was considered as a sort of impromptu fire-works. A splendid ascension was made on one evening, the balloon soaring gracefully away and taking a direction towards Amherst Courthouse. Descending to the earth a few miles this side of that place, it greatly alarmed the inhabitants of the plantation, particularly an old lady, who, fancying that the day of judgment had arrived, mistook the balloon for the angel Gabriel in a chariot of fire.

A short distance above the reservoir, was a long low brick building, which was then used as a place for theatrical performances,* and, though small, it was well adapted to the purpose, having side-boxes and a pit: the scenery, too, was good, and the amateur orchestra, playing for the Thespian Society, was very superior.

Though the writer has since that time seen Hackett, Burton, and other celebrated comedians, yet, putting aside all partiality for residents of

---

* A wooden tenement, opposite the Norvell-House, was first used as a theatre by Thespians—the tickets were presented to friends, and no charge was made; the performance, too, was very good. This house was afterwards "Dandrige's Carriage Manufactory."

Lynchburg, she has seen no performer who had so good a perception of our English comedy, as the late Hardin Murrell. The late Mr. Giles Word and William Digges also had considerable dramatic talents, and the plays of Colman, Cumberland, Sheridan, Foote and Mrs. Inchbald, were well performed by this Thespian Society.

GEORGE P. RICHARDSON, Esq., a resident of Lynchburg, was thought to have a very decided talent for the drama. He often appeared in the company of Thespians, sustaining his parts with ability, and eliciting warm applause from the audiences of Lynchburg. A reverse of fortune occuring, he was induced to resort to the stage as a means of support. He accordingly became manager of the Richmond Theatre, and though his career was a brilliant one, yet it resulted to him in no pecuniary benefit. Soon afterwards he embarked for England, and appearing on the boards of Druly Lane Theatre, he there met with a severe disappointment. His performance was not appreciated, and in a brief time he returned to his native country.* The first strolling players who appeared in Lynchburg were "Brown's Company," who visited the town in 1821. In this company were

---

* It is not remembered whether he took to the stage on his return.

some superior performers. Placide at that time was a young and handsome man, possessing fine manners and a beautiful countenance. Many romantic stories were told of this young actor, and it was said that whilst in Lynchburg he formed a devoted attachment. * * * * * In after years Placide was a distinguished performer in the Northern theatres, doubtless having gained a proper appreciation of himself, and obtaining sufficient confidence in his powers during his performance in Lynchburg.

A few years after, Herbert's Company made a considerable sensation in Lynchburg; but the last strolling company performing in this old theatre was "Cargill's Company," which appeared in Lynchburg during the year 1823, and remained* there

---

* This Company came to Lynchburg in considerable style, being conveyed in carriages and buggies, and their wardrobe, &c., being brought in baggage-wagons. But after remaining there twelve months, they prepared to leave the town by going in batteau boats down the river. An inhabitant of the place enquired of Beverly Snow, a well known free colored man, what mode of conveyance the Company designed taking. Whereupon this well known individual, with his customary deferential manner, replied: "I believe, sir, that the play-actors have concluded to glide smoothly down the stream," which was certainly one of the greatest euphemisms, under the circumstances, ever uttered in Lynchburg. Beverly Snow was a highly respected free colored man, and, with his worthy wife, Judith Snow, kept an oyster-house at the corner house afterwards occupied by Col-

nearly twelve months. These performers were really good, not at all resembling the celebrated one of Mr. Crummles in Nicholas Nickleby, nor was it necessary for them to resort to sending out in person the "Phenomenon," in order to engage tickets. Mr. Cargill was a gentlemanly man, and Mrs. Cargill was said to be lady-like and educated, whilst the beautiful Mary Cargill, their daughter, was universally beloved and respected in Lynchburg. Those good old days have long since passed; the old theatre no longer occupies the spot where it then stood, whilst Dudley and Masonic Halls are now used for such performances. But the great defect in Dudley Hall is, that the audience have all to sit in front of the performance, and rather lower than the stage. The absence of scenery, too, is felt sensibly; and the Avon Troupe neither compares with the companies mentioned above, nor the Thespian Societies which formerly existed in Lynchburg.

---

lins as a saddler's shop. This free man waited, we believe, on Mr. Van Buren whilst President, and he afterwards kept an eating-house in the West.

METHODIST CHURCH IN LYNCHBURG.

"John Wesley was more learned, and, in all respects, better fitted to become the leader and founder of a sect. His father was rector of Epworth, in Linconshire, where John was born in 1703. He was educated at Oxford, where he and his brother Charles and a few other students lived in a regular system of pious study and discipline, whence they were denominated 'Methodists.' After officiating a short time as curate to his father, the young enthusiast set off as a missionary to Georgia, where he remained about two years. Shortly after his return in 1738, he commenced field-preaching, occasionally traveling through every part of Great Britain and Ireland, where he established congregations of Methodists. Thousands flocked to his standard. The grand doctrine of Wesley was universal redemption, as contra-distinguished from the Calvinistic doctrine of particular redemption. Wesley continued writing, preaching and traveling, till he was eighty-eight years of age, his apostolic earnestness and venerable appearance procuring for him everywhere profound respect. He had preached about forty thousand sermons, and traveled three hundred thousand miles. His highly useful and laborious career was terminated on the 2nd of March, 1791. His body lay in a kind of state in his chapel at London, the day previous to his interment, dressed in his clerical habit, with gown, cossack, and band—the old clerical cap on his head, a bible in one hand and white handkerchief in the other. The funeral service was read by one of his old preachers. When he came to that part of the Service, which reads—'Forasmuch as it hath pleased God to take unto himself the soul of our deceased BROTHER,' his voice changed, and he substituted the word *Father*—and the feeling with which he did this was such, that the congregation, who were shedding silent tears, burst at once into loud weeping.* At the time of Wesley's death, the number of Methodists in Europe, America, and the West India Islands, was eighty thousand; they are now above a million, three hundred thousand of which are in Great Britain and Ireland."

CHAMBERS' *Sketch of John Wesley.*

The old Methodist Church of Lynchburg was founded in 1804, and, since that time, it has continued in a high state of prosperity, enjoying the pastoral care of able ministers, and numbering many active, influential members. The first recollection of this place of worship, is in the year 1819 or '20, when the church was principally under the care of the Rev. JOHN EARLY. His constant, untiring labors, have, since that time, never ceased,

---

* Southey's Life of Wesley.

till, by imperceptible degrees, the Methodist church, in upper Virginia, has spread like a great vigorous tree, around whose roots are continually springing up smaller ones. Notwithstanding the active employment and frequent travelling necessary in his profession, Bishop Early has spent a great portion of his ministerial life in Lynchburg, which through time and eternity will continue to feel his influence. A small, beautiful rose, designated as "the miniature rose," was many years since introduced into Lynchburg by Bishop Early, who has always had a great fondness for flowers. A few small shoots were brought by him from one of his circuits, and by him distributed amongst his friends, and from these plants have descended all that numerous family of roses now seen in upper Virginia. Frequently, where other plants would not grow, this tenacious, hardy shrub would flourish, and, in its progress from year to year, eradicating more delicate plants, and sometimes, in its course, wholly uprooting from the soil, weeds, thistles, and even brambles. A strong analogy exists between this simple plant, in its sure, rapid constant progress, and the labors of Bishop Early, which have been arduous, incessant and unremitted, till Methodism in the upper country has become established on a sure basis, other systems, where less zeal has been manifested, giving way before its animating worship.

Bishop Early was married, in 1821, to ELIZABETH

Rives, a young lady of great worth and piety. She was then in all the freshness and bloom of early womanhood, and it might naturally have been supposed that she would sometimes, like other young persons, be allured or carried away, particularly in conversation. But she was grave, modest, dignified—never losing sight of what was due to herself as the wife of a minister, and never forgetting that the great business of a Christian professor was to show forth the beauty of holiness, not only with her lips, but in her life; and, doubtless, much of the prosperity of the Methodist Church has been owing to her influence, together with that of other eminent females. Though only a small child, the writer remembers with peculiar pleasure, an evening spent, at that time, with Mrs. Early,* in company with a few other friends. It was whilst Mrs. Early was a bride—the bright, beautiful flush of health was on her cheek, her mild, thoughtful eye beaming with love and kindness—and her image, as she then appeared, will ever remain deeply engraven on memory; whilst her recent departure from our midst, has tenderly recalled incidents and scenes long past and nearly forgotten,† but now cherished with pensive retrospection.

---

* At the house now occupied by Henry Dunnington, Esq.
† This excellent lady died during the spring of 1857.

About the year 1821, the Rev. GEORGE W. CHARLTON made Lynchburg his residence. He was a man of splendid personal appearance; and, being gifted with great eloquence, he exercised a sway and influence which has rarely been exceeded. His church was crowded, his catechism schools were full, his society was as much sought by the gay and worldly as by the grave and pious. He lived in the house of Mr. John Thurmon; and, though Mr. Charlton might have much contributed to the brilliancy of society, yet he rarely accepted invitations, never to parties, and very rarely would he meet more than a few friends on a social visit. He was, indeed, a zealous young minister; and his sermons were so striking, that the attention even of the most worldly, was arrested. During his residence in Lynchburg, Mr. Charlton was attacked with hemorrhage of the lungs, and the delicate state of his health, at this time, was such as to awaken the warmest interest, not only of members of his Church, but of the affectionate little band of children, whom he taught every Saturday at the Methodist Church. He left Lynchburg, after a residence of two years, during which time he greatly contributed to the influence of the Church, many members being added to its communion during his ministry. A few years after this time, Mr. Charlton married a lady from the lower country, and since that time he has resided almost constantly in Petersburg.

On his last visit to Lynchburg,* he accompanied Miss MILLER, a female Methodist preacher, who was, with her traveling companion, Miss HILTON, making a tour of the State. Notice having been given that a female would preach at the Methodist Church, that building was crowded to overflowing long before the hour fixed for the service. This remarkably interesting lady did not ascend the pulpit, but stood within the altar, taking for her text—"The Spirit and the bride say, Come;" and so profound was the silence which reigned throughout the church, that not a word was lost of her beautiful and touching address; and several of the sentences of that discourse, heard in childhood, are still remembered. At one time, her eloquent appeal being in these words:—"Oh, immortal spirits! bound for the bar of God, what madness hath possessed you?"

At that time, the Rev. WILLIAM A. SMITH was the stationed Methodist minister of Lynchburg. He was a very young man, but even then giving promise of what he has since become. The eloquence of his preaching, his zealous prayer-meetings, his pastoral visits, were all greatly blessed; so that, during the summer of 1828, a

---

* In the spring of 1828.

revival took place in his church, which, for permanency of effect, has never been equalled. The gayest and most careless were led to inquire the way of salvation, many converts were made, and large numbers were added to the Methodist Church; but a part of them connected themselves with the Episcopal Church, continuing to this day its devoted members. In the fall of that year, Mr. Smith was united in marriage to Miss Ellice M. Miller, the female preacher; and since that period, his history and brilliant career have placed this distinguished man so before the public that farther comment is here unnecessary.

Rev. WILLIAM MARTIN resided a few miles above Lynchburg; but, together with his excellent wife, he spent the greater portion of his time in the city. He was a very good, harmless, old man, of middle stature, and not possessing any great intellectual gifts. He used, however, to say, that from *one* certain text he could preach a sermon, in which he would acknowledge no superior. That favorite discourse was from the text:—"Is there no balm in Gilead? is there no physician there?" He described himself as having been in his youth a remarkably handsome man; and he had been heard to say, that, attending at that time a ball, dressed in shorts, knee-buckles, ruffled shirt, &c., he found himself in the dance *vis a vis* to General Washington; and Mr.

Martin alleged that *he* considered *himself* a much handsomer and finer looking individual than the Father of his Country. All of uncle Martin's foibles were innocent, and there is no doubt that he was an humble, sincere Christian, and a man of most upright and exemplary character.

Mrs. ELIZABETH MARTIN,* wife of Rev. William Martin, was a lady of great mental attainments, joined to deep and fervid piety. She was very lovely in personal appearance, and exercised a great influence in Lynchburg, where she was much beloved. The members of the Methodist Church, as well as others, considering it a privilege to have her as a guest—her example was an inestimable benefit, and her prayers a protection to a household. Surviving for some years her venerable partner, she, from that time, made the hospitable mansion of Mrs. Ann Irvine her principal residence. Mrs. Martin died early in the spring of 1831, and those who had the privilege of beholding this sainted woman during the last few weeks of her life, will ever regard that time, when looking back, as a Boca in their earthly pilgrimage. During the whole of her last illness, she sat erect in her arm chair, habited with her customary neatness, and,

---

* This lady was a niece of Edmund Pendleton.

whilst in that position, her gentle spirit took its flight to a heavenly home. Her chamber was at the time filled with a concourse of sorrowing friends, many of whom sent messages to their relatives in Heaven. Some comments were, at the time made on this; but it seems a holy, beautiful thought, mingled with poetical feelings, all of which we find so sweetly embodied in Mrs. Hemans' "Message to the Dead." The funeral of Mrs. Martin was preached at the old Methodist Church, and none can forget, who heard that eloquent discourse, or listened to the sublime words of "The Dying Christian," sung by the choir of the Church, which, at that time, numbered the finest singers in Lynchburg.

About the year 1825, Father HERSEY, "the walking circuit-rider," made his appearance in Lynchburg. He was an eccentric, but really excellent man, of striking appearance, and with a manner of speaking at once most fervid and eloquent. He had unfortunately become involved in debt, and in order to extricate himself, he wore clothes of the plainest kind, made of coarse fabrics, and he walked to all of the different churches within his circuit, appropriating the money thus saved to the liquidation of his debts. By this course of frugality and self-denial, he insured the respect of the community, who were always ready to listen to him attentively, even though he told them the truth with severity. This venerable man survives, and is, we understand, still a member of the Baltimore Conference.

It is proper to mention in this place, the name of Mr. THURMON, who was a devout member of the church, aiding in its extension by his blameless life and example. When very young, he had held, during the Revolutionary war, an employment in the army, and to him were accorded the honor and privilege of residing for a length of time with Washington and La Fayette, in that small stone building in the city of Richmond, now so reverenced on account of its distinguished inmates at that time. When General La Fayette visited Richmond in 1825, Uncle Thurmon* made him a visit at that place, habited in the same clothes which he had worn whilst living in the stone-house with himself and General Washington. The interview was extremely interesting and affecting, La Fayette receiving him with open arms, whilst down the manly cheeks of the brave, gallant Frenchman flowed tears of emotion. Uncle Thurmon possessed nearly, or quite as much influence in his church as a

---

* This venerable man was always spoken of in Lynchburg as Uncle Thurmon.

minister of the gospel. He, with the other elders of the Methodist Church, sat inside the altar, with their faces turned towards the preacher, and whenever a part of the discourse touched them particularly, they expressed audibly their approbation, in such words as "Amen, even so, Lord;" "God grant it." These expressions, uttered fervently, so stimulated and animated their preachers, that truly they might have been styled "Boanerges"— for it was then that those burning words were uttered, which pierced the consciences and entered the hearts of the hearers, so that multitudes would throng the altar, inquiring, with tearful, agonized accents, "What must I do to be saved?" Mr. Thurmon lived to a great age, passing away calmly from earth, and leaving to his numerous descendants, the rich inheritance of his blameless, well-spent life.

JOHN THURMON was a worthy son of this most excellent man. He was by trade a saddler, carrying his piety into the workshop as well as the church. He was a man of most kind, benignant feelings, remarkably gentle and affectionate in his disposition, and at all times showing that love to his neighbor, so enjoined in the Word of God. In no act of his life has more good resulted than in the establishment of the first Sunday school in the State of Virginia. In the year 1817, he was the principal agent in the formation of this Sabbath school, which was held in the old Methodist Church, and from which have emanated all the other Sunday schools in the State, and the immense benefits resulting from the first one will be felt through time and eternity. Several members of Congress owed their first education to the Sabbath school, established first in Lynchburg.

John Thurmon married a daughter of the late Mrs. Essex, and for many years they resided in a neat white house, not far from the Reservoir. He died in the year 1855, leaving a numerous family, nearly all of whom are inhabitants of Lynchburg. Many female members of this Church possessed great influence, being gifted with eloquence in prayer and exhortation, so that they greatly strengthened their minister's hands; but, out of a large number, only two of this class will now be mentioned, both of them eminent for all of the social virtues, as well as for usefulness in the Church.

Mrs. Essex* was, for many years, a resident of Lynchburg. She was married, when very young, to Mr. Simpson; and she was the mother of Mr. James Simpson, and of Miss Jane Simpson, well-known in this community. After the death of Mr.

---

* We think she is a native of Fredericksburg.

Simpson, her first husband, Mrs. Simpson married the Rev. Mr. Essex, at that time a minister of the Methodist church. Her only daughter, Miss Eliza Essex, became the wife of Mr. M. Lyman, now a resident of Lewisburg. Mrs. Essex was a lady of a very strong mind and excellent heart, and was moreover gifted with a remarkable command of language, and a facility of expressing herself both gracefully and eloquently, particularly on religious subjects. She joined to those gifts a knowledge of medicine, which greatly extended her influence throughout Lynchburg and the adjoining country; and so skillful and well-informed was she in her profession, that she might aptly have been styled "The Baudelocque" of upper Virginia. This excellent lady died many years since in Lynchburg, leaving a void in the Church to which she belonged, not easily supplied.

Mrs. MARY BROWN was a native of Bedford county. Her maiden-name was Mary Hancock, and she was a sister of Ammon Hancock, a well known merchant of Lynchburg. Her memory will tenderly be cherished by a large circle of friends in the city; nor can she ever be forgotten by those who have shared her kindness and hospitality. Though passing often through the deep waters and fiery furnace of affliction, she was ever the patient and submissive Christian. Twice was her domestic hearth invaded by death in violent forms—one of her sons being instantly killed, by a loaded wagon passing over him; and a few years subsequent to this heart-rending event, a younger son came to his end in consequence of the accidental discharge of a gun in the hands of a school-companion. Yet, after the first burst of sorrow, she was enabled to see the hand of God even in these mournful casualties. In perfect harmony with her holy, exemplary life, was the triumphant scene in her chamber of death; and, standing on the confines of eternity, she discerned so clearly, through faith, the promised land, that her last words were, "Joy, joy! I am almost home!"

Can we wonder at the growth and prosperity of a Church, which numbered amongst its worshipers such women as Mrs. Mary Brown? Would that her example might stimulate all who remember her, to press onwards to the high mark of their calling in Christ Jesus; so that, at the solemn hour of dissolution, they may, like her, feel, that

> "Jesus can make a dying bed,
> Feel soft as downy pillows are,
> Whilst on His breast I lean my head,
> And breathe my life out sweetly there."

THE EXPERIENCE OF MRS. ELIZABETH MARTIN.

Mrs. ELIZABETH MARTIN* was born September, 1750, in the county of King & Queen, Virginia. She is the daughter of Mr. John Pendleton, who was a man of respectability and a member of the Church of England. Her mother died when she was young, and her father intermarried a second time; but she still continued with him till she was seventeen years of age, when she was married to William P. Martin, her present husband. She tells her religious experience nearly in the following words:

"From my youth I had a propensity for different diversions, particularly for dancing. My fondness for this last was such, that when at a ball I scarcely could even think of taking ordinary sustenance. I was so fascinated with music, company and mirth, that I was entirely led off from thinking of a future state, or making preparation for death and judgment. At sixteen years of age, I enjoyed a remarkable share of

---

* The above article is taken from "The Evangelical Magazine," a religious paper, published in Lynchburg as early as 1810. It was sent in by James Brown, Esq., of that place, after the work was in press; and, to the numbers in upper Virginia, who loved and reverenced this remarkable woman, a perusal of her experience will doubtless be interesting.

health, and was blest with a good constitutien, both of which I sadly impaired by overheating myself at a dance, and then going out into the night air. By One particular instance of this kind of imprudence, I laid a foundation for a long and dangerous spell of sickness, from which I never entirely recovered. My case was thought desperate by the physicians: still, I was not afraid to die, and only regretted the thought of leaving my friends and relations in this world. But I was destitute of religion, and had never once heard that our nature must be changed—that we must be born of the Spirit, before we can have a right to the Kingdom of Heaven. It was a time of great darkness, and I had no one to take me by the hand and lead me into the paths of peace and happiness. I had not, however, the least opposition to religion, or the professors of it—except only, that once I was offended with a preacher whom I thought carried matters too far.

"For several years after my marriage, I still indulged myself in the gaieties and follies of the world. We lived in a neighborhood of dancers, with whom I freely joined, still entertaining the fashionable opinion that it was not wrong. In this opinion I was joined and strengthened by my companion, who also was fond of merriment himself, and played on the violin. Thus we spent our precious time together, in partaking of the frothy and trifling things of this world, unthoughtful of the hand which supported us, and wholly taken up with the 'things that perish in the using.'

"I was awakened to a sense of my lost estate, by nature, by a woman who, from religious motives, had quitted the practice of dancing. I thought she was wrong, and took uncommon pains to convince her. But she turned the scales upon me, and, by a few words, convinced me not only that I was wrong, but, moreover, that I was a vile, ungrateful sinner. She quoted this important truth from Scripture, 'That we must be converted'—a phrase that I had never heard, or, at least, had never considered before. This had the desired effect. It brought about an immediate self-examination, which was attended with Divine light, and I soon plainly discovered that I was far gone from original righteousness—that I was a most ungrateful being, and, although I could not charge myself with any scandalous sins, so called by the world, I found myself destitute of everything truly and religiously good, my life having been devoted to the pleasures and maxims of this poor and wicked world. Immediately, I felt determined, by the grace of God, to seek for true religion, let the consequence be what it might, and engaged in reading, prayer and meditation. The Word of God was my delight: things began to appear in a different light, and I was condemned by the Word of God and by my own conscience. I had violent opposition from various quarters, particularly from my husband, who peremptorily forbid my going to meeting, and often declared that, unless I would quit this new course of mine, he would live with me no longer. Once, because I attended a meeting in his absence, he was so much irritated that he whipped the boy that waited on me to the meeting, and went off for a short season. This was, indeed, a trying time—how to act so as to please God and be obedient to my husband. I expostulated, and told him I had a soul to save, and must do it—that I was willing to comply with all his reasonable commands, and would do everything I could with a clear conscience to please him, but could go no farther. I felt more and more the necessity of heart-felt religion, and was much in earnest to obtain it. I had parted with all my actual sins (as I verily believe), except one, for which I had a great propensity : it was jesting. I had great delight to please the company I then kept, and was of a very volatile disposition. In the meantime I heard of a people called 'The Methodists,' and was very desirous to hear them preach, but was debarred from it for two or three years. I took some pains to make myself acquainted with the different tenets of the various sects, that I might judge for myself; and, from what I could learn, the Methodists held opinions which accorded with mine.

"We were then living in King William county, in the midst of a people much opposed to vital religion and utterly ignorant of spiritual things; and I pray God for them, that they may not still continue in the same darkness. About the beginning of the Revolutionary war, however, we removed up the country, and settled in Halifax county, Virginia, where I had the great gratification to hear a Methodist preacher. His name was John Dickins. It was a comfortable season. His doctrines were edifying, and well coincided with the creed which I had formed for myself. He preached from Second Corinthians, chapter v. verse 17th—'Therefore, if any man be in Christ, he is a new creature'—and his words came with power. Even my companion, who heard in much prejudice, acknowledged he never had heard a man who knew how to preach *extempore*, till then; and, I believe, through the instrumentality of this man, my companion was awakened to seek the salvation of his soul. After reading the Rules of the Methodist Society, he proposed joining members to form a class. I was so captivated with his preaching, doctrine and Rules, that I would gladly have joined him immediately, and partaken of the reproaches of Christ which had fallen upon this little body of people. But my companion did not consent. I was determined, however, to keep the Rules, although my name could not be enrolled on their class paper. After this, I was freed from restraint about hearing them preach; and, in a few weeks, I went to hear a youth of eighteen—Ishum Tatum. Although a mere beardless boy, he spake by the energy of the Spirit; and, whilst he pronounced the words of truth, I was blessed with the spirit of adoption. My load of sin fell off—peace and joy sprung up in my soul—love to God and man flowed into my heart—and I knew that, 'For me, the Saviour died!' My witness was so clear and manifest, that not a doubt of its reality has ever arisen in my mind. I was so overpowered, by divine grace, that, for some time, I forgot my home; and, with truth, I could say, 'Old things are passed away! Behold all things are become new!'

"That day, four weeks, the young preacher came again; and, after his sermon was ended, again proposed to admit members into his Society: and, to the surprise of every one present, my companion went forward and desired to have his name enrolled as a member. This was highly pleasing to me; and I, also, went forward and joined at the same time. This took place about thirty-three years ago. Thus happily placed among the people whom I loved as my soul, I felt inexpressible joy, whilst we sweetly took counsel together. The preaching place was near our house, so that I could conveniently attend the preaching and class-meetings; and we had comfort in helping each other on, in our way towards the peaceful shores of bliss.

"After having been some time in this state of peace with God, through our Lord Jesus Christ, I began to discover there were greater attainments in religion than those I had as yet experienced. Although I felt no condemnation for actual transgression, yet I found my heart was not wholly given to God: I did not love the Lord with all my soul, might, mind and strength. I found remains of the carnal mind, and that the body of sin was not destroyed. Again I began to double my diligence in calling upon God, reading his precious Word, and in hearing discourses on the doctrine of sanctification. It was not long till I was nearly convinced it was my privilege to enjoy this unspeakable blessing. I was then frequently determined, by the grace of God, to seek after it, and not rest till I had found the blessed treasure; and I as often saw with clearness, that, without holiness of heart and life, no one shall see the Lord. Sometimes I had no doubt but that the Lord would bestow it upon me, sooner or later, and began to cry to God to sanctify me throughout soul, body and spirit—to give me that perfect love which casteth out fear!

> ' Oh make me all in Thee complete!
> Oh make me all for glory mete!'

But I was several times discouraged by conversing with some professors of religion in the neighborhood, who declared against the possibility of the attainment, and appealed to their own experience for their own confirmation. At length, however, my conviction of the reality of this grace was still more deepened, and I was brought to cry, mightily too, in earnest expectation of the blessing. And the Lord was good and gracious unto me. He heard and answered my petition. I was enabled, by faith, to trust His great and precious promises; and I knew, by joyful experience, that 'God was faithful and just, not only to forgive us our sins, but also to cleanse us from all unrighteousness.'

"This great and happy additional change took place something more than two years after I had experienced the forgiveness of my sins. From that time, even until now, I feel myself a poor, needy and unprofitable creature—the least of all God's people; but let His name be praised for the revelation of this grace. I do know I love Him with my whole heart. I love His law—I love His people; and I had rather be a door-keeper in His house, than dwell in the palaces of kings. I daily feel that love which passeth all understanding, and is full of glory! 'I reckon myself dead unto sin,' 'and to this world.' I feel universal love and good will to men; and my daily and heart-felt prayer to God is, 'Thy will be done on Earth as it is in Heaven!' I have no confidence in the flesh—and I can say with truth, 'The life I now live, is by faith in Christ Jesus.'

> 'There is my home and portion fair,
> My treasure and my heart are there,
> And my abiding home.
> For me, my elder Brethren stay,
> And angels beckon me away,
> And Jesus bids me come!'

"It may be useful to others for me to state, that I have been much afflicted with sickness, and, for more than twenty years, have hardly experienced one well day. In the year 1780, I went to the Warm Springs, but experienced very little benefit. Several years afterwards, I visited the Sweet Springs, and found some relief; and the last few years of my life have been the most healthy I have experienced for the space of forty years. But, blessed be the name of the Lord, I am bound to say that, under all my pain and sufferings, I never had a murmuring thought. With the Psalmist, I felt 'It was good for me to be afflicted'—and was constanily supported by the words of the great Apostle to the Hebrews: 'Whom the Lord loveth, He chasteneth.'

"I have now been endeavoring to walk in the way of obedience thirty-six years; and it has been something more than thirty-three years, since I was brought to the knowledge of God in the pardon of my sins. And in all this course I have found, that it is by faith alone that I have attained to anything pertaining to true godliness. When I obtained mercy at the first, I was enabled to believe that Jesus Christ, the Saviour of the world, had died for all, and especially for me. I loved the Lord, for He had first loved me. I ventured my soul upon Him, and felt joy and peace in the Holy Ghost. When I was burdened with a conscious sense of inbred corruption, I ventured again to cast myself upon his mercy and his power, believing Him 'able and willing to save to the uttermost, them that believe.' My prayer, then, was, 'Give me a clean heart, oh God! and renew a right spirit within me.'

"From the day that my faith in God became steadfast, even until now, I enjoy a continual peace—a peace which flows like a river. I am still a monument of the Divine mercy; and I feel, as much as ever, disposed to spend my few remaining days to the honor and glory of the Redeemer's grace. The hope of an immortal crown now raises my heart above the trifling toys of this vain world. I am not, however, without my comforts here— for I take the greatest delight in the worship of God, and in the fellowship of the saints. I have joy in seeing the prosperity of Zion. When I first became a member of the Methodist Society, there were not more than three or four thousand on this whole continent, including all the riding preachers, twenty in number. From this little cloud, I have seen the work spread, until I have now lived to hear there are not less than sixteen thousand members, five hundred riding and two thousand local preachers. May God continue to bless his vineyard. Great Father of Light, let Thy kingdom come, Thy will be done, on Earth as it is in Heaven.

E. MARTIN."

THE OWENS FAMILY.

"Ah me! full sorely is my heart forlorn,
  To think how modest worth neglected lies,
While partial Fame doth with her blasts adorn,
  Such deeds alone, as pride and pomp disguise,
  Deeds of ill sort, and mischievous emprise,
    Lend me thy clarion, goddess! let me try
  To sound the praise of merit, ere it dies.

"In elbow chairs, (like those of Scottish stem,
  By the sharp tooth of cankering old defaced,
In which, when he receives his diadem,
  Our sovereign prince and liefest liege is placed,)
  The matron sat; and some with rank she graced,
  The source of children's and of courtier's pride,)
Redressed affronts—for vile affronts there passed—
  And warned them not the fretful to deride,
But love each other dear, whatever them betide."

Extracts from SHENSTONE'S SCHOOL-MISTRESS.

OWEN OWENS and Mrs. JANE OWENS were natives of Augusta county, but soon after the settlement of Lynchburg they removed thither, where they soon became the most prominent of its inhabitants, giving to the newly formed town influences which have greatly tended to advance its prosperity and refinement.

Mr. and Mrs. Owens were well educated and intelligent, possessing, in a high degree, the purest and most refined species of mental culture—for they both had the most enthusiastic love for the beautiful, as seen in creation, particularly in shrubs, plants and flowers, which they cultivated in great perfection, thus investing life with all the poetry of which it is capable, and diffusing through Lynchburg a taste for Botany and Floriculture.

They established in this town a school, which was first kept at the house on the corner opposite to the old Masons' Hall, but removing to the present residence of Dr. William Owens, the school was for many years kept in the basement of that house: and from that room have been carried impressions whose influence will be felt through time and eternity.

The heart expands at the mention of the name of Owens, and there are doubtless many now in Lynchburg, besides numbers scattered throughout the Union, who will sympathize in these emotions. Mrs. Owens was the beloved instructress of nearly every child in Lynchburg, and grateful indeed should the present inhabitants feel, could they command the services of such a teacher. Incredible was the rapidity with which her pupils were brought forward. In those good old days, learning was taken in the natural way; and there were no pleasing series with pictures to allure on the child, but only Webster's* Spelling-Book, in an unmitigated form, with the Bible and Testament as sole reading books for beginners; yet her pupils made more rapid progress than those of the present day, with all of their alleviations, correct spelling and beautiful penmanship being the peculiar forte of our beloved instructress. Having an enthusiastic love for flowers, these simple, beautiful tokens were given out by her on Friday evening as rewards. She had a knowledge of drawing and painting, and gave lessons in these accomplishments. Plain and ornamental needle-work were important branches in her school, and many of her patterns and designs would put to shame those in Godey's Lady's Book. Judicious and impartial, she reigned supreme in the hearts of the loving band of young children who encircled her, and no clouds overshadowed this happy abode, till the death of Mr. Owen Owens; but after this period, Mrs. Owens resumed her labors, continuing them for many years, and relinquishing them most unwillingly on the advance of age and infirmity. She survived her husband many years,

---

* Mrs. Owens was among the first in Virginia who adopted this spelling-book, and at a time when his pronunciation and his manner of dividing words was ridiculed by most persons.

living to an advanced age,* and when full of years and honors, she calmly breathed her last at the residence of her daughter, in the town of Lynchburg.

The taste for flowers, drawing and painting was not all for which Lynchburg was indebted to the Owens family. Many years since they established a circulating library, with a number of choice volumes by the best authors. The works of Madame de Stael, Madame de Sevigne, Madame de Genlis, the works of Lady Morgan, Miss Burney, Monk Lewis, the works of Miss Edgeworth, as many as were then written—all these adorned their bookshelves, in addition to a large quantity of useful and valuable reading, which fostered in Lynchburg a taste for the best writings; and Owens' Circulating Library has been the means of bringing many acquainted with the standard British authors, and stimulating them to pursue still farther their reading, when perhaps their taste for literature might have remained dormant, but for the facilities afforded by this library.

Of this family alone survive Mrs. HENRY LATHAM and Dr. WILLIAM OWENS, both well known and beloved in our community. Dr. Owens is much

---

* Should not her numerous pupils over the United States unite to place a monument over her remains?

esteemed for his excellence, and valued for his skill in medicine; but both of these qualifications are only secondary in comparison with his many virtues as a son and brother; his dutiful and affectionate conduct to his parents in his early youth, his respectful, devoted attachment to them when they were aged and infirm, his tender care of sisters and brothers, to whom he acted the part of a parent—all these it is, which make us admire and respect this good man, and ardently desire that he may experience fully the truth of the *only* commandment with promise. Dr. William Owens married, when a young man, Jane Latham, of Culpeper. She was a lady of great worth and intelligence, and her death many years since, was a sad loss to her husband and young family.

There were two younger brothers of Dr. William Owens—BENJAMIN FRANKLIN and SEPTIMUS D. OWENS. They were young men of fine intellectual gifts, and of great promise, but both of them died young. These brothers were remarkably handsome, and their portraits, beautifully taken in oil, still remain in the family, serving to recall the past in a manner both pleasant and mournful.

After the decease of Mr. Owen Owens, the family continued unbroken till the death of Mrs. HUGHES,* the oldest daughter. Sarah Owens pos-

---

* In 1820 or '21, according to the memory of the writer.

sessed the loveliest traits of character, and was greatly beloved in Lynchburg, where she resided. She had been married for some years to Mr. Hughes, and they lived about a square from the residence of Mrs. Owens. Occasionally we would see her with her sister and mother, and before we could define why it was, we felt better and happier after we had been with them. On a Friday morning in the summer of 1820, we hastened as usual to school, ever anxious, as we were, to meet our beloved teacher, but missing her from her accustomed place, we were told by a domestic that her mistress had been sent for in the night to see Mrs. Hughes, who was dangerously ill.

The heart-rending notes of distress from her young sister up stairs, told us in thrilling accents, that Mrs. Hughes was in the last extremity. Previous to this time, an unexpected holiday had always been a delight, for then we would go off in small bands to roam the adjacent hills for plants and flowers, often stimulated in the pursuit by the anticipated pleasure of presenting some of these simple offerings to our beloved instructress. But on this day no joy could such pursuits afford; we dispersed, it is true, to the hills, but ere attaining the summit of the highest and most beautiful, the mournful notes of the bell announced to us that Mrs. Hughes had breathed her last, and the solemn knell was echoed through glen and valley, till the number of years of the deceased had been tolled.

The following Monday we returned to school, and our teacher, as usual, sat by her little table, the moisture in her eye and slight tremor of her hand alone evincing outwardly the sorrow within; and we knew not, till in after years, what efforts it cost that bereaved mother, so soon to again enter upon the active duties of life. Two lovely little girls, the daughters of Mrs. Hughes, we found domesticated with their grandmother, and, with tenderness and childish sorrow, we gazed on these young children, so early deprived of their mother; and feeling that though we could not recall the dead, we could at least bring more peace to our own hearts, by cherishing the living; and from that hour we all felt bound to those little beings by the strongest cords of love and sympathy!

SCHOOLS ON CHURCH STREET.

> "While some on earnest business bent,
>   Their murmuring labors ply,
> 'Gainst graver hours that bring content,
>   To sweeten liberty,
> Some bold adventurers disdain
> The limits of their little reign,
>   And unknown regions dare descry;
> Still as they run they look behind,
> They hear a voice in every wind,
>   And snatch a fearful joy."
>
> GRAY'S *lines on a distant view of Eaton College.*

The schools on this street were so numerous that it might very properly have been called "School Street." One of these institutions was kept by JOHN REID, Esq., in the house now occupied by Mr. John Cary. Mr. Reid was a younger brother of the Rev. W. S. Reid, and he was remarkable for steady discipline, governing his pupils with all the vigor and energy of "Canny Yorkshire." In the next house above was a school kept by Mrs. LOYD; and the house at the corner, just below the present residence of Dr. William Owens, was occupied by Mr. RAWSON, a native of New England, who kept there, for boys, an excellent classical school. The excellent institution of Mrs. OWENS has already been mentioned in the preceding chapter; and the house, at the corner above, just across the street from the old Masonic Hall, was the residence of Mrs. VICTOR, a venerable, excellent lady, from Fredericksburg. Her daughter, Mrs. Lucy Johnson, then resided with her mother, and long will the former lady be affectionately remembered in Lynchburg, for her kindness to the sick and afflicted. Possessing a very retentive memory, and a fund of anecdote, her society was peculiarly acceptable to the invalid; and so great were her conversational powers, that she would attract the young to her for hours, causing them to forget engagements made to join a gay circle. Her sister, Miss MARIA VICTOR, kept, for many years, an excellent school in the basement of that house, and, being a worthy communicant of the Presbyterian Church, her scholars were principally the children of members who worshiped with that denomination. Miss Maria Victor was the first teacher who introduced medals in Lynchburg, the system having been by her fairly tested, and the results being such as to show that their use tended to stimulate pupils, and to induce amongst them a spirit of emulation. She was an advocate for colonization, liberating some valuable slaves belonging to her, amongst them Tom Dyson, well known in Lynchburg as an accomplished servant and excellent carriage-driver.

Musical instruments, at this time, were very rare in Lynchburg, and an old spinet stood in this school-room, bereft of all its strings, save one, and looking quite as pensive and mournful as Tara's harp. Yet this ancient piano was looked upon with great awe and respect, by the urchins from the different schools in that vicinity.

A school was always kept in the old Masonic Hall of Lynchburg. In the year 1822, one was established there by the Rev. F. G. SMITH; and in a few years, he was succeeded by JOHN CARY, Esq., who then as now exercised a powerful influence in this town. It has been said that one reason that there are not more good male teachers is, that the employment is generally regarded as only a stepping-stone to some of the learned professions, and the time occupied in imparting instructions, is too often regarded as a time of probation, till circumstances permit the teacher to emerge as a barrister or a physician. May not the great success which has attended Mr. Cary in this department, be owing somewhat to his having made teaching his permanent profession? It is highly desirable that there should be more who choose for their avocation that of teaching, and diligently pursue it for a term of years, after the example of Mr. Cary.

There was great rivalry between the pupils of these numerous institutions, none of them being willing to acknowledge a less number of pupils than assembled in the school-rooms attended by their companions. Frequent practical jokes were played off, by way of retort, on those who made insinuations against teachers, pupils and school-rooms; and every opportunity of this sort was greatly prized by all of the scholars on that street, particularly by those attending the boys' school, held in the Masonic Hall.

In the year 1828, a man by the name of WATSON appeared in Lynchburg, with hand-bills and advertisements, affirming that, in sixteen lessons he would give a thorough knowledge of the English Grammar—stating, also, that the years usually spent in studying the structure of the English language was nothing but a wanton and sinful waste of our precious time. The tendency of human nature, in general, has been to find a royal road to geometry, and this disposition was now, with respect to grammar, manifested in the good town of Lynchburg. Accordingly, crowds of urchins, who had never before dreamed of any kinder intention than that of murdering the King's English, were now entered as pupils to Mr. Watson.

This personage was a spare, sedate looking man, his hair ornamented with a queue, and his dress composed entirely of light pea-green cloth. He was the beau-ideal of one of the greatest humbugs that ever gladdened Lynchburg. His school was in the basement of a house owned and occupied by Mr. Schoolfield, situated at the corner of the street leading down to the old post-office. This grammarian kept closed doors, and was particularly annoyed at any kind of interruption, save that of some deluded person coming to enter fresh candidates for this high-pressure grammar system.

SILAS VAWTER* was at that time a pupil at the Masonic Hall, where the system of fagging was, to a degree, kept up, as at Westminster School and Eaton College. A very small boy, named Callaway, generally acted as fag to Mr. Vawter, performing sundry little jobs, by way of saving the aforesaid young gentleman trouble; but, on one occasion, Callaway testifying great unwillingness to bring fresh water, Silas, like a wise statesman, concluded that it was better to promise a reward for the performance, than punish for the refusal. So, in an unwary moment, he agreed to give this small boy the sum of twelve and a half cents. As the promise remained unfulfilled, Silas was soon politely reminded of it by his young creditor; and

---

* The elder brother of Bransford Vawter.

owing, likewise, a small grudge to Watson and some of his scholars, Vawter, with ready humor, gave Callaway an order on the former for the amount, telling him to enter the school-room boldly, and, before showing the written order to Watson, to state to him the business which had brought him there. Accordingly, he stalked up to the Grammar School, knocking loudly at the door, which was opened by Watson himself, who inquired of the boy his errand. Callaway was in the habit of stammering very much, and, being now somewhat embarrassed and intimidated by the august presence of Watson and the grammar-class, he stammered out, "Si-si-si, Vaw-Vaw-Vaw-ter-ter sa-sa-says, that you are in-de-de-debt-ed to him ni-ni-nine-pence!" "What is that you say, you little scoundrel?" Whereupon, the chap again commenced with "Si-si, Vaw-Vaw-ter-ter"—but long before he had half gotten through his tedious narration, up went Watson's cane, and speedily from the grammar-hall disappeared this youthful dun, never daring again to enter this classic abode.

In this neighborhood lived those excellent people and good citizens, the Sumpters, Schoolfields, and many members of the Thurmon family. Mr. Jehu Williams resides a little above. His first wife was a lady of great worth, and she was the mother of many fine women, some of whom reside in this

State; and Mrs. W. P. Bryant, one of them, being an inhabitant of Baltimore. His second wife, was Miss Susan Tompkins, a lady of a most amiable disposition, and a daughter of the Rev. Mr. Tompkins, of the Presbyterian Church. The venerable mother of Mrs. Susan Williams was well known and esteemed in Lynchburg, of which place she was really the oldest inhabitant.

The WALLACE* family lived a few doors above; and nearly opposite was the modest dwelling of the good Mr. Thurmon, the patriarch of the town. Close by the latter dwelling, was the humble abode of Milly Cooper, a free woman of color, who there lived with the unfortunate maniac, her son, Archie Cooper; and just above, was the residence of the excellent Mrs. Polly Brown, which is now occupied by her son, Henry Brown, Esq.

The house at present owned and occupied by Dr. Gilmer, was, in 1818, inhabited by George Tucker, Esq.; and the one opposite, was the residence of the family of Duffel, excellent citizens, of Scottish descent; and the residence of Mr. Richard Tyree stands below this house. He was an honest, good citizen, and the husband of Mrs. Mildred Tyree, a very lovely woman and a

---

* Mrs. Wallace afterwards married the Rev. Mr. Cole, of the Methodist Church, a gentleman of great worth and piety.

member of the Quaker denomination. Just opposite was the dwelling of Captain Peter Dudley, an excellent man and good citizen. He married Miss Davis, the daughter of William Davis, Sr., one of the oldest and most influential of the citizens of Lynchburg. Just above the residence of Dr. Gilmer, lived Mr. James Gilliam, a worthy man; and the next house above, was the residence of Mrs. Eliza Echols, the widow of Joseph Echols, Esq., a well-known citizen of Lynchburg, who died more than thirty-three years since. His excellent wife had then a double duty to perform, in rearing and educating her young family, which consisted of one daughter and three sons; and about the year 1829, she broke up housekeeping in Lynchburg, removing from that place to New Haven, Connecticut, whither she carried her children for the advantage of attending the Seminary of Dr. Dwight. As soon as her daughter had finished her education, Mrs. Echols, returning to her native State, chose, as a place of residence, Lexington, in order that her sons might finish their education at Washington College. This excellent lady survives, and is now a resident of Union, Monroe county, at which place resides her daughter, Mrs. Allen T. Caperton. Her sons are well known and esteemed in Virginia:—Mr. Edward Echols, of Rockbridge; John Echols, Esq., of

Monroe; and Mr. Robert J. Echols, of Richmond.

The house now occupied by Dr. John Patterson, was, in 1819, the residence of Mr. James Stuart, who married a daughter of Major William Warwick, and the house nearly adjoining the Methodist Church, was, for many years, the residence of Mrs. Nancy Tait, a sister of the late George Whitelocke, of Petersburg; and the house just above the Methodist Church, and at the foot of the hill, was inhabited by Mr. Cullensworth and his sister, Mrs. Martin, who resided there many years with her sons and daughter. These good people were members of the Methodist Church, and their abode was ever open to young visitors from the schools on that street, who would resort thither to amuse themselves with Mrs. Martin's fine swing, or to gaze with wonder and admiration at the wax figures of the "Babes in the Wood," sleeping peacefully in death!

> "No burial or covering
> Were given to the pair;
> But little Robin Redbreast
> Did cover them with care."

All of which affecting particulars were read in those days from a large edition, and were religiously believed.

The white house on the cross street, from Dr. Gilmer's to Main street, was (if memory does not deceive), for a brief period, the residence of William and Jane Lynch. It was afterwards the residence of a Mr. Duffy—and it was here that "Duffy's Brewery" was kept. It was afterwards the abode of Green B. Lewellen; and then a man, by the name of Wilson, kept there an "entertainment" for gentlemen, wagoners and hog-drovers.

The house occupied by Dr. Gilmer was also, at one time, the residence of Mrs. ELIZABETH CAMM, of Amherst county. This lady was the wife of Mr. ―――― Camm, well-known and esteemed for brilliant talents. She was the mother of Robert Camm, who was also remarkable for his fine talents, and whose early death was much deplored by a large circle of friends. This venerable lady survives, and, at an advanced age, retains all of her faculties in a remarkable degree. She resides on her estate, in the county of Amherst, managing her domestic concerns with great energy. Mrs. Camm is the mother of Mrs. Donald and Mrs. Anderson, of Bedford; Mrs. William Saunders, of Lynchburg; and Mrs. Dr. David Patterson, of Amherst. Mrs. Camm also resided, for a time, in the house opposite; and in the house on the hill now occupied by Mr. Cabaniss. The house on the hill, now occupied by Mr. Biggers, was the abode of Mr. Roberts, a member of the Friends' Society, who married Miss Lynch, one of the daughters of the founder of Lynchburg; and this house is now occupied by a grand-daughter of this worthy man, Mrs. Mildred Biggers.

Exactly opposite the residence of Dr. William Owens, was a brick cottage, with two doors opening on the street. This spot is invested with a peculiar interest from its having been the residence of John Hampden Pleasants, who lived there with his lovely wife during the brief period of their married life, though this sweet woman was at her mother's house at the time of her sudden death.

In 1826, the house occupied by Dr. Gilmer was the residence of Mr. DAVID PATTERSON, of Buckingham. He was a good man, and honest, useful citizen; and was a younger brother of Mr. Alexander Patterson, who was the first to run stages between Lynchburg and Richmond. This latter gentleman was a person of great energy and enterprise; and, at the time he first started his line of stages, the road between the town and the city of Richmond, was almost impassable, and the "Leathern Convenience" only plied once a week between the two places:—the coaches then were very little better than wagons, and the passengers clambered in, by way of the driver's seat, in front. When the stages began to be made comfortable, and to have side-doors, they were considered as most luxurious conveyances: they then made two trips in one week, and, finally, they made tri-weekly trips, which were thought to be the greatest speed, at which public conveyances could arrive. But since the canal and railroad have been in operation, the pleasures of stage-travelling are now scarce known, whilst all those well known and celebrated stopping places—"Upper Patterson's," "Lower Patterson's," "French's," "Raines' Tavern"—are broken up, and many public houses on the Richmond road untenanted, save by owls and bats.

The house now owned and occupied by Dr. Saunders, was, in 1833, the residence of Dr. GUSTAVUS ROSE, a well known and esteemed physician of Lynchburg. This gentleman was the youngest brother of those remarkable women, Mrs. James Pleasants, Mrs. Spottswood Garland, Mrs. Charles Irvine, Mrs. Landon Cabell, Sr., and Mrs. Copeland, of Cumberland. Dr. Rose married Anna, daughter of David S. Garland, Esq., of Amherst county. No one in Lynchburg can ever forget this lovely woman, so remarkable for all the traits which adorn the wife, mother and friend; and feelings of the past so rush into our heart, filling it with sweet, hallowed memories of her many virtues, that we feel inadequate to give such a sketch of her as would do justice to her memory. About twenty-three years since, Dr. Rose emigrated to Indiana, where his excellent wife died in 1856, leaving a large family settled near Laporte, Indiana.

THE LANGHORNE FAMILY.

> " The same fond mother bent at night
> O'er each fair sleeping brow;
> She held each folded flower in sight—
> Where are those dreamers now?"
>
> HEMANS.

A large old wooden Hotel stood nearly opposite the Episcopal Church. It was formerly the "Bell Tavern," kept for many years by Mr. Wells.* It was afterwards the residence of Mr. and Mrs. Douglass, who there kept a Seminary; then, for a time, it was inhabited by the late Mr. Pleasant Pastier. It was a rumbling old building, reminding one of the "Blue Lion, Muggleton," the "Great White Hart," or "The Great White Horse Cellar." Some years since, this edifice was purchased by Colonel

---

* Are there any surviving, who attended school on Church Street many years since, when a fat boy and girl were exhibited at this place? Their pictures were swung out from the porch, greatly alluring the little folks who passed by; that of the fat boy, with an orange in his hand, and a portrait of the girl with a full blown rose.

Maurice Langhorne, and by him much modernized. It was the happy and hospitable abode of this family for some years, but it has since been pulled down, and in its place now stands a stately building, quite like the style of Philadelphia or New York.

Colonel MAURICE LANGHORNE was a native of Cumberland county, and in early life was united in marriage to Elizabeth Allen, a lady of great worth and loveliness, and for a number of years after this event, they resided in the vicinity of Cumberland Court-house. In the year 1828, removing with his family to Lynchburg, he for a term of years leased the beautiful residence of William Lewis Cabell, the house now occupied by D. Payne, Esq. Their arrival was quite an epoch in the social life of Lynchburg; for the amiable, kindly disposition of the Langhorne family, joined to their hospitality, soon made their abode a favorite place in the town. Mrs. Elizabeth Langhorne was greatly beloved and esteemed, and her memory will ever be fondly cherished by friends, who will look back with admiration on her lovely exemplification of the Christian life. In this house, passed away, in the spring of 1832, one of the fairest and loveliest girls of Lynchburg. SALLY CARY LANGHORNE, the second daughter of Colonel Maurice Langhorne, died at the age of seventeen. Lovely both in person and character, her untimely death spread for a length of time a gloom over the town.* Death could not efface the beauty of this young girl, and very many went to the house of her father to gaze on her lifeless remains, which, in their beautiful repose, resembled an angel.

ELIZABETH LANGHORNE, the eldest daughter, was singularly lovely in appearance. Her form perfectly symmetrical, her complexion pure and beautiful, her bright golden hair actually seeming to gild her youthful features, throwing around them a halo.

Whilst the heart throbs with tender emotion at the recollection of a beloved school-mate, we cannot adequately express the warm appreciation we have of this very lovely woman. She became the wife of Anderson Armistead, Esq., blessing his house hold with the sunshine of her cheerful, loving heart. Rejoicing as a wife and mother, she was called, during the full tide of youth and happiness, to join her beloved sister in heaven; and mournfully do we now record the departure of MARY,†

"The last of that bright band.

---

* The funeral of this sweet girl was preached three times; once at the Presbyterian Church, whither her remains were carried, and on the Sabbath afterwards, it was preached by her affectionate teacher, Rev. F. G. Smith, and the Sabbath following it was preached at the Reform Methodist Church.

† This amiable lady was the youngest daughter of Colonel

She was the wife of J. Kerr Caskie, Esq., surviving her marriage only a short time, and soon following to the grave her infant child.

Colonel M. Langhorne, with a numerous family of sons, resides in Lynchburg, and though somewhat advanced in years, he retains the energy, activity and cheerfulness of youth. Most industrious in his habits, a long course of diligence in his pursuits has been crowned with an ample fortune, which he enjoys in a rational manner, establishing during his lifetime his children and descendants.

Langhorne, and greatly beloved by all. She died several years previous to the death of Mrs. Armistead.

HENRY LANGHORNE—MRS. FRANCES LANGHORNE.

" When I consider how my light is spent,
  Ere half my days, in this dark world and wide,
  And that one talent which is death to hide,
  Lodged with me useless, though my soul more bent
  To serve therewith my Maker, and present
  My true account, lest he, returning, chide;
' Doth God exact day labor, light denied?'
I fondly ask; but Patience, to prevent
That murmur, soon replies, 'God doth not need
Either man's work or his own gifts; who best
Bear his mild yoke, they serve him best; his state
Is kingly; thousands at his bidding speed
And post o'er land and ocean without rest;
They also serve, who only stand and wait!'"
              MILTON'S SONNET *on his own blindness.*

HENRY LANGHORNE was a brother of Colonel Maurice Langhorne, and was likewise a native of Cumberland county. When a very young man he was married to Frances, a daughter of James Steptoe, Esq., of Bedford, who was for more than forty years a clerk of that county.

Henry Langhorne was a man of great energy and strength of character, of ardent temperament, and of a disposition most cordial and affectionate. For many years he resided in Lynchburg and its vicinity, subject to many alternations of fortune, but maintaining throughout his unbounded hospitality. For more than ten years of his life he was the victim of a slow, wasting disease; yet, during the whole of that period, he was closely engaged in the active pursuit of business, amassing, under these trying circumstances, a large fortune, and providing liberally the whilst for a large number dependent on him. A few years since he removed to the county of Roanoke, where he died in 1854.

Mrs. FRANCES LANGHORNE was a very remarkable woman, possessing those high-minded, magnanimous traits for which her venerable father was so remarkable. Passing calmly through a life chequered with vicissitudes, she was at all times the quiet, cheerful Christian. In her youth she was singularly lovely, her large blue eyes radiant with love and hope, shedding the mildest rays to gladden the social domestic circle. But before she had attained the age of thirty, she lost her eye-sight, and in a short time she became totally blind. Yet she retained her buoyancy and cheerfulness, continuing in her habits of industry, and frequently taking from beneath her pillow at night sewing, with which she had provided herself, lest the watches of the night should be tedious.

For some time they resided at Chesnut Hill, the former residence of Judge Edmund Winston, and during the time they were living there, the house took fire whilst Mr. Langhorne was absent, and was entirely burnt to the ground, consuming, too, nearly every article of clothes and furniture. It was a time of fearful panic and alarm—a mother deprived of sight, with her young children in this burning dwelling; yet, to the astonishment of all, this noble woman preserved throughout this trying scene perfect calmness and self-possession, issuing to all directions in an unfaltering voice, going herself to the secretary of Mr. Langhorne, and amidst the crash of falling timbers, the terrible sighing of the raging element, and the broad-side showers of hot coals, she saved every paper of importance belonging to her husband. The house of a kind brother in Lynchburg was, for a time, the home of Mr. Henry Langhorne's family, till a new building could be erected at Chesnut Hill. Returning then to their cheerful, happy home, they resided there for a few years, continuing the exercise of their generous hospitality. In the year 1830, Mrs. Langhorne's health declining, she yielded to the solicitations of her friends, and went to the residence of Colonel M. Langhorne in Lynchburg, hoping that change of air might restore to her cheek its beautiful bloom, and strengthen also her exhausted frame. For a time the interesting invalid seemed to rally, but early in the summer of that year, she breathed her last, at the residence of Colonel Maurice Langhorne, leaving a devoted husband and many children, some of whose faces she had never gazed on in consequence of her loss of sight.

The house now occupied by Dr. Allison was the residence of Wm. Morgan, Esq., Sr., and his excellent wife, Mrs. Elizabeth Morgan; a short distance above, was the residence of Judge Daniel, and across the street was the Western Hotel, kept by John F. Johnson, and a little further on, the Kentucky Hotel, kept by Mr. Mallory, but afterwards by Mr. Feazle; and not far off, the large white house, on the road leading to the graveyard, was the town residence of the good and beloved "Staunton John Lynch," whilst just below the cemetery was a modest white house, where lived Mr. Vawter, with his family, at the time of his death.

Just below the Western Hotel, on a cross street, was the residence of Mr. Matthew Brown, a useful, honest, excellent citizen, who lived there for many years with his family. Of the survivors are Mrs. Mathews, of Lewisburg, Edwin Brown, Esq., of Monroe county, and Howell Brown, Esq., of Amherst, together with Miss Brown, of the latter place; of those gone before, the good Mrs. Samuel Wiatt; and amongst the early called, Eveline Brown, a child of great piety and excellence, who died many years since in Lynchburg.

EPISCOPAL CHURCH IN LYNCHBURG.

Until the year 1819, Episcopacy was quite unknown in Lynchburg. About that time or earlier, Bishop Ravenscroft* visited Lynchburg, preaching in the old Methodist Church. Robed in gown and bands, and walking up the aisle of the church, his appearance excited the wonder and astonishment of the good people of the town, particularly that of the small boys, who verily believed the Bishop to have been an elderly lady in a black morning wrapper.

Notice having been given that this worthy prelate would discourse at the old Methodist Church, those who were interested immediately set about to procure a few persons to respond to the morning service. The Carter and Tucker families, and the ladies of the Byrd family, all possessed prayer-books, and knew how to go through the services;

---

* Having nothing to rely on but memory, the precise date is not accurately known, and indeed the writer is not even certain of the name of the Bishop; it was an Episcopal one—she thinks Bishop Ravenscroft.

but, for the credit of the town, it was deemed absolutely necessary to have at least one male voice in the responses. Accordingly they procured the services of one Meredy, an Englishman, who had a large red prayer-book. He stood in front of the gallery, holding his prayer-book very conspicuously, responding loudly, and surveying the congregation with an air of superiority, mingled with compassion for their ignorance.

After this time, a minister by the name of TREADWAY, occasionally preached in Lynchburg, but the attendance being always small, and the services not popular, Mr. Treadway was discouraged from making any attempt to rear there the standard of Episcopacy. To the Rev. Nicholas Cobbs, now Bishop of Alabama, is Lynchburg indebted for the first dawning of an Episcopal Church. This excellent man was a native of Bedford county, and, in early youth, he adopted the profession of schoolteaching. Soon after his marriage, he made a profession of religion; and, partly through the influence of the late Mr. Seth Ward, he connected himself with the Episcopal Church. Mr. Cobbs was much beloved in the town of Lynchburg, and his well known humility and piety disposed persons to listen attentively to his preaching; and, in time, the morning service, with his earnest manner of reading, became very popular. Though located in his native county, Mr. Cobbs had a peculiar and tender care of the parish in Lynchburg, greatly aiding, by his counsel and sympathy, the first Episcopal minister who settled in that place.

About the year 1822, or 1823, the Rev. F. G. SMITH established himself in Lynchburg, making his home in the house of Thomas Wyatt, where, during the lifetime of that excellent man, he remained. Mr. Smith established in the town, a school of first class for boys, teaching during the week in the Masonic Hall, and preaching in his school-room every Sabbath. Notwithstanding the opposition, at this time, to Episcopacy, Mr. Smith continued to preach under discouraging circumstances, and, for some years, without even the smallest salary. He was a man of great worth and purity of character, exercising at all times that "charity which beareth all things and is not easily provoked." His uniform mildness and gentleness effected in Lynchburg more than could be imagined—the Church members increased, and the use of the prayer-book became common throughout that little band of worshipers in the old Masonic Hall. He caused great improvements to be made in church-music, and the chants were, under his instruction, beautifully sung, with all the different parts. It was at length determined to build a church. Mrs. Sarah Cabell, the wife of the late Dr. George Cabell, presenting them with the ground, the corner stone was laid in the year 1825—the work progressing rapidly, the pastor aiding by liberal donations from his own small store. The Thespian Society, headed by the late Hardin Murrel, Giles Ward and William Diggs, had, during the summer of that year, a series of entertainments at the old theatre, the proceeds being applied to the benefit of the Church.

Mrs. Sarah Cabell was a lady of great elegance and refinement, a devoted member of the Episcopal Church, and fondly did she look forward to the time when she could worship in the Church of her adoption; but early in the spring of 1826, she died after a short illness. At this time the Church was quite in an unfinished state, but it was pressed forward with great eagerness, as the first Episcopal Convention in upper Virginia was to hold its meeting in this new church during the month of May. A great concourse of visitors assembled at this time in Lynchburg, whilst the august body of lay-delegates and ministers made a strong impression on the good people of the town. It had been arranged that the funeral of Mrs. Sarah Cabell should be preached, by the Rev. F. G. Smith, the last Sunday evening of the Convention. This lady had been greatly attached to her pastor, and it was fitting that he who so well appreciated her shining traits and lofty character, should preach her funeral sermon. But it was a task too trying to his heart;

his feelings of friendship for that excellent lady were of too sacred and tender a nature to allow him to speak of her in public. A terrific thunder-storm coming on during the sermon, many of the congregation expressed audibly their fears. Mr. Smith had been greatly affected whilst delivering this funeral discourse; and whilst the storm continued to rage, a scene most touching occurred. Overpowered by his feelings, he descended from the pulpit, unable to speak; and the congregation, though awed and alarmed at the tempest, could not but sympathize with this young pastor in those tears shed for one whom he looked upon in the light of a mother.

After the completion of the Church, an organ was purchased; and, in the summer of 1828, a fair was held at the Franklin Hotel, for the benefit of the Church. This was the first fair ever held in Lynchburg: it was a brilliant, beautiful scene—such a one as has never since been witnessed in that city,—the late John E. Norvelle directing and assisting with his taste in all the arrangements, and, during the nights of the exhibition, bringing a large band of amateur-musicians to enliven the scene. How many bright recollections are associated with this Fair! How many who there presided, have long since been called away; how many around whom clustered the tenderest hopes, have lived to see those hopes blasted, and to mourn the loved ones who stood by their side in all the pride and buoyancy of youth. James W. Pegram had but recently been married to the lovely Miss Virginia Johnston. She presided at one of the tables, and near her stood the manly form of her young husband. Of all who then gazed on these two, so happy in mutual love, and blest in the possession of all the world can give, not one could have foreshadowed the mournful termination which fifteen years would bring to their happiness. The last night of the Fair was finished with an auction—George Whitelocke, Esq., acting the part of an auctioneer, and dispensing his witty comments and remarks to the great amusement of the bystanders. The amount more than equalled the greatest expectations, and the proceeds were immediately applied to liquidating the debts of the Church.

By slow degrees, the Episcopal denomination increased; and, during the summer of 1828, a general revival taking place in the Churches of Lynchburg, considerable numbers were at this time added to the Church, continuing its most valued and devoted members. Amongst these was Mrs. Saluda Norvelle, wife of Edmund Norvelle, Esq. Her bright example was felt throughout a large circle of friends and relatives, who remember her with tender affection, mingled with deep regret at her untimely death in 1835.

Mr. and Mrs. SETH WARD were members of this Church, having at a very early date enjoyed the privilege of attending the ministry of the Rev. Mr. JARRAT, who was one of the first Episcopal Ministers who attempted to revive that Church subsequent to the American Revolution. Mr. Ward was a native of the lower country, and when a young man he was united in marriage to Miss Martha Norvelle, a sister of Captain William Norvelle, of Lynchburg; and a few years after that event, they settled in New London. His heart was ever deeply engaged in the cause of religion, and the Church of his youth; and, during the time of his prosperity, his money was liberally expended in furthering this darling object, and, in the days of his adversity, he gave far beyond his means. Soon after settling in Bedford county, Mr. Ward built, pretty much at his own expense, a small Church, known as Chax-creek Church, in which Mr. Crawford officiated. That Church has long since gone down, and Trinity, through the instrumentality of the Rev. Nicholas Cobbs, was built near the original Church. Mr. Ward took an active part in first procuring for Lynchburg the services of the Rev. William S. Reid, of the first Presbyterian Church, the former being at that time the only Episcopalian in town, was of course unable to procure the services of the Church of his choice. He was very influential in building the Church of

St. Stephen's in Bedford county, near which he lived; and, though not at that time residing in Lynchburg, he took a very active interest in procuring a minister, joining the congregation and building the Church.

An extract from a letter written by the Rev. William Norvelle Ward, a son of this excellent man, thus feelingly speaks of his venerable father: "I think my parent, in life, could say from the heart

> 'I love Thy kingdom, Lord;
> The house of Thine abode!'

And, I am sure, that fond regard for the memory of my father is not carrying me too far, when I say, that the services of the Church in that country, owes as much, perhaps more, to him than to any other, either clerical or lay. He laid the foundation on which such men as Bishop Cobbs and others built their spiritual temples. 'He rests from his labors, and his works do follow him.' "*

The establishment of Mr. F. G. SMITH's school was a new epoch in Lynchburg, he being one of the first who wisely governed by rewards instead of punishment. Acquiring an influence over the minds

---

* Mr. and Mrs. Ward emigrated some years since to Tennessee, where they both died. Several of their daughters reside there—Mrs. Williams, Mrs. Kerr, and Miss Ward.

and hearts of his pupils, he gently led them on, encouraging the weak and gently restraining the most ambitious, he insensibly diffused amongst them a love of literature, causing them to be desirous of mental culture, and inculcating the doctrine, that a school routine is not the finish, but the mere commencement of an education, to be carried on in after life. In the year 1829, he established in Lynchburg, a female school, on a high basis. The happiest results attended his system, and, a few years later, marrying Sarah, the second daughter of Henry Davis, Esq., the plan of the school was much enlarged—the one formed by Mr. and Mrs. Smith was the most superior school ever known in Lynchburg. The best teachers were provided, and, whilst in full operation, Mr. Smith being urgently solicited to take charge of a literary institution in Tennessee, he left Lynchburg to the regret of his friends and parishoners. A series of resolutions, of a most affectionate and respectful nature, were drawn up by his congregation, and, in the fall of 1837, he left Lynchburg for Columbia, where he for many years carried on, with zeal and energy, a most extensive course of learning. He is, at present, the able and valued principal of the Athenæum near Columbia. Assisted by his excellent wife, and provided with a corps of competent teachers, this institution is undoubtedly the best of the sort in the United States. The extensive library, the splendid paintings, the numerous musical instruments, the beautiful walks,—all these render the place most desirable, not to mention the privilege of associating intimately with persons so excellent and highly cultivated as Mr. and Mrs. Smith.

FRANKLIN GENET SMITH is a native of one of the New England States, and is a son of Judge Smith, of —— State. In very early life he emigrated to Virginia, establishing himself in the county of Prince Edward, where he, for a time, pursued the business of school-teaching. Completely naturalized in his adopted State, he secured the esteem of all, particularly that of the Presbyterian Church, with whose members he was at that time so intimately associated.* A finished scholar and literary gentleman, the wonderful success of his teaching in Lynchburg has already been mentioned. His manner of reading the Morning Service was peculiarly beautiful and touching. His sermons were perfect in style and finish—eloquent thoughts being often in a few words condensed,—Mr. Smith being remarkable for simplicity and conciseness. Passages from many of his sermons are remembered, and with

---

* It would seem that this brief memoir should have been inserted several pages earlier, but it could not be done without interruption to the sketch of the Episcopal Church.

peculiar feelings one of his most striking, from the text, "The night is far spent and the day is at hand." This sermon was preached several times by request, and is still remembered by the old inhabitants of Lynchburg.

After the removal of Mr. Smith to Tennessee, the Church for some years enjoyed the pastoral care of the Rev. Mr. ATKINSON, at present Bishop of the diocese of North Carolina. The congregation are now most happy under the ministry of the Rev. William Kinckle, well known and beloved in our community. How blessed has been this Church, which has been so favored for thirty-seven years, as to have alternately the services of three such excellent pastors as Mr. Smith, Mr. Atkinson and Mr. Kinckle.

MASONRY IN LYNCHBURG.

BALL ON ST. JOHN'S DAY.—IRISH JOHN ROBERTSON.

"The trowel is an instrument made use of, by operative masons, to spread the cement which unites a building into one common mass; but we, as Free and Accepted Masons, are taught to make use of it for the more noble and glorious purpose of spreading the cement of brotherly love and affection; that cement which unites us into one sacred band, or society of friends and brothers, among whom no contention should ever exist, but that noble contention, or rather emulation, of who can best work and best agree."

WORK ON MASONRY.

The old Masonic Hall of Lynchburg stood on the spot where the new one now rears its head. It was a common two-story building, without device or ornament to distinguish it from the surrounding houses; yet it was held in great awe by the children, who generally avoided that side of the street, under the firm impression that his satanic majesty was kept chained in the cellar below, and it was also believed that up stairs there were piles of coffins, a skeleton, and horrors sufficient, with tolerable economy, to have lasted Mrs. Radcliffe through at least one romance.

Yet Masonry flourished in Lynchburg, processions were numerous, and, as they generally paraded, Church Street, the sound of wind instruments, by which they were always preceded, was hailed with joy by the numerous candidates for learning who sat within the different schools of that section. A most wholesome interruption and innocent amusement was thereby afforded to the youth of this good town,* and they would return to their labors refreshed by the pleasing sight of the whole Masonic fraternity marching two and two, with blue scarfs and Masons' aprons. Captain Tardy, in crimson scarf, with Bible in hand, Colonel Holmes by his side, with other insignia, the Master Masons, with striking symbols of the craft—all of these being gazed upon with that species of awe and admiration, known only in early childhood.

These halcyon days are past, celebrations seldom occur, and even the great pageantry of a Masonic funeral is seldom witnessed. It is a pity that so ancient and honored an institution should be ne-

---

* Quite as much so as that afforded by the military of Rochester, mentioned by Mr. Pickwick.

glected; for a conscientious Mason is obliged, at least outwardly, to conform to the rules of Christianity, and one who is truly one of the disciples of Hiram, is not far from the kingdom of God.

In the month of December, 1827, a Masonic ball was given at the Franklin Hotel, on the day of St. John the Baptist—such a ball and supper as only Mrs. Robert Morriss knew how to provide. Strange it seems that there should have been a sumptuous entertainment on the birth night of him whose "meat was locusts and wild honey;" but so it was, and so brilliant a display of beauty and fashion had never before been seen in Lynchburg. The Bible, the compass, the trowel, the mallet, and all the other appropriate symbols of Masonry were arranged round the spacious ball-room, amidst festoons of evergreen. None but ladies were admitted, till the folding doors opening, the Masons in full regalia entered the room, forming a circle. The citizens then followed, the grand Master Mason then taking out a book, read therefrom a short address; then was sung a Masonic ode by the Fraternity, concluding with a tribute to the ladies. The whole of this imposing scene now appears as a brilliant panorama; and mingled with pleasing recollections of that evening, how many sad thoughts arise, filling the heart with mournful retrospections of the past! The gay, the brave, the beautiful, so many now lie mouldering in silent dust, or live to mourn the broken ties of that joyous time. The late Maurice Garland, on this evening so full of youth and hope, the life of the little circle at that end of the room, and so gallant and imposing in the becoming regalia and crimson scarf; the lovely Sarah May, of Buckingham, in all the freshness and beauty of girlhood: a few years later, we beheld her as a wife and mother, not with the blissful expression of these sacred relations, but with the wan and fevered look of the invalid, hastening home to take a last farewell of a young family, and then meekly resign her gentle spirit to Him who gave it.

At this ball was JOHN ROBERTSON, usually known by the soubriquet of "Irish John Robertson." His broad forehead, his gold spectacles, his portly form, habited in the old-fashioned garb, with short breeches, long stockings and knee-buckles—all these made him, in outward appearance, a fac simile of Pickwick, though he was widely different from that worthy gentleman in bland manners and social traits, for Irish John Robertson was an isolated man.

Emigrating from Ireland when very young, he had chosen Lynchburg for his home, where, by a long course of frugality and industry, he had accumulated quite a large fortune. He was a singular man, mingling little in society, and seeming to regard Masonry as his sole tie to mankind. Whence was it, that thus he passed through life, without forming near connexions, or without seeming to feel that in the city of hills he had found a resting-place? Had a great disappointment in early life caused him to feel the vanity of worldly objects, and taught him to centre his hopes on a more sure basis, in the Celestial city? It was a different motive which actuated him—which had caused him "to rise up early, to sit up late, to eat the bread of sorrow." It had been the hope of his youth, the determination of his manhood, the comfort of his age. It was an intense desire to return to his beloved Emerald Isle, and there, amidst the cherished scenes of his boyhood, to pass his remaining days, and then to be laid quietly in the old church-yard by the side of his parents, not far from the grave of sweet Kathleen Mavourneen, for whom in childhood he had gathered the pratees and cut the bog, and whose taper fingers he had watched, as she spun the flax by the evening fire, whilst her low, sweet voice gently murmured the song of his native land.

In the autumn of 1830, arranging his affairs, he bade adieu to the old musty counting-room, and left Lynchburg buoyant with expectation of again beholding Ireland. Proceeding by rapid stages to New York, he embarked from that city to his native land, but on arriving at his old home, he found none there remaining who remembered him. The friends of his childhood and youth were no more, his father's dwelling had been levelled to the ground; even the household graves could not be identified, and in bitter disappointment the stern man wept.

In a brief time he re-embarked for America, and returning to Lynchburg, he sought his old counting-room, endeavoring to again interest himself in the pursuits of business. But, alas! the motive was at an end; the day dream of his youth was effaced; and in the scene of his early struggles, he lingered out for a few years a mournful existence. His remains were followed to their last resting-place by the Masonic Fraternity, who there rendered a last solemn tribute to him who for years had been a worthy and prominent member of the Lynchburg Lodge.

"When silent time wi' lightly foot
 Had trod on thirty years,
I sought again my native land
 Wi' mony hopes and fears—
Wha kens gin the dear friends I left
 May still continue mine,
Or gin I e'er again shall taste
 The joys I left behind.

As I drew near my ancient pile,
 My heart beat all the way,
Ilk place I passed seemed yet to speak
 O' some dear former day.
Those days that followed me afar,
 Those happy days of mine,
Which made me think the present joys
 A' naething to Lang Syne.

The ivied tower now met my eye,
    Where minstrels used to blow,
Nae frend stepped forth wi' open hand
    Nae weel kenned face I saw.
Till Donald tottered to the door,
    Wham I left in his prime,
And grat to see the lad return,
    He bore about Lang Syne.

I ran to ilka dear friends' room,
    As if to find them there,
I knew where ilk ane used to sit,
    And hang o'er mony a chair,
Till soft remembrance threw a veil
    Across these e'en a mine,
I closed the door and sobbed aloud
    To think on Auld Lang Syne.

Ye sons to comrades of my youth,
    Forgie an auld man's spleen,
Wha midst your gayest scenes still mourns
    The days he once has seen.
When time has past and seasons fled,
    Your hearts will feel like mine,
And aye the sang will maist delight,
    That minds ye of Lang Sync."

BLAMIRE.

THOMAS ESTON RANDOLPH.

"Lord, who shall abide in thy tabernacle? Who shall dwell in thy holy hill?

He that walketh uprightly and worketh righteousness, and speaketh the truth in his heart?"—*Psalm* XV.

THOMAS ESTON RANDOLPH was a native of Bristol, England, descended from the poet Thomas Randolph. He was also nearly connected with the family of Gifford, a name well known in the literary circles of Great Britain and America.

Mr. Randolph was a wealthy English gentleman, one of those merchant-princes who plough the main, bringing to our shores the luxuries of the old world, carrying in return the materials from which the skill of the Britons produce those beautiful textures, which, for so many years, was the sole dress of the Americans. Whilst in Virginia, after one of his voyages, he visited the different members of the Randolph family, and, during a sojourn at the hospitable mansion of Thomas Randolph, of Tuckahoe, captivated by the beauty aud loveliness of Jane Randolph, a daughter of that gentleman, he determined to settle in the Old Dominion, after having made seventeen voyages across the Atlantic. A gentleman of great worth and piety, Virginia may justly be proud of this her adopted son, who was shortly after married to Jane Randolph. Removing to a splendid estate, he there resided for a number of years in affluence and elegance, practising all the hospitality and living in all the ease and comfort of a wealthy planter and slaveholder.

At the time of her marriage, Mrs. Jane Randolph was a very beautiful woman; and, though remembered by the younger members of her family, only as a pale, feeble invalid, still her appearance, even at this time, was very lovely, and through all those years of sickness, she was the mainspring of the family—its order, comfort and happiness, depending on her. Though confined to her chamber six months of every year, yet from that spot emanated an influence gentle, yet so strong—practical, yet so beautiful—that its results are seen and felt now, and eternity will reveal the whole. To her daughters, she set an example of all a woman and Christian should be, showing woman's true place and teaching them to love it and its duties, because its lot was appointed by a Heavenly Father. She taught them to desire the love of God above all other things—and she was, herself, a living example of Christ, where all might read the beauty of holiness and the power of vital piety.

A sudden reverse depriving Mr. Randolph of nearly the whole of his estate, it was at this period that the grace of God was found sufficient to support, under trying circumstances, those who put their trust in Him.* Cheerfully relinquishing his elegant mansion, with all the comforts and luxuries to which they had been accustomed, and retaining only a small number of his faithful servants, he bade adieu to the beloved homestead, which had to him been the scene of unalloyed happiness. For a short time this family resided in New London, but in the autumn of 1827 they moved to Lynchburg, taking possession of the house formerly occupied by Robert Morriss, Esq., but recently the residence of Chiswell Dabney, Esq.

Sweet, indeed, are the uses of adversity! Such latent qualities it developes—such hidden good it brings to light! The daughters of this family, then in the full tide of youth and beauty, availed themselves of their talents, proving the superiority of their education, by now coming forward to aid those parents who in infancy and childhood had so kindly nurtured them. They immediately established a boarding-school of the very first order, and procuring a music teacher, the success of this youthful trio was unprecedented in Lynchburg, and the

---

* The Randolph family were devout Episcopalians.

and the establishment of this institution* was the dawning of a new era in the town; for with the usual school routine, there was excited in the scholar a taste for literature and a desire for mental cultivation. After continuing about eighteen months, the school was broken up by the removal of the family to Florida, where it was thought the health of Mrs. Randolph would improve, whilst breathing the mild, genial atmosphere of this sunny land. The first year after their removal to Florida, a decided improvement appeared to take place, but soon again she failed, and gradually, through patiently borne suffering, with words of love and counsel to each child, she passed away from earth.

Mr. Randolph survived his excellent wife for many years, his health and comfort being the especial care of his beloved youngest daughter. Beautiful was his old age!—so fervent and earnest in his devotions, so gentle and loving to all around him—patient under the failure of strength and hearing and all the powers of life. He was only confined to his bed a few days, and then he fell asleep, like an infant on his mother's bosom, on the day he attained the age of seventy-five; and, as a shock of wheat, fully ripe, is gathered into the

---

* This was about two years previous to the establishment of the Female School by F. G. Smith.

garner, so was he called to the mansions prepared for him.

Of the members of this family, there survive Mrs. Lucy Parkhill and Mary Page Randolph, who reside in the vicinity of Tallahassee, Florida; Dr. James Randolph and Arthur Randolph, Esq., of the same place. Elizabeth Randolph, the oldest daughter, was singularly lovely in character and appearance. She became the wife of Francis Eppes, Esq., of Poplar Forest, a grandson of Thomas Jefferson. Emigrating with her husband and family to Florida, she survived only a few years after their establishment in the South. Harriet, the second daughter, was also a very beautiful woman, endowed with every grace and accomplishment which could add a lustre to a well-cultivated mind and noble heart. During her residence in Lynchburg, she exercised a great sway and influence over the circle in which she moved, giving a tone to society, and embellishing it by her queenly appearance. Soon after their removal to Florida, she was married to Dr. Willis, but surviving only one year this event, her untimely death cast over her friends a dark shadow, which time, with its healing balm, cannot wholly dispel.

ANN LEWIS, who remained in this family during the period in which their school was in operation,

We can feel no surprise at the great success of Dr. was a native of Philadelphia, and a member of one of the first families in the City of Brotherly Love. Her mother was Miss Hartshorne, a relative of the distinguished physician of that name; and her father was at one time a wealthy gentleman, but failing in business whilst his children were all young, Mrs. Lewis wisely reared them, so that each might aid in the prosperity of the other. Ann, having a great genius for music, was educated as a teacher of this science, whilst the others were brought up just as their talents gave promise of success in any particular department. Just as Ann had reached the age of twenty, she was recommended to the Randolph family, by a lady from Virginia; and, bringing with her the warmest letters of introduction, this lovely and intelligent young lady met with a reception worthy of the Old Dominion; for kindness and hospitality were literally showered on her, so that she was the life of the social circle in Lynchburg, who will long remember her for her bright, cheerful wit and delightful music.

On leaving Lynchburg, she accepted a situation as music-teacher in Princeton, New Jersey, and shortly after, marrying Mr. William Clay of Philadelphia, she accompanied her husband to New Orleans, where they for several years resided. During the prevalence there of yellow-fever in

1833, William Clay was claimed as its victim, and from that time Ann Clay lost all desire for life, feeling that existence was in future a blank to her; so that those who knew and loved her best, could not selfishly grieve when in a brief space she was called hence to join her husband in another world.

The house occupied and owned formerly by Robert Morriss, Esq., was, in 1823, the residence of Mrs. BROWN, of Amherst, wife of Dr. James Brown,* who was a brother of the distinguished Dr. Thomas Brown of Edinburgh, formerly Professor of Moral Philosophy, the successor of Dugald Stewart, and the predecessor of the great and good Wilson.

This excellent lady was a valued resident of Lynchburg, for several years; and she is well-remembered, together with her family, by all of the old inhabitants of the town. She was the mother of Mrs. Archer Robertson, of Amherst, and Dr. John Brown, of Charlotte Courthouse, who received his education in Edinburgh, under the immediate care of his distinguished uncle.

A brief tribute must here be offered to THOMAS BROWN, second son of Dr. James Brown, of New

---

* The remains of Dr. James Brown repose in the Presbyterian graveyard of Lynchburg.

Glasgow, Amherst county. This young man was a resident of Lynchburg for some years, where he was greatly esteemed. He was a lawyer of fine talents and great promise. He married Miss Coleman, of Orange, or Caroline county, when he removed from Lynchburg. His untimely death in 1835, was a great sorrow to his relatives and numerous friends.

This house was for a brief period the residence of Col. Maurice Langhorne: it was then purchased and greatly improved by the late Maurice Garland, who was there residing at the date of his death, which occurred, in the prime of manhood, in 1841.

MISCELLANEOUS CHARACTERS.

Many persons in Lynchburg doubtless remember an unfortunate man, whose name was JAMES MOSELEY, but more commonly known and recognized by that of "Molly Peckerwood." But, few are aware that James Moseley was of respectable parentage, and gently reared and nurtured under the influence of the quiet doctrines of Quakerism. He was a native of Bedford county, passing his childhood and youth in the vicinity of Goose Creek, having been placed, when a mere boy, in the store of Christopher Anthony, Sr., where he for some years performed the offices of clerk and book-keeper. On removing to Lynchburg, Mr. Moseley married a young lady of an excellent family; but soon after that time he became intemperate, and continued to be so till the day of his death, with only a few brief intermissions. He had been a man of amiable disposition, and considering the period in which he lived, his education had been quite well conducted. His hand-writing was a very elegant one, and very proud was he of this accomplishment, never omitting any opportunity of making a display in chirography. The style of his letters was extremely like that of Wilkins Micawber, particularly in the manner of concluding them, and in the final flourish attached to his superscription. He was principally supported by a gentleman of Lynchburg, who placed him at the house of Captain Benjamin A. Philips; and every few days would Mr. Moseley send a note, elegantly gotten up, telling the particulars of his residence with that well known personage, and generally winding up by saying, " Captain B. A. Philips has shown me much attention and respect." On visiting the office of a gentleman, if no one were within, he would seat himself at the writing-desk, and with many ornamental strokes of the pen, he would write: " Sir, permit me to wonder that you should thus leave your office;" and about twice a year he would go to Bedford, where he established a writing-school, the proceeds of which he usually applied to furnishing himself with breakfast and "*trimmings*," as he designated his glass of brandy.

In the month of October, 1835, information being giving to James Moseley that Mr. Anthony was no more, he was greatly affected, and was instantly sobered. He attended the funeral, and followed the remains to the grave, where he remained till every one else had left the spot, and as he turned away, tears flowed down his furrowed cheeks, for he felt that he had lost his only friend. He survived this event some years, and died in the town of Lynchburg.

About the year 1819, Lynchburg was the abode of many distinguished loafers and beggars, some of whom would have been considered eminent in their profession, even in these days of progress. A family by the name of KIDD were the most prominent of this class, and systematically, in the town, did they levy a species of black mail on the more benevolent housekeepers. BALLAD KIDD, the head of the family, was by profession a house-painter; and should even a doubt be thrown on this fact, the following lines, from the poems of our townsman, TANDY BOGUS, set the matter beyond any dispute:

> "Ballad Kidd, indeed he did
> Agree to paint the church,
> Which, when he had done,
> He thought it poor fun,
> That he should be left in the lurch."

There was a material difference between Mr. Kidd and the bricklayer in Bleakhouse, the latter being visited in "due order" by Mrs. Pardiggle, whereas, Mr. Kidd himself called at regular intervals on his neighbors for such articles as were wanted for his domestic arrangements. Various excellent ladies were, like Mrs. Pardiggle, anxious for his soul's good, and tracts, books and religious newspapers were not unfrequently sent to this worthy house-painter; and, like the bricklayer, might have asked of himself, "Did I read that little book you sent me? no"—and he might have added, "nor the large book either;" for, after all their missionary efforts, the ladies were mortified and discouraged to learn that Mr. Kidd only used the large Bible sent him, as a sort of portfolio, or undisturbed place of safety in which to deposit some gaudy colored pictures which he possessed.

Like most eminent men, though, the capacious mind of Mr. Kidd found itself too much circumscribed in the quiet business of house-painting, and on a summer's eve, throwing off the shackles thus imposed on him, he might have been seen wending his way to the best fishing places on the river, accompanied by his sons, Baldwin and Jennings. When rewarded by a good string of fish, the family would fare sumptuously for a few days, only exacting from their neighbors bacon, lard, flour and pepper for the purpose of frying their fish. But if, on the contrary, the fishermen were unsuccessful, then were the boys and girls of the family sent out in various directions for the purpose of begging articles for supper and breakfast. Being very fond of molasses, they had their regular days for going out to beg that article; and on molasses days, they placed a large jug in the branch, partly concealing it with sand, and six or seven of the family would take the different wards of the town, and meeting at the place of rendezvous, they would deposit their sweet treasures in the earthen vessel, and jointly convey it to the dwelling of their respected relative.

Several of the females of the family were distinguished in the annals of the town. Miss Cecilia, having traveled to Richmond at the public expense, spending there several years in that large brick building, invidiously called the Penitentiary.

Miss Isabella suffered from ennui, and owing to this peculiar temperament, she became addicted to the use of spiritous liquors, often in a fit of absence removing from the counter those articles without paying for them; and for these offences, as well as for disorderly conduct, she was often escorted to jail by her assiduous attendant, that terror of evildoers, Mr. Mason.

About the year 1820, Captain EPPS SPAIN resided in a small brick house on Diamond Hill. This dwelling had been several times struck with lightning, and met with an accident of that sort during the sojourn there of Captain Spain. He was a humorous man, somewhat eccentric, paying considerable attention to the culture of flowers, and being fond of children, he not unfrequently had calls at his gate from the little folks on their way to school, and they always received from Captain Spain bouquets of pinks and roses, neatly arranged after the good old fashion, with a small bunch of thyme in their midst.

He owned a great many servants, and they all seemed to lead together a very easy life; but determining to remove to the Western country, for this purpose Captain Spain purchased a large old-fashioned yellow carriage, bordered with a wreath of blood-red roses. Perceiving that his preparations were nearly completed, the community began to wonder about his carriage horses, and to enquire when he designed getting a pair. The gentleman never gave his friends any satisfactory information on the subject; but about 10 o'clock one morning, the question about the quadrupeds was satisfactorily answered by Captain Spain coming out of the house, having his baggage put on the carriage, locking the door, and taking out of his pocket a piece of chalk, with which he wrote for "For rent." Finally, he seated himself in his carriage, taking out for perusal the morning's paper; then emerged from the kitchen, Sam, Pete, Bill, and a host of others. A part took hold of the carriage in front, and the rest at the back—and when last Captain Spain* was seen, he was sitting reading on the back

---

* Whether he really went all the way to the West in this

seat, a basket of apples by his side, of which he was liberally partaking, with as much non-chalance as Micawber in the stage eating walnuts out of a paper bag.

There were in Lynchburg many colored persons, both free and slaves, who possessed very good characters, and some of them were remarkable for good sense as well as for moral virtues. There were uncle Cato and aunt Sophy his wife, Arthur Holcombe, Armistead Pride, who was liberated by his master as a reward for his faithful services; Isaac Harrison, who was at one time a slave, but who purchased his freedom, sustaining an excellent character, and managing his bathing establishment with comfort and neatness. He was universally respected in Lynchburg, where he died suddenly a few years since.

There was BLIND BILLY, who will long be remembered, though the soft clear notes of his flute are now no more heard. Like all blind persons, he possessed a great talent for music, and at balls, parties, and military parades, he was a most important personage. Billy was a slave, owned by the late Dr. Howell Davies; and there was not an in-

---

manner, is not recollected, but it is certain that he thus left Lynchburg.

habitant of the town who would pass Blind Bill without at least a kindly word. His remembrance of voices was so remarkable, that he would by that means recognize an acquaintance whom he had not seen for fifteen or twenty years. His death, occurring a few years since, left in the musical world a chasm not easily supplied; for who can now play so sweetly for us those touching old Scotch airs, which tearfully recall the loved, the lost—or who can so gladden us with the sounds of merry music as poor Blind Bill!

THE CABELL FAMILY.

"WILLIAM CABELL was a native of Warminster, England, and was a surgeon in the British Navy. He arrived in the colony of Virginia in 1720, and, having taken up lands on both sides of James River in the present counties of Amherst, Nelson and Buckingham, he laid in that region the foundation of his fortune. He was a good scholar, and soon surrounded himself in his forest home* with a noble library. He was skilled in his profession, which he practiced within a wide sphere— was sagacious in business, was fond of rural sports, and revelled in the play of a sportive fancy, the sallies of which yet afford amusement at the firesides of his descendants. Dying at an advanced age in 1774, he did not live to hail the advent of Independence; but, like his contemporary John Lewis, he contributed four sons to the eventful contest in which it was won. Of these four sons, the eldest was William, the second was Joseph, who at various times was a member of the House of Burgesses, especially in 1769, when that body, dissolved

---

* Liberty Hall, now the residence of N. F. Cabell, Esq., Nelson county.

by Botetourt, adopted, in the Raleigh Tavern, the agreement already alluded to, and to which his name is attached; and, in 1770, when the Burgesses uniting with the merchants, organized the mercantile association which also bears his name. He was a member of the Convention for March, of July and of December, but gave place in May, 1776, to Gabriel Penn, and was subsequently a member of the Assembly. The third son, John, was a member of the Convention of 1775, and of the Convention of which we are now treating. The fourth, Nicholas, engaged in the military service of the Revolution, served under the command of La Fayette, was a member at various times of the Assembly, and an active politician. Thus did three sons of the elder Cabell serve in the respective Conventions, which were held before the Constitution went into effect."

Hugh Blair Grigsby.

Dr. George Cabell, eldest son of Col. John Cabell, mentioned above, was born at Green Hill,* Buckingham county, about the year 1766. He was reared in great hardihood, practising from earliest childhood all those athletic sports so well adapted for strengthening the constitution. Evincing a very decided talent for medicine and surgery, as soon as he had attained the proper age, he was sent to Philadelphia to attend the medical lectures. At that time, Philip Syng Physick was at the zenith of

---

* The present residence of Lewis W. Cabell, Esq.

his fame, and Dr. Cabell proved himself a disciple worthy of his distinguished master: and it was said in Lynchburg and the adjacent country, that Dr. Cabell's skill in surgery was unsurpassed; so that he was never known to display the smallest tremor or agitation, even whilst performing the most trying and difficult operations.

Those were the days of calomel and jalap—these medicines then being given without limit, followed by immense doses of tartarized antimony, and ipecachuana, when the suffering patient was only permitted the use of drinks luke-warm, and in small quantities; and, although Dr. Cabell did not entirely alter this state of affairs, yet he effected a considerable reform in these particulars; and, long ere the name of Broussais was known in America, Dr. Cabell advocated, in a great measure, the system introduced by that distinguished Frenchman, beginning by greatly diminishing the large portions of mercury then administered without any limitation, by allowing the use of ice and cooling drinks, and relying greatly on diet and abstinence, to reduce inflammatory symptoms.

The reputation of Dr. Cabell became so great, that he often found himself placed in painful and difficult positions—for, being regarded with awe and superstitious reverence, the patient and friends expected him to perform miraculous cures, keeping at bay even the great tyrant Death. There can be no doubt, however, that the strong faith felt in Dr. Cabell, was often beneficial to the sick, buoying up the exhausted spirits of the suffering, and thus permitting them to rally under disease.

At this time Dr. SAMUEL K. JENNINGS* was a resident of Lynchburg, being eminent for his skill in medicine; and, with his profession, combining the holy calling of a Minister of the Gospel, he was often during his practice called upon to pray for those who were ill, and to point the way to that great Physician, the Saviour of mankind.

On one occasion, both Dr. Cabell and himself were the medical attendants of a gentlemen dangerously ill. The symptoms of the patient were very bad, life appearing to be fast ebbing, so that even Dr. Cabell, with his sanguine disposition, feared that the sufferer would soon enter the confines of eternity. Overpowered by the solemnity of the scene, and having nearly abandoned all hope, Dr. Jennings sank on his knees by the bedside, pouring forth a prayer both touching and eloquent. A sudden ray of hope dawning on Dr. Cabell, he arose from his seat to try some fresh remedies, calling out to Dr. Jennings, "That's

---

* Many of our old inhabitants, doubtless, remember Dr. Jennings's "Steam-Bath"—an invention serviceable for rheumatism.

right, Brother Jennings*—you for his soul and I for his body!" The prayers of this excellent man, and the healing remedies of Dr. Cabell were blest: a perspiration appearing on the brow of the sick man, was pronounced by some, the dew of death; but, ere long, a gentle slumber being induced, so gentle, that

"They thought him dying when he slept!"

But, on awaking, the crisis of the disease was past, and, in a short time, the patient was entirely restored to health.

In early life, Dr. George Cabell was married to Sarah, the eldest daughter of Judge Edmund Winston. Mrs. CABELL was a lady of great elegance, beauty and refinement, dignifying and adorning the high station which she occupied. Their residence was, at one time, the house now owned by Mr. A. Armistead. They afterwards resided at "The Point of Honor," the handsome mansion now owned by D. Payne, Esq. Of a large family of sons and daughters, only two members survive—J. Breckenridge Cabell, Esq., of Greenbrier county, and George Kuhn Cabell, Esq.

This family were remarkable for their mental culture and accomplishments, particularly that of music, the three daughters performing, on different

---

* This anecdote is related by a connexion of Dr. Cabell.

instruments, in a manner that would excite astonishment and admiration even at the present day. Elvira, the eldest, was the wife of Spottswood Henry, Esq.; Alice, the second, married Walter Carrington, Esq. Marian Fontaine Cabell was a very superior woman, gifted with wit most refined, and a temperament highly poetical and imaginative. Long will she be remembered in her native town, with just pride, and her early, mournful fate deplored. The thrilling tones of her music still vibrate on the tender chords of memory, though her beautiful hands have long lain in the silent tomb. She married Dr. Landon Cabell, of Amherst, surviving only a few years this event.

The high-minded, warm-hearted WILLIAM LEWIS CABELL was the youngest son of Dr. George Cabell. His early death, and that of his young wife, has already been mentioned; but, in this place, naturally the retrospective thought carries us back to that period when the greater part of our community assembled with downcast looks and tearful eyes, to listen to their funeral sermon, preached at the same time by the Rev. F. G. Smith, at the Episcopal Church of Lynchburg.

DR. JOHN J. CABELL.

John Jordan Cabell was the second son of Colonel John Cabell, of Buckingham, and he was born at Greenhill, where his parents at that time resided. He studied medicine in Philadelphia, where he graduated with high honors; and, establishing himself soon after in Lynchburg, he rose rapidly in his profession. His reputation as a surgeon was not so great as that of his brother; but, in the practice of medicine, he occupied a standing equally high. Dr. John Cabell had an impediment in his speech, which made him appear to disadvantage in society, yet he was a man of enlarged and cultivated mind, wielding the pen with power, particularly on political subjects:* but the trait for which John J. Cabell was most remarkable, was an untiring perseverance in the most arduous pursuits, and a recuperative energy in the most trying emergencies of life; and prominent as are those dispositions in the Cabell family, yet in no instance have any of its members excelled Dr. John Cabell. An anecdote related of him when a boy, may be here introduced to display the resources possessed by him, even at that tender age.

---

* He established, in Lynchburg, the paper called the "Jeffersonian Republican."

His father was a man of wealth, and was possessed of great energy and industry. One morning coming in from a very busy scene on his plantation, somewhat tired and impatient too, in consequence of the delay of his customary cup of coffee, he upbraided John most unjustly for being idle—a charge quite undeserved by the subject of this sketch, and which might have been shared by many other young men, previous to their obtaining a profession, or being settled on plantations of their own. Stung to the quick by these reproaches, John determined to go to the county of Monroe, where, at that time, his father owned a large body of land. When arrived there, finding that the inhabitants of that secluded spot desired a little polish, in the way of a dancing school, he immediately offered himself as a teacher, and was gladly accepted by those primitive people. On the day appointed for the opening of his "Terpsichore Hall," accompanied by a fiddler, he proceeded to the place of rendezvous. The tardy country mails, even in those days, sometimes brought letters, and just as the first strain of music had been played, preparatory to commencing evolutions, a letter was handed to the youthful amateur dancing-master. The lines were from his father, urging his speedy return to the paternal roof, and promising to settle him on a plantation, or to send him to Philadelphia to study medicine. With his characteristic taciturnity, John Cabell merely remarked, in a laconic manner, "This school is dismissed"—and directly he set out on his return to Buckingham.

Soon after graduating in medicine, Dr. J. Cabell married Harrianne Davies, of Bedford, a lady of great worth, and whose kind acts and amiable disposition will never be forgotten by her friends throughout the State. Dr. Cabell accumulated a large fortune, and, purchasing a valuable estate in Kanawha, when somewhat advanced in life, he established himself there permanently, carrying on with great energy and perseverance an extensive salt manufactory. It is related of him, that soon after purchasing this property, and when comparatively a young man, he ascertained that, for carrying on his salt works, a certain piece of machinery was absolutely necessary. At this time, there were no steamboats on the Ohio and Kanawha Rivers, and it was impossible to purchase this piece of machinery nearer than Cincinnati; so Dr. Cabell went from Kanawha to that place on horseback, purchased the desired article, took it on his shoulder, and thus returned to the salt manufactory. The piece of machinery was an immensely long iron pipe, extending a distance, both in advance and in rear, so that it was visible long before the rider, and left a trace when he was partially out of sight.*

---

* This anecdote is related by the late F. Sydnor, Esq.

J. Cabell in life, when we hear of his brave combat with its troubles and difficulties. In the year 1830, he removed his family to Kanawha; and, during the summer of 1834, he died very suddenly from the effects of exposure whilst attending to his business. His excellent wife survived him many years, dying in Lynchburg in the year 1842.

Of a large family, Mrs. HENRIANNE EARLY, of Lynchburg alone survives. She is the wife of Samuel Henry Early, Esq., and they occupy the old family mansion, in which for many years Dr. Cabell resided, and where his good wife so kindly and gently dispensed her hospitalities. As we look back and contemplate the departure of that household band, we are tempted to wish that we could turn aside to the paths of fiction, making a pleasing record of blooming health and long life. Mary, the oldest daughter, possessed a mind of the highest order: she was poetical, and contemplative, and, from childhood, she was remarkable for her deep and fervent aspirations for a higher and nobler state of existence. When she was very young, her father became a convert to the doctrines of Emmanual Swedenborg—the diffusion of which he prosecuted with all the fervid zeal of his nature,— and this favorite daughter deeply sympathized with her beloved parent in these spiritual views, seeming to understand all of his feelings, and to be aware of his thoughts almost before their utterance; but this sacred intercourse was broken up, Death claiming for his own the loving, gentle, intellectual Mary.

Mrs. Richard Cralle, Mrs. Henry Ward, and Mrs. Thomas Friend, were all gifted with superior minds and most kindly dispositions. Paulina, the most beautiful girl of Lynchburg, joined the sacred throng on high, in the month of May, 1835: the touching beauty of her death-scene, was tenderly recorded by one who stood beside her and has long since joined her in Heaven:

> "There is no death—what seems so is transition:
> This life of mortal breath,
> Is but a suburb of the life elysian,
> Whose portal we call Death!"

Of the members of the Cabell family in Lynchburg, Mrs. WILLIAM LEWIS, of Mount Athos, may properly be mentioned. She was one of the daughters of Joseph Cabell, mentioned in the extract from the speech of Hugh Blair Grigsby, Esq. She was a faithful and affectionate friend, and possessed a warm, generous heart. Her husband belonged to the Lewis family, of Augusta and Monroe, and he was one of the sons of the brave, gallant William Lewis, of Augusta, who so nobly participated in the revolutionary struggles. She survived her worthy husband many years, making her home principally in Kentucky, with her sister, the venerable Mrs. Breckenridge, who was also a daughter of Joseph Cabell.

Mrs. BRECKENRIDGE was the wife of Attorney General Breckenridge, who received that appointment from General Washington; and, during the lifetime of her husband, she emigrated to Kentucky, where her descendants reside. She was the mother of the distinguished Presbyterian ministers of that name, and grand-mother of John C. Breckenridge, the Vice President of the United States. She was also the mother of Mrs. General Porter, of Black Rock, a lady distinguished throughout the Union for her worth and excellence, as well as for her elegant manners and appearance. Not a great many years since, Mrs. Breckenridge visited her native State, calling on many friends and relatives, and captivating all who met her by her warm-hearted sincerity.

LANDON CABELL, Esq., resided for many years in the vicinity of Lynchburg, in the county of Amherst. He was a grandson of William Cabell, of Warminster, England; and a son of William Cabell, of Union Hill. He made his home, also, in Lynchburg for a period of eighteen months. He was a high-minded, chivalrous man—a true gentleman of the old school, with impulses most generous and feelings most kindly. Of liberal education, he continued through life to derive pleasure from the use of an extensive library. He died in 1834, leaving a widow and three children, of whom Dr. R. H. Cabell, of Richmond, and Mrs. E. Preston, of Missouri, survive. Many little incidents might be recorded to show the generous nature of this excellent man, and the delicacy of feeling which governed all his actions. Residing for some years in the mountains of Nelson county, he was chosen magistrate—an office but little adapted to his kind, sensitive disposition. He, however, discharged its duties with great zeal and faithfulness, and when compelled to render a verdict, or judgment, against a poor man, Mr. Cabell invariably paid the costs for him.

Mrs. PAULINA DANIEL, the second wife of Judge Daniel, was a sister of Dr. George Cabell, and Mrs. George Whitelocke was a daughter of Samuel Cabell, Esq., of Soldier's Joy. She was also a sister of P. H. Cabell, of Lynchburg, well esteemed in the town, and who died in 1838. Mrs. Whitelocke was a lady of most excellent disposition, and of fine personal appearance; and her domestic management was the most superior in Lynchburg. She resided in the house owned by Mr. Whitelocke, just below the house of the Rev. W. S. Reid. In

1827 this excellent lady departed this life, leaving only one daughter, Mrs. Dr. Bohannan, of Richmond.

Mrs. EMELINE SCRUGGS, so well beloved in Lynchburg, is the youngest daughter of Colonel Samuel J. Cabell, of Soldier's Joy. This lady is the widow of B. E. Scruggs, Esq., a well known and esteemed citizen of Lynchburg, who died in the winter of 1856, and whose remains repose in the Presbyterian graveyard.

Nor can this chapter be closed without a brief tribute to the memory of Mrs. John Morriss, of Lynchburg. She was the oldest daughter of Dr. Samuel J. Cabell, of Bedford. Her lovely, amiable disposition, and bright, beautiful face, are indelibly impressed on memory; and, whilst we deplore her mournful, untimely death, which took place ere the bridal wreath had withered on her fair brow, we yet feel every assurance that she now rejoices in Paradise, crowned with never-fading flowers. Her remains repose in the extreme corner of the Presbyterian graveyard, where a most elegant, simple and appropriate monument marks the spot.

THE WINSTON FAMILY.

> " He kept a brave old mansion,
> At a bountiful old rate,
> With a good old porter to relieve
> The old poor at his gate.
> Like a fine old English gentleman,
> All of the olden time."

With the name of Cabell is intimately associated that of Winston, not only from their occupying the same position in society, but from the circumstance of two of the sons of Colonel John Cabell, of Buckingham, marrying daughters of Judge Edmund Winston, of Chesnut Hill, Campbell county. Dr. George Cabell was united in marriage to Sarah Winston, and some few years later, Frederick Cabell, Sr., of Nelson, became the husband of Alice, the second daughter.

Judge EDMUND WINSTON was a native of Hanover county, and when a young man he chose for his wife Alice Winston, his first cousin. Settling in the latter part of the last century near Lynchburg, his abode was the seat of that genuine old Virginia hospitality, which, in this age of steam and telegraph, is so fast departing from our midst. Of the high talents and legal abilities of this eminent jurist, it is not here the intention to make a record, but only to recall a few incidents connected with this family, alike distinguished for moral worth and high mental attainments. Sarah, the accomplished and excellent wife of Dr. George Cabell, has already been mentioned. ALICE, the second daughter, was a very superior woman, her mind being of a fine order, and in the highest degree cultivated; and it is related that the late Joseph C. Cabell, on his return from a European tour, where he had access to the most brilliant and enlightened circles of the old country, was heard to say that he in Europe had seen few ladies equal to Alice Winston, and none superior.

On becoming the wife of Frederick Cabell, Sr., and leaving the paternal roof, this lady entered on a life entirely new to her, in a county at that time thinly settled, and the inhabitants primitive in their habits; yet she found herself perfectly at home amid those simple scenes, carrying on with zeal and energy the manufacture of domestic fabrics, continuing to improve her mind, and in after years assisting in the education of her children, from whom she was taken suddenly in 1814, whilst the greater part of them were in infancy.

The members of the Winston family are all distinguished for that calm self-possession and dignified composure, which would cause any one of them to be at perfect ease in the presence even of a crowned monarch. One of the younger daughters married Mr. Moseley, of Bedford, and this excellent woman resided for many years in the vicinity of Liberty, where she led a most useful, happy life, and where many of her descendants still live, cherishing the memory of her virtues as a sacred legacy. MARY, the youngest daughter, married Colonel John Johns, of Buckingham, and dying five years since, she was interred at Chesnut Hill, their former residence. GEORGE WINSTON, the oldest son, married a daughter of Patrick Henry. Emigrating some years since to Alabama, his descendants reside in that State, one of his sons being at present Governor of Alabama. Of this large family, EDMUND WINSTON, Esq., of Amherst, alone survives. Well known and beloved throughout a large circle of friends, who have partaken of his noble hospitality, this excellent man is now calmly passing the evening of his days, patiently waiting the time when his broken household shall be happily re-united in a heavenly home. More than half a century since, Mr. Winston married Caroline, the daughter of Colonel John Wiatt, and who still survives; and this venerable couple have lived to witness many changes.

Numberless anecdotes are related of Judge Winston, all tending to show that high-minded, chivalrous disposition which so adorned the Cavalier gentlemen of the Old Dominion. During the violence of the French Revolution, a family of French refugees accidentally made Chesnut Hill their temporary home. They were perfect strangers to Judge Winston, and the hospitality tendered to them was such as a Christian would, in its broadest sense, exercise, without any interested motives whatever. They proved to be persons of great elegance and refinement, and Madame Laporte and her daughters enlivened much the social circle of Chesnut Hill; and though so recently from a scene of blood and carnage, yet, with all the buoyancy and versatility of the French nation, they related anecdotes of the Tuilleries, Versailles, and many incidents connected with the gifted, but ill-fated Madame Roland, and the lovely, unfortunate Marie Antoinette. After a short time, Judge Winston established these ladies on a plantation owned by himself, in the neighborhood of New London, and from that place they often visited Chesnut Hill, exhibiting all those courtesies in which the French nation so excel all others. On the death of an aged relative of the Winston family, Madame Laporte and her daughters came down on a formal visit of condolence, and very soon after, a large chest was by them packed with brocades, French fans, slippers, laces, silks, &c., and sent to the Misses Winston. The contents, being viewed with great delight by the young ladies, a distribution was about being made, when their father, entering the room, caused a stop to be put to these proceedings, by having the chest nailed up again and returned, with many polite messages to the French ladies, deeming that it was not right to accept such favors in the position which he occupied to them. A part of Madame Laporte's fortune having been rescued and remitted to her, these ladies, leaving the upper country, selected for themselves a home in the neighborhood of Petersburg. Victoire, the oldest daughter, married a Virginian by the name of Campbell, and settled in the town of Petersburg. Many years after this time, Judge Winston was attending one of his courts in that town. He had gone thither in his carriage, and whilst there, one of his horses having died, the Judge was much troubled about returning home, for in those days there were no public conveyances. Delighted to have an opportunity of repaying her many obligations to Judge Winston, Mrs. Campbell had insisted on his making her house his home during his stay in Petersburg, and the death of his carriage horse was, to this lively French woman, a positive pleasure, as it afforded her the great gratification of lending him one of her carriage horses, and sending with him a servant man to bring the horse home. By a singular coincidence, the oldest son of Mrs. Campbell, many years after this time, accidentally met with Mary Moseley, a granddaughter of Judge Winston, and being mutually pleased, the acquaintance led to a marriage between them. Mr. Campbell was a well known and esteemed minister of the Presbyterian Church. They resided for some years in Bedford county, but removing to the West, both himself and his lovely wife there died, leaving several orphan children. An incident, touching from its simplicity, will be recorded of these sisters of the Winston family. Like the five sisters of York,* these four daughters of Judge Winston together wrought with diligent hands a large piece of embroidery, each one laying off her appointed portion, and anticipating the time when the survivors would tenderly and mournfully gaze on the record which would recall so much of joy and sorrow. It was kept in the family, and often brought forth by these sisters, when they met, till the last remaining sister would contemplate it, and by her this piece of embroidery was a map or chart of memory, every bud and flower bringing before her the past, and vividly recalling the times of hope and youth, when these four sisters encircled the family hearth, gladdening with innocent mirth their happy home.

---

* Incident of the five sisters of York, related in Nicholas Nickleby.

Colonel JOHN WIATT, for many years a valued and beloved citizen of Lynchburg, was a native of the lower country. He was a most gallant gentleman, combining all the courtesy of the old Cavalier of Virginia, with feelings the most ardent, generous and affectionate. When a young man he married Wilhelmina Jordan, a sister of Mrs. William Cabell, of Union Hill, and Mrs. John Cabell, of Buckingham. Colonel Wiatt served with bravery in the Revolutionary war, and was present at the battle of Guilford Court-house; but shortly after the termination of the war, he came to reside on his plantation in the county of Amherst, and a few years later he removed to Lynchburg, where, to the day of his death, he continued a useful and revered resident.

Mrs. MINA WIATT was a lady of great beauty and vivacity, possessing a fund of wit, refined by good humor, and such an acquaintance with human nature as enabled her in a short time, with ready tact, to form a just estimate of all with whom she came in contact. She was, in old age, very lovely and graceful, and her appearance as a young bride was thus described by a lady* who met her at her

---

* Mrs. Anne Cabell, at that time Miss Carrington, and afterwards Mrs. Wm. Cabell, of Union Hill.

bridal party at Union Hill: "Mrs. Wiatt was a blooming, beautiful woman, with brilliant black eyes and a profusion of dark hair. She was habited in pink brocade trimmed with silver, with a double skirt of the same; her hair was dressed with pink and silver, and done up in cushions; and her sparkling jewelry set off her elegant appearance, when slowly going through the dignified, graceful movements of the minuet."

Colonel Wiatt and his excellent wife, doubtless, in a great measure led and directed the taste of the infant town of Lynchburg, of which they were the earliest settlers. Of cultivated minds and of great skill in horticulture and gardening, and perfect adepts in every sort of domestic manufacture, Col. and Mrs. Wiatt, by their wise and prudent counsels, greatly assisted housekeepers younger than themselves.

They had been reared under the usages and observances of the Church of England; but after the Revolutionary war, that denomination becoming nearly extinct, they worshiped with great liberality in other churches, and from the establishment of the first Presbyterian Church of Lynchburg, they regularly attended there and communed. Col. Wiatt being deaf, was accommodated with an elevated seat, nearly on a line with the pulpit; and those accustomed in their childhood to see there his venerable form, in wrapt attention, feel, on entering that old church, something wanting, when they gaze on the vacant spot where sat Colonel John Wiatt.

This excellent couple lived to great age, Mrs. Wiatt surviving for some years her husband, who died in 1827. Of this large family alone survive Mrs. Caroline Winston, of Amherst, and Colonel Samuel Wiatt, both of whom are well known and appreciated in our community. Captain Wiatt is a worthy, high-minded gentleman, possessing a warm, affectionate heart, joined to wit of a high order, which, together with a fine memory and habits of great observation, render his experience of life truly amusing and interesting, and such as would make him an invaluable aid to Dickens and Thackeray.

Captain Wiatt was first married to Mary, a daughter of Benjamin Brown, Esq., of Amherst. She was a lady of great personal beauty, and her mind equally lovely. She died in the summer of 1825, at the residence of Edmund Winston, Esq., of Amherst. A few years later, Captain Wiatt was united to Miss S. Brown, of Lynchburg, a daughter of our good citizen, Matthew Brown, Esq. This lady, for moral worth and mental superiority, was unrivalled in her native town. Studious and diligent from early childhood, to her husband's house she carried these dispositions, which, together with her energy and industry, made her a rare combination of all that was excellent in woman. She died in 1842, and her death scene will never be forgotten by her friends, whose faith was thereby strengthened in the power of religion to make bright the dark valley of the shadow of Death.

THE NORVELL FAMILY.

"The world is filled with the voices of the dead. Sweet and solemn voices are they, speaking with unearthly authority; coming back to us in the messages of angels."
INFLUENCE.

Captain WILLIAM NORVELL, Sr. resided for many years in the large mansion-house, at present occupied by John M. Otey, Esq. Previously to the time of his coming to Lynchburg, Captain Norvell resided in the county of Amherst, where he married Anne, the second daughter of Colonel John Wiatt. Captain Norvell was an excellent, high-minded gentleman, possessing great energy and industry. Accumulating a large fortune, and ably for many years filling the office of President of the Bank of Virginia, he died long before attaining old age, leaving a numerous young family, the care of whom devolved on his widow, Mrs. ANNE NORVELL. This lady was a very lovely and remarkable woman, inheriting much of the grace and personal beauty of her mother, Mrs. Mina Wiatt, together with that elasticity of disposition and buoyancy of character, which contributed towards forming one of the finest characters with which Lynchburg has ever been adorned.

Remarkably cheerful and even gay in early life, as soon as Mrs. Norvell became religious, she gave up all worldly pleasures; joyful in the Lord, she ever found His service a pleasant one, and into her religion were infused the buoyancy and hopefulness of her disposition, causing her in her daily walk to show forth the beauty of holiness, thereby proving to the worldling, that

> "Religion never was designed,
> To make our pleasures less."

Thus did Mrs. Norvell live, in all the ordinances of the Lord blameless, perfecting holiness in the fear of God. An active member of the Dorcas Society, a zealous member of the Methodist Church, dispensing aid to the suffering and relief to the sick, encouraging and stimulating her minister by her active performance of duties, and wisely governing and guiding her own household, so that when "at midnight the cry was heard that the Bridegroom cometh," she arose like the wise virgins, and went forth to meet him.

> "Rise, saith the Master, come unto the feast;
> She heard the call and came with willing feet;
> But thinking it not otherwise than meet
> For such a bidding to put on her best,

> She is gone, as for a few short hours,
> Into her bridal closet, there to await
> For the unfolding of the palace gate,
> That gives her entrance to the blissful bowers.
> We have not seen her yet, though we have been
> Full often to her chamber door, and oft
> Have listened underneath the porter's gate,
> And laid fresh flowers, and whispered short and soft;
> But she hath made no answer, and the day
> From the clear West is fading fast away."
>
> ALFORD.

Many of the members of this interesting family survive. Captain William Norvell, of Lynchburg, Mrs. John M. Otey, and Mrs. John Warwick, also, of that place, and well known and esteemed in this section of country; Mrs. Daniel Warwick, of Baltimore, Mrs. Maria Waller, and Fayette Norvell, Esq., of Shelbyville, Ky., and Samuel G. Norvell, Esq., of Cincinnati. The first distinct recollection of this family commences only a few weeks previous to the death of Mrs. Emeline Trent, second daughter of Captain William Norvell. This lovely lady was, whilst very young, married to Dr. Trent, of Cumberland, and in less than two years she was the bride, the widow, the childless mother and the lifeless corpse. Her happiness thus in the very day-spring of life crushed and withered by accumulated sorrows, she yet, with all the fortitude of a strong mind and a gentle heart, endeavored to rally and cast aside somewhat the heavy weight of woe which had so overshadowed her youth. After preparing for a visit to the relatives of her husband in Cumberland, she came to make a parting visit at the house now occupied by Henry Dunnington, Esq. With what warm, childish admiration was her fair face gazed on, her golden hair so beautifully contrasted with her deep mourning habit. As she sat by the window, the sunbeams danced around her, playing in her bright tresses, thus throwing around her a halo, and giving to her face that angelic expression it was so soon destined to wear in Heaven.

In a brief time after her departure were the tidings of her death received, and the day on which her lovely remains were brought to Lynchburg will ever, by her family and friends, be remembered with tender and mournful interest; for a two-fold sorrow might now be said to attend the house of Captain William Norvell. Several years previous, Martha Ann, the eldest daughter, had married Chiswell Dabney, Esq., and ere two years had elapsed of her happy married life, the young wife was suddenly called hence, just as she had for a few weeks only rejoiced in the sweet dream of her motherhood. Tenderly had she been laid to rest in the garden of her parents, where her grave served constantly to remind them of their irreparable loss. But on the death of Mrs. Trent, Mrs. Martha Dabney was disinterred, and these two lovely sisters were together borne a few miles from the town to the plantation of Captain William Norvell, which, from that period, became the burial place of the Norvell family.

We cannot close without a brief tribute to the memory of JOHN E. NORVELL, second son of Captain William Norvell. He was born in the town of Lynchburg, and principally educated in that place, where he was greatly beloved. Elegant in person and manners, and gifted with feelings the most amiable and honorable, John E. Norvell will ever be remembered with affection and admiration by those with whom he was associated in his native place. Possessing exquisite talents for music, from this art he derived no selfish gratification, frequently making a sacrifice of his own ease and convenience in order to administer to the pleasure and cheerfulness of others. A D'Orsay in polished elegance, without the heartlessness of fashion; and in the perfect taste of his attire—a Brummel, devoid of the cringing servility of that "master of the Prince Regent," John Norvell will ever live in the remembrance of his friends, and will be cherished as a bright, sunny spot in the memory of bygone days!

THE WARWICK FAMILY.

MAJOR WILLIAM WARWICK.

Major WILLIAM WARWICK, for many years the revered and excellent visitor of our town, was a native of the county of Buckingham,* where was passed his boyhood. Settling whilst a young man in the county of Amherst, and occupying the station of a prominent bank officer, Major Warwick may be justly claimed by our town as a citizen, particularly as through life he was a constant worshiper in the churches of Lynchburg. Major Warwick was a gentleman of the most honorable feelings. His integrity and uprightness were so conspicuous, and so unswerving was he in the prosecution of what he deemed the right, that many were heard to say that these qualities invested him with a moral sublimity.

---

* Buckingham or Nelson, the writer is not certainly informed.

Major Warwick was thrice married, and the children of all these marriages are good and prosperous. May not this be traced, in a great measure, to the immediate hand of Providence, who has promised that the children of the righteous are blessed to the third and fourth generation. The family of Warwick are all long-lived, the venerable mother of Major Warwick attaining the age of 102, and dying in the county of Nelson a few years since. The traits of filial piety have, in this family, been conspicuous from generation to generation, and we now witness a fulfillment of the promise to those who honor parents, "that it may be well with thee, and and that thou mayest live long in the earth." This excellent man died some years since, at an advanced age, leaving to his descendants a sacred legacy in a name untarnished, and connected only with "such things as are pure, lovely, and of good report."

Of the members of this large family are John M. Warwick, Esq., a prominent citizen of Lynchburg, Messrs. Corbin and Abram Warwick, of Richmond, Daniel Warwick, of Baltimore, and Mrs. Saunders and Mrs. Thomas Leftwich, of Bedford county.

The remains of the first wife of Major William Warwick repose in the yard attached to the residence of H. Dunnington, Esq., which, at the time of her decease was the only burying ground* in the newly formed town of Lynchburg. An aspen tree stands at the foot, placed there by the hand of her affectionate daughter, Mrs. Stuart. A very large spreading tree formerly cast its shade over this quiet resting-place, but in the year 1820 it was torn up by the roots during a violent storm, leaving alone the quivering aspen tree, with its beautiful alternations of white and green, reminding us of the living green of the courts above, surrounded by shadowy forms robed in spotless white!

Captain JAMES WARWICK, a brother of Major Warwick, was for a number of years a respected resident of Lynchburg. His residence was exactly opposite to that of Colonel John Wiatt; and with this excellent man did he "oft take sweet counsel, walking together to the house of God." Captain Warwick was a devout member of the first Presby-

---

* On this spot was the first Church of Lynchburg, to which this cemetery was attached. Many of the bodies were moved to the Methodist burying ground, but others were left, and the spot where they reposed identified by their friends. A barracks was at one time held in the part of the house nearest the Court-house. This place was at one time the residence of the Rev. Mr. Tompkins and his family. They were the earliest settlers, and Mrs. Tompkins lived to great age, dying only a few years since.

terian Church of Lynchburg, and conspicuous for the ardor of his attachment to his beloved pastor, adhering closely to him in the division of the church, regardless of the changes of those around him. This excellent man died some years since in the town of Lynchburg.

ROBERT MORRISS.

"Is any sick? the man of Ross relieves,
Prescribes, attends, and medicine makes and gives."
POPE'S MAN OF ROSS.

Thirty-eight years since, the large dwelling opposite the residence of Dr. Robert Early was owned by ROBERT MORRISS, Esq. At that time Mr. Morriss was a man of wealth; his home was the abode of the most genuine hospitality, and the refuge of many whom poverty and death had made desolate. A sudden reverse depriving him of his fortune, himself and his excellent wife there established a house for receiving boarders. But not with the prosperity of Mr. Morriss departed that kind spirit which had succored so many in their hour of adversity. The success of this good couple in hotel keeping was very great; the "bread they had so freely cast on the waters," was now returned, and they were still enabled to pursue charities the most enlarged.

Was the mother of a helpless family called suddenly hence from her young children? Then would

Mr. and Mrs. Morriss take charge of the little ones till a permanent asylum could be provided for them. Did want or sickness invade the dwellings of those surrounding them, then who so prompt to render assistance as this worthy couple, the counterpart of Pope's Man of Ross, save that Mr. Morriss was blest with a good wife, in which he had the advantage of the Man of Ross.

> " Thrice happy man, enabled to pursue
> What all so wish, but want the power to do;
> Oh! say what sums that generous hand supply,
> What mines to swell the generous charity.
>
> Of debts and taxes, wife and children clear,
> This man possessed five hundred pounds a year;
> Blush, grandeur, blush; proud stars, withdraw your blaze—
> Ye little stars, hide your diminished rays!"
>
> POPE'S MAN OF ROSS.

For a number of years, Mr. and Mrs. Morriss continued to supply the temporal wants of many. They educated a number of nieces and nephews, rearing them as their own children, and placing them in independent situations. In the year 1824, Mr. Morriss took possession of the Washington House, which he kept with great success for several years; then he moved to the Franklin Hotel, of which he was the worthy and beloved proprietor for a length of time, dispensing to all around him his unbounded kindness, having in his establishment boarders whom he had kept for a number of years without compensation. This excellent couple survive, residing in Lynchburg. Long may they enjoy health and happiness, experiencing in full the promise made to the charitable: "Blessed is he that considereth the poor: Thou shalt make his bed in sickness."

THOMAS WIATT, Sr.

"In the heraldry of Heaven, goodness precedes greatness."

Bishop Horne.

Thomas Wiatt was a gentleman of great worth and excellence, and a younger brother of Colonel John Wiatt. They were descended from an English family of that name, conspicuous in the days when our State was a colony. In the year 1827, Mr. Wiatt resided in the house owned and occupied by Dr. Robert Early. When a young man, Thomas Wiatt was united in marriage to Sarah Miller, a daughter of one of Lynchburg's earliest and most estimable settlers. A few years since, the ancient dwelling of Mr. Miller remained a short distance above the place where now stands Mr. Jesse Hare's stately building. It was a long, lone dwelling, with shelving porches, but its place is now doubtless supplied by some more modern structure.

Mrs. Wiatt was very congenial to her husband,

in the possession of a disposition most cheerful and buoyant, together with a lively wit, tempered with great sweetness of temper and good humor. Passing through various alternations and reverses, they yet preserved, unharmed, these happy dispositions. Active and useful members of the Methodist Church, they proved by their walk and profession of religion, that

> "Her ways are ways of pleasantness,
> And all her paths are peace!"

This good man died in the summer of 1828, leaving a large family, several of whom survive. His worthy and venerable wife still continues on earth her pilgrimage, having for many years survived her three daughters.

MARY WIATT became the wife of D. Hoffman, Esq., and carried into her married life all those gentle, lovely traits of character which so caused her to shine as friend, sister and daughter. Greatly beloved in Lynchburg, her memory is deeply enshrined in the hearts of friends, who cherish the remembrance of her goodness with a desire that they too may, like her, merit the commendation bestowed by our Saviour on Mary of old: "She hath done what she could."

MARTHA, the youngest daughter, was the brightest girl in Lynchburg—and her sweet smile and joyous countenance are vividly remembered along with her many virtues, though she has long since laid in the silent tomb. She married William Massie, Esq., of Pharsalia, Nelson county; and, surviving her marriage only a few years, she left one daughter, who is now Mrs. Ellen Warwick, of Nelson county.

THE DABNEY FAMILY.

C. DABNEY—MRS N. DABNEY.

CHISWELL DABNEY, Esq. is a native of the county of Hanover. About the year 1812 he settled in the town of Lynchburg, and, soon after commencing the practice of the law, he has since that time continued to add constantly to his legal reputation, and to secure the regard and esteem of the community in which he resides. His talents as a lawyer, and his ability as an efficient bank officer, are too well known to need here any eulogy; but it is a great gratification to associate the name of this gentleman with that of Mrs. Nancy Dabney, his wife, who was the oldest daughter of Thomas Wiatt, Esq.

This lady was a native of the county of Amherst, where were spent her childhood and youth; yet she was educated in Lynchburg, and our town naturally feels desirous to claim as one of its own daughters, this bright, talented, and excellent lady. She was a very superior woman, endowed with a mind of the highest order, and gifted with wit most brilliant, though ever tempered with gentleness and good humor. A strong resemblance in character, manners and disposition, existed between Mrs. Dabney and the family of James Pleasants, of Goochland—both possessing those warm-hearted dispositions, that happy gift of extracting from passing scenes interest and amusement, and of enlivening the fireside by those happy sallies of wit and humor; thus keeping at bay all the minor, worrying cares of life, which so often corrode and canker the heart, even more than those heavy afflictions in which the hand of Providence is immediately recognized. Many early recollections of Mrs. Dabney now fill the heart, blended with days of childhood, when she with other loved forms surrounded the cheerful family hearth; and words then spoken are still fondly cherished, and often called to mind, though the voices which uttered them have long been silent in the grave. This excellent lady died in the summer of 1834, leaving five daughters, at that time a lovely unbroken household. About sixteen years since, two of these daughters were called hence to join their mother in Heaven, a week only intervening between the departure of these beautiful girls. Three of these sisters survive: Mrs. John S. Langhorne, of Amherst; Mrs. Lucy Otey, of Campbell; and Mrs. Dr. Walker, of Lynchburg.

CAPTAIN THOMAS A. HOLCOMBE.

"Mark the perfect man, and behold the upright, for the end of that man is peace."

Captain THOMAS A. HOLCOMBE, for many years a useful and beloved citizen of Lynchburg, was a native of Prince Edward county, and a son of the venerable Philemon Holcombe. He was born on the 18th of August, 1785, and was educated at Hampden Sydney College, where he graduated; and, soon after studying for the bar, he made such rapid progress, that, in a brief time, he obtained a license and removed to the State of Georgia, with the intention of there pursuing his profession. But, very soon after his settlement in that State, his plans were entirely frustrated by a violent spell of fever, which was near costing him his life. Obeying then the urgent entreaties of his parents, he returned to his native State, where he for several years had charge of a classical school, after which he returned to the profession of law, which avocation he pursued until he became a Christian and joined the Presbyterian Church, of which he was a ruling elder. His having conscientious scruples in continuing the practice of the law, was the occasion of his resigning that profession; and he then became Marshal of the Chancery Court; but after that system was abolished, he became a merchant, in which occupation he continued till his death.

His temperament being most ardent, and his mind active and energetic, Captain Holcombe carried with him through life these distinguishing traits, infusing them into all of his undertakings. In his youth, he had been united in marriage to Mary Royall, a lady of great excellence, and in every way worthy to have been the wife of such a man. It is said that, when a young man, Captain Holcombe was remarkably gay in his disposition, fond of pleasure, and enthusiastic in the enjoyment of music and dancing; but the one penning these lines, has no other recollection of him than as an ardent, devout member of the Presbyterian Church of Lynchburg, where he greatly aided his minister by the interest he manifested in public worship, and by the zealous assistance he rendered in the Sabbath School, which, both in this Church* and in the old Methodist denomination has been so much blessed.

---

* In the division of the Presbyterian Church, Captain Holcombe joined the new side, of which the Rev. Mr. Russell was first pastor, and the Rev. Mr. Mitchell the second.

The dwelling of Captain Holcombe was the abode of the most genuine old Virginia hospitality; nor did he at one time think it wrong to press on his guests the cheerful invigorating glass of wine. But his attention being drawn to the subject of temperance, he was led to see that there was no safety in a middle course; and that precept and example would better operate, if the system of total abstinence was practised by himself; accordingly, he, in his household, abandoned the use both of wine and spirituous liquors, warmly urging his friends and the community to do the same. At that time there were no Temperance Societies* in Virginia—an attempt though having been made to institute such a society by the venerable Micajah Pendleton, of Amherst county—so that Captain Holcombe may properly be denominated the Father of Temperance in our State. He formed a temperance society in Lynchburg—he made public speeches, distributed tracts, and he traveled thousands of miles preaching the wholesome doctrines of Temperance. Zealous, also, in the prosecution of his secular employments, prompt in thought, liberal in his household, and ever holding in view the service and glory of God, Captain Holcombe passed through a most useful life, blessed by hun-

---

* Such is the impression.

dreds whom his influence had rescued from the grasp of the demon of intemperance.

In the month of October, 1843, Captain Holcombe left his happy home for a brief period—business requiring his presence in Montgomery county. As soon as he had arranged everything to his satisfaction, he returned to Lynchburg, where he arrived on the evening of Tuesday, the 31st of October, 1843. On his return home, he met his devoted family with even more than usual tenderness. His health seemed perfect, his spirits were buoyant and cheerful; but in one short hour from the time of entering his own house, his sainted spirit winged its way to realms of bliss,* to enjoy,

---

* Extract from a letter received from a gentleman of Lynchburg a few days after this mournful event:

" Such a sensation I have never known produced by any death, as by that of Captain Holcombe. He had been absent in the Western section of the State a short time, and returned in the stage Tuesday evening, a few hours before his death, in fine health and spirits. I believe that the true cause of his death is unknown; but it is conjectured that the immediate cause was the rupture of a blood vessel. The shock was so sudden and unexpected, that, although no lesson has been oftener or more solemnly taught, that the thread which suspends the sword overhead, may be cut at any moment, scarcely any one at first could believe it was so. The Societies paid extraordinary marks of respect and grief at his funeral and burial, which were also attended by a great number of citizens, and for several hours, during the passing of the funeral and procession, all the stores on Main street were closed. All this must have been gratify-

through all eternity, the presence of that Saviour he had so faithfully served whilst a pilgrim and sojourner of earth. A splendid monument stands over his remains in the Presbyterian graveyard, but his memory is deeply enshrined in the hearts of devoted friends; and, to those who knew and loved him, a simple stone, with the name of "Thomas A. Holcombe," would speak of the past more tenderly than the most costly marble structure.

It may truly be said of this excellent man, that "He delivered the poor that cried, and the fatherless, and him that had none to help him. The blessings of him that was ready to perish came upon him, and he caused the widow's heart to sing for joy." Many interesting incidents might be recorded of his numerous charities, but the recollection of them is yet fresh in Lynchburg; and only one little incident will here be mentioned, touching for its pathos and simplicity. Every Saturday evening it was the custom of Captain Holcombe to have some little boys come to his office to receive their weekly supply of provisions. The father of those boys

---

ing to the relatives of the deceased, and was, I think, very creditable to the people, and raised them considerably in my estimation. It proves that they can justly appreciate the worth and feel the loss of a man who had, with the greatest enthusiasm and activity, devoted a large portion of his life wholly to benevolent and charitable objects."

was given to inebriation, and Captain Holcombe would always caution them not to allow their father to pawn any part of the provision given for liquor; but he would add, "Tell your mother, when your father comes home drunk, to take care of him, and when he sobers off, give him some bread and meat to eat and some strong coffee to drink; and tell him, that a gentleman who desires to save him from a drunkard's grave, has provided these comforts for him."

The day after the death of Captain Holcombe, a gentleman was standing in the front door of the residence of the deceased, when he noticed three or four little boys approaching. They came up to the gate and inquired, "Is Captain Holcombe dead?" The gentleman answered in the affirmative; and they then asked, "Could we be permitted to go in and look at him?" He gave them permission, and they, with noiseless steps, entered the chamber of death. They stood around his lifeless body, and, as they gazed on that marble forehead, one of them, with a swelling heart and tearful eye, exclaimed—"Who will now give us bread!"

Of the members of this family, survive Mrs. HOLCOMBE, the beloved wife of Captain Thomas A. Holcombe; Mrs. Walter Henderson, of Lynchburg, and William and Royall Holcombe, Esqs., of the same place. Of those gone before are

Thomas Philemon Holcombe, the oldest son of the deceased, who died many years since—the sweet remembrance of whose manly, loving heart and many virtues is warmly cherished by his numerous friends in his native town—and Lucy Anne, the youngest daughter, the lovely wife of Dr. Scott, who died a few years since, having been suddenly called hence from her husband and young children, to join her father and brother in Heaven.

ROYALL FAMILY.

WILLIAM ROYALL, Sr., was one of the oldest settlers of Lynchburg after its formation. He married Miss Royall, a first cousin, and a sister of Mrs. Thomas A. Holcombe; and this excellent couple for some years resided in the house now occupied by Charles L. Mosby, Esq. In easy, prosperous circumstances, and blessed with a numerous family, few advanced to the summit of life under such favorable auspices, as Mr. and Mrs. Royall. This domestic happiness was invaded about the year 1818 or '19, by the death of Mr. Royall; and like a far distant, indistinct dream, is faintly remembered the mournful procession of Masons bearing the deceased to his last resting-place, which was situated in the grounds attached to his dwelling house. Since that period many of that family have been removed, till, of all that circle, none survive, save the excellent wife of William Royall, Sr., one son, and a daughter, Mrs. Charles L. Mosby, of Lynchburg.

Around WILLIAM ROYALL, jr., third son of Mrs.

Judith Royall, linger the most pleasing and grateful memories of long ago, blended with happy scenes of childhood, when with those, too, who have since passed away, we received instruction from the same good man, Mr. Richardson,* and when on a summer's eve, with careless glee, we traversed Ivy Hill or roamed to Richardson's springs. William Royall spent his boyhood in Lynchburg, and was then sent to Amherst College. With a heart most warm and affectionate, and a soul formed for friendship most lasting, William Royall possessed a fine mind, well cultivated—a taste for reading and study rarely met with. About eighteen years since, emigrating to the South-west, he died suddenly, far from home and friends, who, though years have elapsed, still speak of him with emotion, deeply regretting his untimely departure:

> "One midst the forests of the West
> By a dark stream is laid;
> The Indian knows his place of rest,
> Fast by the forest shade."

Rev. JOHN ROYALL was the eldest son of William Royall, Sr.; he was a native of Lynchburg, where he too passed his boyhood under the influence of a

---

* This excellent man and first-rate teacher was a brother of Mr. James Benagh, of Lynchburg. He died of consumption in 1823.

pious mother. Sent at an early age to Hampden Sydney College, he made sure and rapid progress in his studies, laying at this time the foundation of what he was in after years—the faithful, laborious, self-sacrificing minister of the gospel.

Soon after entering college, a great revival of religion taking place, Mr. Royall became deeply impressed on the subject, and for a time even his efforts to study were frustrated by the intense and overwhelming desire to find out the way of salvation. Soon after, making a public profession of religion, he united himself to the Presbyterian Church, devoting himself to the ministry, and by his walk and conversation adorning the Christian profession, and so showing forth in his. life the beauty of holiness, that all who saw him could "take knowledge of him that he had been with Jesus."

Mr. Royall was, when very young, united in marriage to Anna Keith Taylor, daughter of the distinguished lawyer, George Keith Taylor, and a niece of Chief Justice Marshall: and for the last few years of his life, Mr. Royall resided in the county of Fauquier, where he occupied a post of usefulness, preaching acceptably to a large congregation, who were greatly attached to him.

In the month of February, 1856, notwithstanding the inclement weather, Mr. Royall had set out to fulfill a ministerial engagement; but on the way to church he was stricken down, and entered his eternal rest on the Sabbath. Did we compute age by the number of years Mr. Royall had lived, we should say that he had died young, for he could not have attained his fiftieth year; but when we consider his life of active usefulness, his constant efforts to advance the Redeemer's kingdom; when we reflect upon the many whom, by his pious example, he induced to become disciples of Christ; bearing in mind, too, the constant comfort he diffused, not only in his own family, but in that of his widowed mother, we should say that in amount of good works Mr. Royall had passed a long life, and had doubtless finished his allotted task, departing at the time and in the manner appointed for him by the Wise Disposer of Events.

"Blessed is that servant whom the Lord, when he cometh, shall find watching."

"Be ye therefore ready also, for the son of man cometh at an hour when ye think not."

MR. AND MRS. BARNES,

FROM BUFFALO, NEW YORK.

THEIR CRUELTY TO ANN HINDERSHOT, THEIR WHITE SERVANT—SINGULAR TERMINATION OF THE AFFAIR.

During the year of 1828, a man by the name of BARNES settled, with his family, in the town of Lynchburg, taking possession of the white house whose gable end fronts Main street, and divided from the residence of Captain Pleasants Labby by a cross street. They were from the State of New York, and Mr. Barnes was a portly, good-looking man, with a grave, dignified exterior, and when he basked in the sunshine before his shop door, with folded arms, his appearance suggested the idea of a domesticated Alexander Selkirk, or a modern Diogenes, particularly when resting on a large nest of tubs on the sidewalk. Like all model artistes, Mr. Barnes had evidently studied attitudes, for all of his tableaux were imposing. For instance, his favorite one was to place himself by his door, surrounded by a group of his beautiful children, thereby producing on passers-by the impression that he was a gentleman of admirable domestic traits.

Mrs. BARNES was a fashionable looking lady, speaking contemptuously of the slow ways of doing things in Virginia, and when the family appeared on Sunday going to church, their appearance excited the admiration of the primitive Lynchburgers, drawing from them the remark, "what a fine-looking family, and how they *do* walk amongst us with such a city air!"

Mrs. Barnes had often been heard to express disgust at the idea of a colored servant. "She would not have one of the ugly creatures with their slovenly ways. She was well provided with a help, who could do more in one day than a negro would perform in a week." She had brought with her from New York an indentured white servant, whose name was Ann Hindershot, and the neighbors had noticed and commended the diligence of the girl, observing, however, that the child wore a timid expression of countenance, as if she thought some one was coming up behind to strike her. The next neighbor, Mrs. Labby, had for several days missed Anne from her accustomed duties, but had made no comment on the circumstance. On entering her parlor one morning and throwing open the window, she beheld in the attic of Barnes' house a sight from which she recoiled with horror. She saw the pale, emaciated form of Ann Hindershot tied to the bed post, her thin hands raised in a supplicating attitude, whilst the cruel Mrs. Barnes was inflicting on the child heavy blows with a stick, the barbarous woman ending the morning's torture by throwing over the sufferer a shovel full of hot embers. Ann Hindershot was, by famine, so reduced, that she could only utter a feeble cry, before falling across the foot of the bed in a swoon. Mrs. Labby, going immediately for her husband, informed him of what she had seen, and that good citizen, with his customary promptitude, lost no time in procuring a warrant for the arrest of Barnes and his wife. They denied, of course, the allegation of cruelty, but were exceedingly unwilling for Ann Hindershot to be seen; but Captain Labby, insisting on the execution of the warrant, the officers and himself forced their way up stairs, where lay, in a fainting fit, the exhausted frame of this unfortunate young girl. Capt. Labby dispatched a message for the late Christopher Anthony, and procured the attendance of several physicians, and whilst remedies were being administered to the sufferer, Mr. Anthony demanded of Barnes a history of the case. Barnes was evidently a timid man, after the order of Mr. Bumble, much afraid of the savage wife, and decidedly "more of a philosopher than a warrior." He stated that the girl had been bound to him by her father in Buffalo, New York, and the exhibition of the indentures fully confirmed the truth of the statement. Barnes and his wife were held to bail,* and after the child had recovered from the deep swoon, and her many wounds had been dressed, she was placed in a carriage and conveyed to the residence of Mr. Jones, exactly opposite the dwelling of Major James B. Risque. Receiving every kindness from the citizens of Lynchburg, she was visited by more than a thousand persons, to ascertain whether the horrible story could be true; and there are many who recollect the wretched appearance of this poor girl, whilst she to them narrated the persecutions by her undergone whilst living with the Barnes family. What a strange contrast was her ghastly face and attenuated form, to the blooming beauty and fashion by whom she was often surrounded. Had Ann Hindershot been a slave on a Southern plantation,† this incident might have done admirably as a fresh horror for Mrs. Beecher Stowe to add to "Uncle Tom's Cabin;" but as Ann Hindershot was only a white servant, and her master and mistress natives of a Northern State, it is not likely that Mrs. Stowe would venture to interweave such a narrative in any of her productions. A large

---

* A suitable accompaniment to the story of "Prue, the Rusk woman," in New Orleans.

† Having nothing but memory on which to rely, perhaps some of the old inhabitants can state the fate of Mr. and Mrs. Barnes.

subscription having been taken up for Ann, it was by some of the most judicious citizens suggested that she should be returned to her parents in Buffalo; but this scheme was not carried into effect, and some of the more visionary were not willing to receive as true the statement given by Barnes, but they desired for her a more romantic history. A gentleman of Lynchburg, recollected that some years previous he had seen the advertisement of a Mrs. Allen, of New York, stating that her only child had been lost or stolen whilst conveying some work to the Sing Sing prison, for which she was as a seamstress employed. This advertisement contained a description of Susan Allen, the lost child, and it earnestly called upon all humane persons throughout the United States to assist her in the recovery of her daughter.

The gentleman above mentioned, hastily summoning a council of his friends; they unanimously came to the conclusion that Ann Hindershot was no other than Mrs. Allen's "Wept of Wishton Wish;" so they accordingly wrote to that lady, urging her immediate presence in Lynchburg, saying to her that her lost treasure had been recovered. Mrs. Allen, soon appearing, was most hospitably received by many of our citizens, but more particularly by those belonging to the Methodist denomination. She was informed of all the circumstances, and told of the large donation which had been given to the child;

but on meeting Ann Hindershot, there was no simultaneous rush into each other's arms, and no adjuration in the true style of novels, of "Living Image of my departed Theodore;" for, greatly to the disappointment of the good people of Lynchburg, Mrs. Allen was compelled to acknowledge that the child did not resemble the one she had lost—that the color of the eyes differed, and that the age did not correspond. Whilst in this state of doubt, fresh eclat continued to be thrown around this pair, and additional sums of money were contributed for the benefit of Ann Hindershot; so that one day, whilst Mrs. Allen was gazing on her, she exclaimed passionately, "Susan Allen, my long lost, vainly sought, dearly loved child, embrace your mother, for the voice of nature in my heart assures me that in that sacred relationship do I stand to you!" The town was thrown into a state of delight and enthusiasm; the soubriquet of Ann Hindershot being now no longer recognized, the names of Susan Allen and her mother were only heard from the lips of the admiring throng; the hospitality of the town was tendered to them so abundantly, and Susan Allen so feasted on its good things, that, like Grettel in the German story, she would frequently say, "who am I; am I Grettel or am I not?" The contrast was so great between the scant fare at Barnes's and the rich viands by which she was now tempted, that Miss Allen got to thinking that extremes were bad, and that a medium between the two was best.

Mrs. Allen and her daughter left Lynchburg early in the winter of 1830, in the house-boat which was to explore the river previously to laying off the James River and Kanawha Canal. This boat was accompanied as far as Smith's well by the mayor and a band of music, and after giving three cheers for Mrs. and Miss Allen, and three more for our good town, the civil functionaries and the band of music returned. The public conveyances throughout the State were requested to make no charge for Mrs. Allen and her daughter, so that their journey through Virginia was one great ovation, and Mrs. Allen, on regaining the Empire State, found herself with a daughter and a purse well filled with money. But living in New York was decidedly more expensive than a residence in Lynchburg, and the lady soon found that the subscriptions raised in that town were not inexhaustible.

The novelty of the case having worn off, fresh supplies could not be obtained from the City of Hills, so that the scales fell from the mental vision of Mrs. Allen, and not Cinderella, escaping from the ball, was more suddenly transformed, than was this poor indented servant; and now, instead of the long lost, vainly sought daughter, Mrs. Allen saw only before her plain "Ann Hindershot," in almost as great need as when rescued from the hands of

Barnes and his wife. The poor child was then sent to Buffalo, and her subsequent fate is not known, though it is to be hoped that the kindness of her real parents made her some amends for the trials and sufferings of her childhood.

The house at present occupied by Wm. Saunders, Esq., was the residence, in 1819, of Mr. and Mrs. James Bullock; then it was the residence of Micajah Lynch and his young wife, Anne Moorman. It was afterwards the residence of John Smith, Esq., and his lovely wife Martha, the eldest daughter of John Bullock, Esq. Just opposite to Dr. Early's present residence, was the dwelling of H. M. Didlake, Esq., a most excellent and highly prized citizen, whose wife was one of the most estimable ladies in Lynchburg. Just up the cross street lived Mr. Newhall, one of Lynchburg's earliest settlers, a native of Lynn, Massachusetts. This worthy man kept for many years a shoe-store, and we well remember the intense admiration with which his sign was contemplated—a man as large as life having his boots pulled off by a colored boy; and the feelings of approval at this picture were only second in degree to those experienced on viewing the sign of the good Mr. John Thurman's saddlery, which then, as now, was a small, inane looking horse, standing on his hind feet.

Mr. Newhall was an excellent citizen, and for years he filled the office of constable of Lynchburg. He was fond of gardening and horticulture, and to him is the upper country indebted for the introduction of the large Scotch gooseberry. His lovely daughter Antoinette became the wife of Mr. Sublett, of Richmond, where, a few years since, she died. His son, Mr. Mortimer Newhall, is a worthy successor to his father in his shoe establishment.

THE MURREL FAMILY.

The family of Murrel came from Mount Holly, New Jersey—a good old town, endeared to many in our State who trace their descent from some of its inhabitants. Many years since, emigrating to Virginia, Mr. and Mrs. Murrel made their home in the town of Lynchburg, where, for a long time, they occupied a place as useful and prominent citizens. Mrs. Murrel was a lady of great energy and industry; and, doubtless, the success of her sons in life, was in a great measure owing to her wise and prudent counsels.

JOHN and HARDIN MURREL were, for many years, the able and efficient postmasters of Lynchburg, administering its affairs with an energy and diligence in the United States unsurpassed. The new post-office, of Lynchburg, though of far nobler proportions, yet fails to impress the beholder, as did the old one, with the extent of Uncle Sam's power. The latter, situated on a retired cross-street, the mail was there received and the doors closed, a very small aperture then being the only means of communication, letters being given out thence, seemingly, by an invisible hand.

What words of weal and woe, of love, of disappointed ambition, of blighted hopes, would come forth from this place, whilst the quiet officers within were noiselessly performing their duties, and thus distributing joy and sorrow, ruin and success, to those without! What a moral in this scene! Those poor frail mortals outside, on whom a few lines could produce all the gradation of feeling, from the most ecstatic to the most agonizing.

When not engaged in the duties of the post-office, John Murrel was occupied as a merchant in the front part of the establishment; and, by a long course of patient diligence, accumulating an immense fortune, he did not, like the generality of millionaires, wait till his death to benefit his relations; but, settling handsomely his aged parents, providing for his sister and other relations, he had the satisfaction during his lifetime of seeing comfort and affluence abound through his instrumentality.

Of this family, several survive. Mrs. Claytor, a daughter of Mrs. Murrel, being a resident of Lynchburg; and Mrs. G. W. Turner* is also one

---

* Since penning the above, this lady has had to mourn the untimely death of her son, Maurice G. Turner, a young man of most exemplary character, and greatly beloved and deeply lamented by all who knew him.

of this family, being a niece of Mr. Murrel, and having come to Lynchburg to reside whilst in early childhood. A few years since, Mrs. Murrel, of Mount Holly, mother of Mrs. Turner, dying in Lynchburg, her remains were interred at the Presbyterian graveyard, where a most appropriate tombstone or tablet is placed over her, headed with this simple inscription: "To our Mother!"—an inscription so touching, and more impressive from its very simplicity, than the monument and inscription over the tomb of Madame Langhans, at Berne, Switzerland.

SAMPSON DIUGUID.

SAMPSON DIUGUID was a native of Appomattox county, from which, many years since, he removed, making his home in Lynchburg, where, till the time of his death, he resided, an honored and beloved citizen. Whilst John and Hardin Murrel were diligently employed on one side of the street, dispensing from the post-office good and ill, Sampson Diuguid, on the other side, was equally occupied in another department of life and death. Combining the occupation of cabinet-maker and undertaker, he industriously pursued his avocations for the benefit of the living and the dead; and his services to the former, will long remain visible throughout the whole section of country around Lynchburg, in that beautiful, durable furniture, by him manufactured, differing so widely from those slight showy articles procured from the Northern cities.

Whilst visible to the passers-by at his occupation, slowly and surely would the last solemn messenger, Death, render it often necessary for the services of Sampson Diuguid to be called in requisition for the departed. His office of undertaker, so frequently placing him amid scenes of distress, it might naturally have been supposed that even a very tender heart would become habituated to such things. Yet often has the fine manly face of Sampson Diuguid been seen suffused with tears on funeral occasions, and frequently at the grave he has with difficulty been able to command his feelings. How different from men of this occupation described by Dickens. Witness the hard, obdurate heart of Sowerberry, and the easy, careless levity of Oram and Joram.

Sampson Diuguid's upright, useful life was closed during the winter of 1856, and this brief notice cannot be more appropriately closed than by a few words treasured up in memory from the editorial of the Lynchburg Virginian, announcing his death— "And, after having consigned many thousand to the narrow chambers of death, he was himself borne to the county of Appomattox, there to repose beneath the clods of the valley!"

A few doors below the establishment of Sampson Diuguid was the quiet bachelor abode of Irish John Robertson, with its gable end fronting the Main street; and where now stands the elegant estabment of John G. Meen, Esq., was a small wooden building kept by that gentleman, but giving, even in those days, a promise of the beauty and elegance for which his store is now so remarkable. Just opposite stood "Upper Kyle's;" and the house on the same side, divided by a cross-street, was called "Lower Kyle's"—for at that period these well known Irish merchants were in the zenith of their prosperity. A number of excellent residents lived below, on either side—the Truslows, Valentines and other members of the Methodist Church.

The family of Todd occupied at one time a dwelling opposite to the Banks. Mr. Todd was of a good family, well known near the regions of tide water; and Mrs. Todd was a lady of great amiability and refinement. Having been placed in pecuniary difficulties, this lady, with the heart of a true woman, exerted all her powers to aid in maintaining a large family, performing most cheerfully her arduous duties, providing for the education of her daughters, and all this time occupying a high place in the esteem of all with whom she was associated.

Mrs. Todd was a sister of those eminent merchants, the Messrs. Dick of New Orleans; and, as soon as their fortune was reared,* they acted with a nobility and generosity worthy the imitation of all brothers. They sent for their sister and her family, settling them in one of the Western States, in circumstances of ease and comfort.

The large brick house just opposite the establish-

---

* This circumstance was said to be as stated above.

ment of Strother & Whitehead, was the residence of the venerable WILLIAM DAVIS, a member of the Friends' Society, and occupying one of the highest stations in Lynchburg; for he was by all sects greatly reverenced. The building called "Friends' Warehouse," was built by him, and was under his peculiar jurisdiction.

Of the members of this excellent family, survive Henry Davis, Esq., Mrs. Peter Dudley, and the Misses Davis, of Lynchburg; all of these ladies are well known, and distinguished by minds of fine order, highly cultivated, and, in an eminent degree, possessing all those virtues of integrity, sincerity and truthfulness, for which their honored parents were so remarkable.

Mrs. CONSTANCE BOUDAR was a native of France, and was at one time a resident of the city of Paris; but, removing to the island of St. Domingo, it was said that she was there at the time of the insurrecrion, having been for several days concealed in a large brick oven.* Many years since, Madame Boudar removed to Lychburg, where, by the assistance of her amiable and intelligent young daughter, Mercie Hyacinth Boudar, she made a comfortable

---

* This was always told and believed, but the writer does not vouch for the truth.

support by the sale of toys and confectionary. She was a polite, well-bred lady, truly French in appearance, with her large hoop ear-rings and her handsome snuff-box.

An excellent, honest-hearted woman, well-cultivated in the literature of her native land, Mrs. Boudar resided for many years in our town, beloved and respected. A zealous and enthusiastic Roman Catholic, Mrs. Boudar always, with joy, hailed the rare pleasure of seeing a priest of her own denomination; for at this period the services of the Roman Catholic Church were quite unknown in Lynchburg.

Miss MERCIE BOUDAR, possessing considerable musical talents, aided her mother by giving instructions in that accomplishment. In their neatly kept parlor sat the piano, and the choice books constituting their library, whilst the bed, like the one described in Goldsmith's "Deserted Village,"

"—— contrived a double debt to pay,
A bed by night—a chest of drawers by day!"

Thus happily and peacefully lived this good mother and daughter, their departure from Lynchburg being a source of real regret; and long will the oldest inhabitants and their children remember, with satisfaction, those good primitive times, when this courteous French woman presided over the *sweet* tastes of the community of Lynchburg.

In the year 1819, there lived a young man not far from the establishment of Samuel Thurmon, whose name was PARHAM ADAMS. He was a confectioner, and at one time resided on Bank Square, and at another, his store was a few doors above Hollins's corner. His establishment boasted a very fine soda fountain, and being excessively anxious to possess the best soda water in Lynchburg, he had been heard to say that he would continue to put on gas till this end was accomplished, even if he should be blown up along with his soda fountain.

To use the expression of Mr. Dowler of the Pickwick, "This was a rash vow"—for one morning, after he had fixed the fountain to his satisfaction, it was really blown up with a tremendous explosion, carrying along with it the unfortunate man, striking his head against the ceiling, and, in his descent, actually with his features indenting the marble. Medical aid, though instantly procured, of course failed to re-animate him, and by strangers' hands was this young man arrayed for burial, and, on the following day, borne to his grave by the company of soldiers to which he belonged. A neat marble tablet, in the old graveyard, marks the place of his interment.

The "Cabell House" now stands partly on the

site of the shop and residence of the late Mrs. SALLY THURMON; and, to old inhabitants, this part of the city looks unnatural without that humble dwelling, its gable-end fronting the street—its benignant hostess, with smiling face and honest countenance, standing behind the counter, giving away, in charity, nearly as much as she disposed of for money.

Mrs. Thurmon was a Miss Lewellen before she became the wife of Richard Thurmon; and she was a most remarkable woman, of fine, generous traits of character, joined to great magnanimity. Her charities were numerous and large, many poor persons being entirely supplied with food from her bakery. Placed at one period of her life in great poverty and difficulties, she by a course of patient industry, energy and economy, not only retrieved the affairs of her husband, but reared for herself a fortune. Many of her benevolent acts might here be recorded, but the recollection of them is still bright in Lynchburg, where her memory will long be cherished with feelings most affectionate. "Uncle Dick," as her husband was familiarly called, was a good-hearted, well-disposed old gentleman, whose greatest pleasure consisted in shooting game and squirrels for sick persons; and vividly to memory does his image now arise, with gun in hand, on his cream-colored horse, his coat laid across the neck of the quadruped. Mrs. Thurmon died in the winter of 1840, her husband and two children surviving her, of whom Mr. Samuel Thurmon is now the only remaining member. An ably written sketch of Mrs. Thurmon appeared at the time of her death, the authorship being attributed to Richard Cralle, Esq., and this admirable piece should have been preserved and inserted in a permanent form, amongst the annals of the best and worthiest who have departed this life in the town of Lynchburg.

The *Eagle Tavern*, in the vicinity of the market-house, was kept by Charles Lewellen; and it was there that wax-work shows and other such exhibitions were held in this good town. There were the Quaker beauty, the sleeping beauty, the Virginia beauty, General Washington, and the ferocious Indian killing the white man, whilst music was ground from an excruciating organ. Could we now witness this scene, we should look around the room for the "genuine and only Jarley" and "George;" and, in the back ground, the sweet pensive face of dear little Nell, by the side of her grandfather. Our *fine* market-house, so much admired by the editors of the Virginian, occupied the place where now it stands, its fair preportions being adorned and increased by a second story.

The house next below the Eagle Marble Works, was at one time the residence of Mrs. MARY KING, a Jewess, whose very lovely daughter married a Jewish gentleman named Andrews,* for many years a merchant of Lynchburg. Mrs. Andrews was extremely interesting in appearance, and might have served as a model for Rebecca the Jewess.

Just opposite was the chair manufactory of that good, useful citizen, CHESLEY HARDY, whose faithful work, executed more than thirty years since, will far outlast chairs manufactured in these days of Young America. A glimpse of him, a few years since, exhibited so little change in his appearance, that we thought it a pity that Rip-Van-Winkle, on waking from his long sleep, could not have been so fortunate as to find a single one of his acquaintance as little altered by the hand of time as Mr. Chesley Hardy. A dim recollection exists of seeing exhibited, ages ago, in that chair establishment, a pair of lions and two royal Bengal tigers; and, together with the noise of drums and cymbals in this small place, the roar of these animals was terrific.

The house on the hill, just opposite the residence

---

* The Messrs. Andrews removed to New Orleans: it is said one of them was drowned in the Lake there, a few years since.

of Henry Dunnington, Esq., was built by Christopher Winfree, Esq., and was for many years his hospitable, kind abode. In the autumn of 1827 it was taken by HUGH MONTGOMERIE, Esq., who lived there for some years. This gentleman was a native of Scotland, but early in life emigrated to Virginia. Possessing kindly dispositions and most brilliant talents, he will long be remembered by friends who have enjoyed the pleasure of listening to his conversation, so full of wit and vivacity. Mr. Montgomerie married, some years since, Anne, the daughter of Thomas Colquhoun, of Petersburg; and this lady is well beloved by friends in this community, surviving her husband, who died in 1855.

THOMAS COLQUHOUN, Esq., was for several years a resident of Lynchburg. He was also a native of Scotland; but, emigrating to this country, he was united in marriage to Miss Wilhelms: and shortly after that event, he went to reside in the city of London, where he was for many years a prosperous, wealthy merchant. But in about fourteen years from that time, again returning to Virginia, he made Petersburg his home, till about 1827, when he came to reside in Lynchburg. Mr. Colquhoun was a gentleman of fine mind and most excellent heart, and greatly endeared himself to many during his residence in Lynchburg, where his manly, handsome appearance, and strict integrity and uprightness are still most warmly remembered by the old inhabitants. He died suddenly in 1831, and his remains are interred in Lynchburg. His excellent and venerable widow survives him, with the powers of her mind undimmed and unimpaired by time.

REFORMED METHODIST CHURCH

OF LYNCHBURG.

About the year 1826 or 1827, a division occurred in the Methodist Church of Lynchburg. Of the causes leading to this separation, it is not here necessary to write; sufficient is it to remark, that no doctrinal points were involved in it, and only a diferent view of some of Wesley's opinions on church government, causing the division, they parted with little or no unkind feelings.

The Society worshiped for a time in the old Masonic Hall,* and as soon as the basement of their own Church was completed, they there held a Sabbath school, and carried on religious services several times during the week. The first minister of this denomination was a man of gigantic frame, the Rev. Mr. McKane; then for a time the services of the Rev. Mr. Jennings were procured. He was a son of Dr. Samuel K. Jennings, already mentioned, an eminent physician and exemplary minister of the Gospel, and one of the most worthy and efficient

---

* If memory is right.

preachers, who formerly belonged to the Society worshiping in the old Methodist Church of Lynchburg. Then for a time the Rev. Mr. Latimer was their esteemed minister : but their great stronghold and most able minister, was the Rev. WILLIAM J. HOLCOMBE. He was a son of the venerable Philemon Holcombe, of Prince Edward, and a younger brother of our beloved townsman, Captain Thomas Holcombe. Graduating at an early age in medicine, Dr. Holcombe settled in Lynchburg, where he became the husband of Miss Clopton, one of the loveliest girls reared in the town. A few years after his marriage, becoming deeply impressed on the subject of religion, he earnestly sought and found that pearl of great price, and studying for the ministry, he made such rapid progress that he was in a short time ordained as a minister of the Methodist denomination; continuing since that time to adorn that sacred office, carrying into his religious profession all that fervid zeal and all those ardent feelings so characteristic of the Holcombe family, and which are the true sources of eloquent preaching.

As a practitioner of medicine, Dr. Holcombe's reputation is well known and widely spread; and after having followed for many years his profession, gaining the entire confidence of the community, Dr. Holcombe, with the humility of a great mind, went on for a season to Philadelphia, attending again the medical lectures, and thereby perfecting himself in the knowledge of his profession. Combining the sacred calling of a minister of Christ with that of a physician, he, like the venerated Dr. Samuel K. Jennings, has often had it in his power, whilst administering to the suffering frame, to lead, guide and direct the sick man to the Great Physician and Saviour of souls. About nineteen years since, emigrating to Indiana, Dr. Holcombe there made a home, from which emanated the bright Christian example of himself and wife, who ensured to themselves the respect and affection of the community in which they lived. But the climate of Indiana, ill suiting the feeble, delicate temperament of Mrs. Holcombe, they have since returned to Virginia, choosing for their home a farm in the vicinity of Lynchburg. Shortly before settling at his present residence, and whilst making arrangements to do so, he preached in Lynchburg to a large congregation of his own denomination, together with many belonging to other churches; and this discourse, for simple, touching eloquence, mingled with real feeling, was said never to have been surpassed in Lynchburg. The moving allusions to the past, connected with many whose seats were vacant, and their places no longer known—all these, united to the pathos of the discourse and the spirituality of the sermon, drew tears from the eyes of the sternest. Several of the sons of Dr. Holcombe are residents of Virginia, and amongst them Professor James P. Holcombe of the University of Virginia.

Of the many valuable members of the Reformed Methodist Church, only a few names will here be recorded. CHRISTOPHER WINFREE, for many years a devout member of the old Methodist Church, went over to the Radical Church at the time of the separation. He is a native of Chesterfield county, and a gentleman of great private worth, and as a friend and neighbor, unrivalled for excellence. In early life he married Mary, a daughter of Major William Warwick, of Amherst, and a very lovely woman was Mrs. Winfree; but surviving only a few years her marriage, Mr. Winfree was, whilst a young man, left a widower with four small children. In a few years he again married, choosing for his wife Cornelia M. Tilden, a very beautiful girl, the daughter of Dr. Tilden of Winchester. This lady was all that a Christian wife and mother should be, steering wisely her course in the narrow and difficult path of step-mother, avoiding all those shoals on which so many have been wrecked.

Adorning the doctrines of God her Saviour, and over her household presiding with a sway wise, mild and gentle, Mrs. Cornelia Winfree passed a life most blameless in Lynchburg, where her memory will long be tenderly cherished; nor will those who there knew and loved her, ever forget her, though they are now removed from their native place.

This excellent lady died about the year 1837, leaving a numerous family, all of whom survive her, with the exception of Robert Nelson, her youngest, whose early piety and beautiful death are assurances that he has in the spirit-land joined his mother.

JOHN VICTOR was a member of the same Church, and was a connection of the Winfree family, having married Mary, the oldest daughter of Dr. Tilden. Mr. Victor was a native of Fredericksburg; but removing with his parents to Lynchburg when very young, he was for many years the principal jeweller and silversmith of the upper country; and an old-fashioned spoon, marked "Williams and Victor," forcibly recalls the period when, with wonder and admiration, the windows and show-cases of this establishment were contemplated; bringing to mind also the time when, with his sweet, excellent wife by his side, he might be seen entering the house of God. When there, his zeal in the services of the sanctuary, and his mild, holy countenance, showed that his thoughts were far withdrawn from worldly concerns, and centred wholly in contemplation of heavenly things. Mr. Victor died many years since, leaving a widow and children who reside in Lynchburg.

EDWARD WILLIAM VICTOR, the second son, was a young man of fine personal appearance, and of great promise. In early manhood he had been united in marriage to Margaret, the daughter of

Mrs. Cole,* of Lynchburg, and a touching incident is connected with the death of this young couple. Fearing that he was threatened with pulmonary disease, Edward William accompanied to the South a kind friend, hoping that a short residence in a warmer climate would arrest the disease, and restore in full health, to a young family, the husband and father. But a sudden and fatal change occurring in his disease, he was hurried into eternity, whilst to his friend remained the painful task of informing his wife and family of this mournful event. A few days previous to the arrival of the letter in Lynchburg, Margaret Victor died unexpectedly, and thus was she spared this great sorrow. Can we imagine anything more blissful than their joyful re-union in Heaven, free from the pains and sorrows of mortality, without having even suffered the pangs of parting, and each till that moment ignorant of the death of the other!

Mr. WILLIAM BURD and his good wife were natives of Ireland, but early in their married life emigrating to America, they became residents of Lynchburg, where they so ensured the love and respect of all with them associated, that they will long, with pleasure, be remembered in the city. Mr. Burd was a gentleman of most gentle, honest and amiable feelings, practising, with great zeal and energy, his

---

* The daughter of Mrs. Wallace, who afterwards married Rev. Mr. Cole.

profession, which was that of an extensive tin manufacturer—and with what honesty and faithfulness, it may well be computed, when it is told that articles manufactured at their establishment more than a quarter of a century since, are even now far superior to those purchased only a few months since from our present manufactories. They were zealous members of the Methodist Church, to which denomination a large family of daughters were attached.

EVELINA BURD, the eldest daughter, a very lovely girl, was, at the age of fifteen, married to Richard Swift Tilden, Esq. This lady was greatly beloved in Lynchburg, and, on her removal to St. Louis, she left a name eminent for domestic virtues, energy and industry. In her new home she rapidly made friends, and occupying a prominent position in society, her tranquil disposition and well-ordered mind exercised a great influence over the affectionate little band of Lynchburgers then resident in St. Louis. The health of Mrs. Tilden becoming impaired, she sought for a time a more northern climate, procuring the advice of the eminent medical men of Philadelphia. Returning home, her friends believed her restoration to health complete; but, late in the year 1839, these hopes were blighted, and the beloved invalid calmly sunk to rest, whilst sorrowing ones stood around her bed of death, hymning for her those sacred words to which she had so loved to listen, as she sat within the sacred walls of the old Methodist Church in the home of her early youth.

One of the three daughters survives their excellent mother. Mrs. Mary Jane Robbins, wife of Z. C. Robbins, Esq., is at present a resident of Washington city, D. C., and though only a child when her parents left Lynchburg, Mrs. Robbins is most affectionately remembered in that place and its vicinity, by classmates as well as by those some years her senior.

AMANDA BURD, the second daughter, married Mr. Patterson, a native of Ireland, and in a brief time this gentleman died in Lynchburg. About the year 1827, a young man by the name of Shelton settled in Lynchburg. He possessed a fine appearance, good sense, and habits of great application to business, so that he soon became very prosperous. This young man was a native of the lower country, and connected with the Shelton family of Hanover, one of whose members was the first wife of Patrick Henry. In the month of December, 1827, Ann Burd, the third daughter, was united in marriage to Mr. Shelton, the wedding taking place on the same night of that of Eliza Daniel and William Lewis Cabell, the carriages to the different places of festivity meeting and intersecting each other constantly. In after years, emigrating to St. Louis with her husband and father's family, Mrs. Shelton, for a length of time after the death of that young wife and husband, rejoiced in the sacred ties of wife and mother, but about twenty years since she died in St. Louis, her husband and family surviving her.

FORTUNATUS SYDNOR.

There are few of the old inhabitants of Lynchburg, who can ever forget FORTUNATUS SYDNOR—his fine, manly form; his bright, intelligent face; his ready wit, so tempered with good humor; his cheerful hilarity; his genuine, old Virginia hospitality. For many years cashier of the Virginia Bank, his playful wit lightening his own labors, as well as those of others; and long will that side-walk appear as though it were still gladdened by the genial presence of this excellent man; for that locality is inseparably joined with pleasing memories of the past, to which Mr. Sydnor is closely linked.

United in marriage to Lizzie Royall, a lady of great worth and loveliness, the measure of his happiness would have been complete, but for the constant feeble health of that lady. The death of his noble-hearted son, Royal Sydnor, just as he had attained manhood, the loss of his second son, followed by that of several infant children—all these teachings of mortality were sent to this family in the brief space of a few years. With fortitude Mr.

Sydnor bore these afflictions, raising the drooping spirits of his wife, for whom was ever dreaded a fatal attack of pulmonary disease. But, alas! for the uncertainty of human life! the strong man was cut down in the prime of life, in the year 1840, whilst the feeble wife was left alone to combat the troubles of earth.

Mrs. SYDNOR possessed a deep, fervid, vital piety, and the knowledge that she was, at any moment, liable to enter eternity, had been present to her for many years, causing her "conversation to be in Heaven;" so that a few years since, when the summons came, she arose with willing feet and "went forth to meet the Bridegroom." A devoted member of the Presbyterian Church, Mrs. Sydnor's Christian demeanor was such, that all who saw her "could also take knowledge of her that she had been with Jesus."

> "Calm on the bosom of thy God,
> Fair spirit, rest thee now,
> E'en while with us thy footsteps trod,
> His soul was on thy brow.
>
> Dust to its narrow house beneath,
> Soul to its place on high,
> They that have seen thy look in death,
> No more may fear to die."

THE BYRD FAMILY.

DAVIDSON BRADFUTE.

Mrs. ANN URSULA BYRD was the wife of William Byrd, Esq., of Westover, a son of the gallant Colonel Byrd of the olden time. Her maiden name was Munford, and after the death of Mr. Byrd, she came to Lynchburg to reside with her married daughters, Mrs. Bradfute and Mrs. Alexander Tompkins. Of a family of five daughters, Mrs. Ann O. Wright, of Lynchburg, is the sole surviving member.

DAVIDSON BRADFUTE, Esq., was a native of Bedford county, and from the name, it may be inferred that the family of Bradfute are of Scottish descent. Few men in Lynchburg occupied, in the regard of friends, a higher station than Mr. Bradfute, and justly did he command the respect and affection of a large circle with him associated. Upright, kind, and industrious, the many virtues of Davidson Bradfute shed over his family and connections a lustre, and his death, occurring in 1829, was a heavy calamity.

Mr. Bradfute married Maria, the daughter of Mrs. Byrd, and for many years they resided in the house at present occupied by Alexander Tompkins, Esq., their abode being the scene of the most constant, generous hospitality. The remembrance of this family is much cherished in Lynchburg, particularly on account of the extraordinary beauty of its seven daughters. In the year 1854 Mrs. Bradfute died, having followed to the tomb many of her lovely daughters.

With what love and tenderness is the memory of EVELYN CARTER BRADFUTE regarded by friends and associates in her native place. She was born in the month of June, 1814, and in early childhood gave promise of the great loveliness of her more mature years. She was, indeed, perfectly beautiful—the mild, bright intelligence of those exquisite dark eyes being the index of a heart and soul most amiable, generous and self-sacrificing. After receiving the meed of admiration from many suitors, she was, in the autumn of 1833, united in marriage to Alfred Penn, Esq., of New Orleans; but ere a few years had flown by, in her early bloom she had passed away, her resting-place far from friends and home; yet, in some faithful, loving hearts, is deeply cloistered a most affectionate remembrance of this lovely woman, and the sweet, gentle influences of her character will ever continue to act on those who were with her associated. During the winter of 1842, she breathed her last in the city of New Orleans, in the 27th year of her age, and her loved remains repose in the cemetery near the city, where a touching and appropriate inscription on her tomb tenderly recalls to passers-by the sweet time of her girlhood in her native place. To this sacred spot do Virginians oft resort, and pensively bend over the grave which contains the "early called," the dearly loved friend of long ago, Evelyn Carter Penn.

> "A star has left the kindling sky,
> A lovely northern light,
> How many planets are on high,
> But that has left the night.
>
> I miss its bright familiar face,
> It was a friend to me,
> Associate with my native place,
> And home beyond the sea."

The dwelling over the druggist establishment of Robinson Stabler was for some years the residence of THOMAS McKINNEY, Esq., an excellent citizen, who, with his amiable wife and family, were highly esteemed in Lynchburg. Mrs. McKinney was a daughter of the good and venerable Mrs. Dupuy, of Richmond, and soon after her marriage, connecting herself with the Episcopal Church of Lynchburg, she continued, till the day of her death, a most valued, beloved member and communicant.

With this family, in the year 1828, came to reside MARTHA LOUISA MCKINNEY, only daughter of William McKinney, Esq. She was a niece of both Mr. and Mrs. McKinney, as her father had also married a Miss Dupuy, who, dying early, had left three children, of whom Peter D. McKinney, Esq., Richmond, is now the only survivor.

Martha L. McKinney was one of the most amiable girls that ever resided in Lynchburg; generous, warm-hearted and affectionate; gifted with a fine, vigorous mind and playful fancy, united to great simplicity of character and perfect naivete of manners, it is no wonder that Martha McKinney should have occupied a high place in the hearts of a large circle of friends. In the spring of 1831 she was married to David Bridges, Esq., now of New Orleans; and this wedding was remarkable for the age of this youthful pair, who then pronounced their vows. The bridegroom was not twenty years old, and the bride just seventeen. Mrs. Bridges passed through various alternations of fortune, but whether in prosperity or adversity, she was the same loving, disinterested friend. Full of life, the dark clouds of adversity could only, for a brief period, overshadow the delightful sunshine of her disposition.

Removing to Richmond soon after her marriage, her shining qualities soon reared around her a numerous circle of friends, who dearly love now to speak of her with affection and admiration. A great misfortune visited her family, at the time of her death, which occurred in the spring of 1844. Her death, as her life, was most beautiful, her gentle, lovely traits being conspicuous even in that solemn hour. Her husband survives her, together with five children, Mrs. Roy and Miss M. Bridges, of Richmond, William Bridges, of New Orleans, and two younger sons residing in the city of Richmond.

>Fair with my first ideas twined,
>Thine image oft will meet my mind,
>And while remembrance brings thee near,
>Affection oft will drop a tear.
>
>What tragic tears bedew the eye,
>What deaths we suffer e'er we die;
>Our broken friendship we deplore,
>And loves of earth that are no more.
>
>No after friendships e'er can raise
>The endearments of our early days,
>And ne'er our hearts such fondness prove,
>As when we first begin to love.
>
>   ANON.

The *Franklin Hotel* was built by Samuel Harrison, Esq. It was thought at the time a stupendous undertaking, and it remains a lasting monument of the energy and judgment of the remarkable man by whom it was planned. Very soon after its completion, this Hotel was leased to Mr. Hoyle, and by this gentleman was the establishment kept for many years in a style superior to anything of the sort in the State of Virginia. This excellent and venerable man was a native of Ireland, but for a number of years previous, he had been an inhabitant of Lynchburg, and a proprietor of the old "Indian Queen," kept on Main street. In his native country, Mr. Hoyle occupied a high standing amongst the Irish gentry; but circumstances rendering it necessary for him to emigrate, he, with his wife, son, daughter and nephew, embarked for America. Mrs. Hoyle was a lady of amiability and refinement, and long will this excellent couple be remembered in Lynchburg by the old inhabitants. The superiority of the table, the perfect order of the establishment, the handsome antique furniture, the fine pictures, the kindly bearing of the host and hostess—all these assisted in making such a public house as we can never more see in this age of steam and telegraph. Amassing a large fortune at this model Hotel, Mr. Hoyle retired from business, his head perfectly frosted by age, and leaving in the hearts of countless friends a lasting remembrance. He survived his good wife many years, and at his death divided his honestly gained estate between his daughter, Mrs. Mary Brown, and his nephew, Mr. George Hoyle, both of whom reside in St. Louis, Missouri. The Franklin Hotel was then leased by Robert Morriss, Esq., and for many years himself and his worthy lady presided over the establishment with a skill and wisdom comparable only to that of the venerable Mr. Hoyle. The name of this Hotel is now changed to that of the "Norvelle House;" and with all the expense encountered by its proprietors, with all its gorgeous, showy furniture and many parlors, this house has never been what it was in the days of Mr. Hoyle and Robert Morriss, Esq.

AN OLD COUPLE.

"Woodman, spare that tree—
Touch not a single bough."

In the year 1819, Dr. HUMPHREYS resided in our town, on Main street, and his dwelling was a long, low cottage-looking building, afterwards the residence of Samuel Bransford, Esq. At that time, this house was deeply shaded by a row of beautiful catalpa trees, which, at the earnest entreaties of Mrs. Humphreys, had been permitted to remain by the town authorities. Dr. Humphreys was of Scottish origin, and was amongst the earliest and most respected of the first settlers of Lynchburg, where, with considerable reputation, he practiced the medical profession; his druggist store, at that time, with the exception of Dr. Enfield's, was the only establishment of the sort in town. Mrs. Humphreys was a high-born, polished lady, of comely appearance and gentle manners. Of great energy and industry, she thus materially aided her husband in his affairs, as well as by her prudence and foresight.

Many young ladies from the country were placed at the residence of this worthy couple for the purpose of attending the schools of Lynchburg. The parents confiding them to their care, felt every assurance of confidence in the kindness and discretion of Dr. and Mrs. Humphreys.

Two lovely daughters gladdened the old age of their parents—Isabella, the eldest, became the wife of James Bullock, Esq., and Jane, the younger, was married to Wm. Lynch. The druggist establishment of Dr. Humphreys was kept in the house afterwards occupied as such by the late Dr. Howell Davies, and being somewhat deaf and near-sighted, Dr. Humphreys was often the recipient of many ill-timed jokes from the numerous school-boys of the town; for instance, one of them would often stand at the corner of the street above, beckoning to Dr. Humphreys as though on urgent business; and before this worthy disciple of Esculapius could possibly reach the spot, the person beckoning would have vanished.

He employed in his establishment a young Scotchman, who was a great mimic, as well as a ventriloquist, and when sent down into the cellar, this Caledonian lad would appear to be carrying on a conversation with several others; and, oh horror! Dr. Humphreys could distinctly hear them uncorking bottles and decantering wine from a cask of his very best and oldest vintage. Precipitating himself down the steps after the delinquents with such rapidity as to endanger life and limb, on entering the subterraneous apartment, Dr. Humphreys would find no one there save the young Scotchman, who would look up with a demure countenance, innocently surprised at the speed and excitement of his employer. Nor was this the only annoyance at this druggist's store; for the Doctor possessed a colored man, named Bob, who was also an incomparable mimic; and so perfectly could he imitate the voice of Dr. Humphreys, that frequently he would cause a great tumult amongst the young men, by coming suddenly to the door and beginning to scold and grumble like his master. In the habit of putting his pen behind his ear, Dr. Humphreys endeavored to enforce amongst his clerks this custom, together with that of putting bottle stoppers and spiles in that same convenient place; but failing in this one day, it is said that Dr. Humphreys lost gallons of fine molasses, not finding the spile in its usual resting-place, and in his confusion entirely forgetting where it was laid.

At this time Dr. Humphreys had in his employment a young man by the name of Richardson, who was also by birth a Scotchman, and who professed to be a nephew of Burns' Highland Mary, thereby investing himself with some of the romance which surrounds that sweet and beloved dream of the Ayrshire ploughman's youth.

Dr. Humphreys was a good man and a useful

citizen, his peculiarities being perfectly harmless. He survived for many years his wife and children; and truly touching was it in his decline of life to witness his loneliness at his desolate hearth, relieved only occasionally by visits from a few grandchildren.

MRS. TALIAFERRO.

This venerable lady resides in Lynchburg, continuing to occupy the same house in which she lived nearly half a century since. Her maiden name was Price, and she was a sister of Mrs. Meredith Lambeth, of the vicinity of Lynchburg. For some years, Mrs. Taliaferro was the wife of Roderick Taliaferro, Esq., an excellent man, who, dying about the year 1819, left her a widow, with the sole charge of a young and helpless family. Conscientiously discharging these arduous duties, she has had the comfort and gratification, in her old age, of seeing her children rise and prosper around her; proving that the good seed, by her sown, had fallen into honest hearts, which, in due season, have brought forth their fruits. She was the mother of the late Judge Norborne Taliaferro, who was reared in Lynchburg, and who studied for the bar under the auspices of the late Christopher Anthony, of that place. Judge Taliaferro was an eminent lawyer, and, when a young man, he married Miss Lucy Jones, an interesting young lady of Lynchburg. Surviving for some years his beloved wife, he was appointed Judge of the Henry and Patrick District. Discharging with great ability these duties, and whilst in the midst of his vigor and usefulness, Judge Taliaferro died a few years since, leaving his aged mother to mourn the loss of her excellent son.

In a small wooden house, not far below the old "Cross Keys," lived Mrs. WOODROW. A lovely face, commanding figure, together with fine sense and much suavity of manners, gave to this lady great influence at one time in Lynchburg. An active member of the Methodist Church, possessing great fluency of speech and a perfect command of her pen, she occupied in that denomination a prominent station, and, by her practical skill in nursing and administering medicines, she greatly aided their society, for visiting the sick and indigent. Her maiden name was Fitzhugh, and that of her first husband was Brent, and her daughter, Mary Brent, was a young lady of great beauty and gentleness. Mr. Woodrow, the second husband, was an amiable man, but of a family widely differing from her first aristocratic connection. Her daughter, Henrietta Woodrow, was just expanding into womanhood at the time they left Lynchburg.

Mary Brent married Tipton Harrison, of Lynchburg, and emigrating with her husband and her mother's family to Pensacola, in a brief time, she with her husband, brother and sister, all fell victims to the yellow fever; and the letters of the bereaved mother, written in all the eloquence of woe, were read with great sympathy and interest by many in Lynchburg. Shortly after this time, Mrs. Woodrow removed to New Orleans with her sister, Miss Nancy Fitzhugh.

Many little incidents connected with the latter personage might be here recorded, but as both herself and her repartees are well remembered by the old inhabitants, it is needless to mention them. The fate both of Mrs. Woodrow and her sister is involved in some obscurity. A few years since, a gentleman of Lynchburg received a long and singular letter from Miss Nancy Fitzhugh, proposing to engage him in a law suit, and laying claim to a considerable property in the town of Lynchburg; and for some time this lady was constantly expected in the city; but as no subsequent tidings were ever received from her, it may be inferred that Miss Nancy Fitzhugh has long since left this lower world.

THE TUCKER FAMILY.

MRS. MARIA TUCKER—ROSALIE TUCKER.

"Beneath every domestic roof," says an American writer, "there are more than are counted by the eye of a stranger. Spirits are there which he does not see, but which are never far from the eyes of the household. Steps are on the stairs, but not for common ears, and familiar places and objects restore familiar smiles and tears, and acts of goodness and words of love, which are seen and heard by memory alone."

Mrs. MARIA TUCKER, eldest daughter of Charles Carter, Esq.,* was a native of Culpeper county. She was in early life married to George Tucker, Esq., a native of the Island of Bermuda, and many years since they settled in the town of Lynchburg.

---

* The wife of this gentleman was a lady of great goodness, refinement and elegance. Her maiden name was "Betsy Lewis," the favorite niece of General Washington. Mrs. Eleanor Brown, wife of the late Henry Brown, Esq., and Mrs. Otwayanna Owens, the second wife of Dr. William Owens, were likewise her daughters. These two last ladies will long be most affectionately remembered in Lynchburg. They were highly gifted with moral qualities, and remarkable for most sprightly imaginations and minds of the highest order.

Posssessing a very lovely face, beautiful form, a mind highly cultivated, perfect command of language, united to most enthusiastic eloquence, Mrs. Tucker adorned the polished circle in which she moved, contributing to its gayety and cheerfulness, by the most refined wit, perfectly tempered with good humor. For some years the family resided in the house owned by George Whitelocke, Esq., in the vicinity of the Rev. William S. Reid's residence, the daughters a lovely household band, till death claimed for its own, ROSALIE, the fairest and loveliest of the sisterhood.

This remarkable young person was born in Culpeper on the 8th of May, 1804; and, from the earliest stage of her existence, her mother had formed the most favorable presages of her future excellence; and, though naturally sanguine, Mrs. Tucker seems, on this occasion, to have been inspired with more than her ordinary enthusiasm.

Extracts from a Memoir of ROSALIE, *written by her Father.*

"From her earliest infancy she was distinguished for a feeling, generous heart; as she grew up, it exhibited itself in a thousand amiable forms of affection, kindness, humanity and benevolence. The tenderness of her nature was not confined to her relations. She was all kindness and sympathy to her young companions—to the poor, to the servants, of whom there is not one who cannot bear testimony to her beneficence and generosity."

"Even in her last illness, worn down as she was by weakness and pain, there was not a day, and scarcely an hour, in which she did not form some plan, or make some request, which showed that she was often insensible of her own suffering in her affectionate solicitude for the happiness of others."

"Warm hearts are apt to be united with irritable tempers. They both seem to be the natural effects of a more than ordinary sensibility. It was not so with Rosalie: she had the temper of an angel. One eternal sunshine of good humor and placidity beamed from her brow. She was never seen angry, and the meekness and patience with which she bore the sufferings of her last illness, have never been surpassed. The fact is, a happy nature, aided by good precepts and good habits, had so subdued all selfish feelings, that they seemed to be subordinate to her sympathy for others, and their ease and accommodation constituted her chief pleasure—it might be said, her ruling passion. Hence it was, that this generous disinterestedness did not wait for great occasions to show itself, or require the stimulus of applause for its support, but was excited in the little concerns and privacy of domestic life, when the character is seen in its true colors without affectation or disguise."

This gifted young person[*] died in Lynchburg, December, 1819, in the fifteenth year of her age;

---

[*] About the time of her death, many young children were called after this lovely girl, and the name Rosalie, has since then become quite common in the vicinity of Lynchburg.

and, though little more than four years old at the time, a perfect recollection of her lovely appearance is preserved—and would that the tender feelings of childish admiration could be eloquently penned as they are felt. The memory of Rosalie Tucker is sacredly cherished by her class-mates, as well as by the oldest inhabitants of Lynchburg; and, in her early death, we have a striking exemplification of the broken alabaster box, whose ointment, though so precious, was unhesitatingly yielded to the Saviour; and whose perfume, though at first confined to that humble Hebrew abode, has now gone forth to the world, conveying a lesson both practical and beautiful. So, after the lapse of thirty-nine years, may the present generation be instructed and stimulated to press onwards, to "be ye therefore perfect"—as much by the tranquil death, as by the exemplary life, of this young girl.

She was very beautiful in person—and a portrait of her, taken after death, serves in a measure to recall those angelic features. Though much younger than Clementina Cuvier, a striking parallel exists between Rosalie and this exemplary young Frenchwoman, not only in rich mental gifts and perfect loveliness of character, but in the peculiar devotion cherished towards Rosalie by her gifted father—which, in its intensity, resembled the affection cherished by Baron Cuvier to his daughter, Clementina. A few years subsequent to this mournful event, Mrs. Tucker was, during the absence of her husband, suddenly called hence, leaving her house lonely and her young family desolate; and, without doubt, in that solemn hour, she could appropriate to herself the truth of our Saviour's words: "What I do, thou knowest not now; but thou shalt know hereafter;" for she could not but be assured that her beloved daughter, the angelic Rosalie, was waiting to receive her on the shores of Eternity.

Mrs. Tucker left an assurance of peace, and met death with great calmness and composure. She had evidently had presentiments of her death, from many little memoranda found, and from particular passages which she had noted and marked in her book of hymns—one of which was sung at her funeral, which took place at the Presbyterian Church, being preached by the Rev. William S. Reid, as soon as Mr. Tucker reached his desolate home:

> "My hope, my all, my Saviour thou,
> To Thee low now my soul I bow:
> I feel the bliss Thy wounds impart,
> I find Thee, Saviour, in my heart!
>
> Be Thou my strength, be Thou my stay,
> Protect me through my life's short day;
> And if I would from Thee depart,
> Then dwell Thou, Saviour, in my heart.
>
> In fierce temptation's darkest hour,
> Save me from sin and Satan's power:
> Tear every idol from Thy throne,
> And reign my Saviour, reign alone.

> My suffering time will soon be o'er,
> Then shall I sigh and weep no more ;
> My ransomed soul shall soar away.
> To sing Thy praise in endless day."

Of the members of this beloved family, Mr. Tucker survives, together with his daughters, Mrs. George Rives, of Sherwood, Albemarle county, and Mrs. Gessner Harrison,* of the University of Virginia. Lelia Tucker, the youngest daughter, died some years since at the residence of her sister, Mrs. Harrison. She was a lady of great goodness, possessing, in an eminent degree, all those qualities of mind and heart, for which the other members of her family were so remarkable. She died as she had lived, the meek, cheerful, devoted Christian; and she is surely now united in Heaven to her sainted mother and sister.

---

* The recent death of Mrs. Broadus, the young and lovely daughter of this lady, whilst awakening affectionate sympathy, tenderly recalls the past, blending the excellencies of the young wife and mother, with those of the lovely Rosalie, whose example had doubtless been held up to her in childhood.

THE TOWLES FAMILY.

COLONEL OLIVER TOWLES.

" How sleep the brave who sink to rest,
By all their country's wishes blest;
When Spring with dewy fingers cold,
Returns to deck their hallowed mould,
She there shall dress a sweeter sod,
Than Fancy's feet have ever trod.

By fairy hands their knell is rung,
By forms unseen their dirge is sung;
There Honor comes, a pilgrim gray,
To bless the turf that wraps their clay,
And Freedom shall awhile repair,
To dwell a weeping hermit there."

COLLINS.

The family of TOWLES were originally from Wales—settling first in the Northern Neck of Virginia, where some of their descendants continue to reside. Colonel Towles, the subject of this brief memoir, was, prior to the Revolution, a lawyer of eminence in the county of Orange; but, as soon as the struggle with England commenced, Colonel Oliver Towles abandoned the law, entering with his whole soul into the contest for liberty. He was, indeed, a patriot and a brave officer, taking an active part from the beginning to the end of our Revolutionary struggle with Great Britain. He was made prisoner at one time, and suffered many hardships as such, on Long Island, where he was for some time kept in captivity.

Colonel Towles* was in several actions, and was taken prisoner at the battle of Germantown, where he received a wound, which was found out by letters from his brother officers to their friends—for he, himself, never alluded to the circumstance. The inhabitants of Philadelphia, particularly the ladies, distinguished themselves by their kind attentions to the prisoners of war. But the British generals behaved very ignobly: they taunted our officers with General Washington's want of military skill in losing the battle, and they spoke of him as "Mr. Washington;" at which Colonel Towles was greatly incensed, and said that "he knew no such man, and that if they meant the American commander-in-chief, and called him so, he would then answer them." At which one of the British officers replied, "These American officers are quite spunky."

Colonel Towles had a son, called HENRY TOWLES,

---

* Colonel Towles was a member and Secretary of the Cincinnati Society.

who was a Captain in General Wayne's engagement with the Indians, and who was killed in the battle. A letter from his commanding officer to his father, shows feelingly in what estimation this brave young man was held; and, amongst the papers left by Colonel Towles, were many letters from General Washington—one of them saying, that "if he was solicited he would take the command of the American forces, but that he would not electioneer for it, and would give it as his opinion that General Andrew Lewis was the fitest man in the country for commander-in-chief." Colonel Towles was present at the surrender of Cornwallis at Yorktown, and he often spoke with enthusiasm of this most imposing scene. He was premoted to Lieutenant-Colonel, which commission he held to the end of the war; and, when Edmund Pendleton* was made Judge, Colonel Towles was solicited to become a candidate for that office, but, owing to his personal friendships, he refused to be put in nomination. Indeed, this venerable patriot was a most remarkable man, possessing great conversational powers, and by his wit and vivacity attracting both old and young.

---

* On his removal to Lynchburg, Colonel Towles called on "Aunt Martin," who was a niece of his old friend, and he remarked that "it cost her no effort to be good, as she was so constitutionally and by inheritance,—that all the Pendletons had good blood flowing through their veins."

He was enthusiastically fond of the British poets; and his reading of Shakspeare was so superior, that it might have borne comparison with that of Mrs. Siddons or Fanny Kemble Butler. He corresponded with most of the leading men of his day, and many of their letters, preserved in the Towles family, will, doubtless, hereafter be valuable as historical references.

This venerable man lived to be upwards of eighty years old, retaining to the last his wonderful faculties; and, on the day of his death, which occurred during the winter of 1824, in Lynchburg, he read, without spectacles, a chapter of small print in his Bible. The remains of this brave and good man are interred in Lynchburg, where he was beloved and reverenced by a large circle of friends and relatives.

Major OLIVER TOWLES, a son of Colonel Towles, was a gallant Virginia gentleman, though too young at the time of the Revolutionary war, to take part in the contest with England. He became the husband of Agatha Lewis, the name of a family which has adorned the annals of our political and military history, and which is also equally eminent for the more quiet virtues of domestic life. Tall and commanding in person, Mrs. Towles inherited from her illustrious ancestors all of that beauty and elegance of manner for which they were so remarkable. This lady was gifted with a fine mind and excellent heart, and long will her good influence be felt amongst her own descendants and those of the warm friends she so strongly attached to herself during her residence in Lynchburg. She was an ardent, sincere Christian, a devout member of the Presbyterian Church of Lynchburg, and she was most tenderly attached to the beloved pastor of that denomination.

Surviving for many years her affectionate husband, she passed through many alternations of fortune, all of which she sustained with the dignity and cheerfulness of a Christian lady. Out of a family of eight children only four survive: Dr. William Towles, of Caira, Cumberland county; Mrs. Caroline Simms, a resident in the vicinity of Caira; Dr. Alfred Towles, of Missouri, and Mrs. John Blair Dabney, of Campbell county, Virginia.

The daughters of Major Towles will ever be remembered with pride and pleasure by those who knew them in Lynchburg. They were queenly looking ladies, gifted with most cordial, affectionate dispositions, which served to endear them to friends, even more than their brilliant minds and great personal beauty. MARIA TOWLES, the oldest, was a very gifted and elegant woman. She became the wife of Dr. Landon Rives, of Nelson county; and, many years since, with her husband and family, she emigrated to Cincinnati, where, for a length of time, Dr. Rives ably filled a professorship in the Medical College of the Queen City. About seventeen years since, Mrs. Rives was taken suddenly from her devoted family. A portrait of this lovely lady is at Oak Ridge, the country seat of Miss P. Rives in Nelson county, but it fails to convey to the beholder an idea of her beautiful, ever-varying countenance.

Mrs. JOHN BLAIR DABNEY, the second daughter, was well known and beloved, in Lynchburg, by the sweet name of Bessie Towles. She was a lady of splendid personal appearance, and it was related by one present at the time, that, on one occasion, appearing in Washington City at a Presidential ball, in simple, elegant attire, her beauty and freshness, her unaffected, sprightly and graceful manners, attracted throughout that large assemblage the most unqualified admiration.

About the year 1822, this lady became the wife of John Blair Dabney, Esq., an eminent lawyer of the upper country, and a son of the late Judge Dabney: and the family reside at their country seat, not very distant from Campbell Courthouse.

Colonel WILLIAM LEWIS, of Mount Athos, who married Miss Cabell, was one of the brothers of Mrs. Agatha Towles; and he was for a length of time a resident at Mount Athos, nine miles below

Lynchburg. This gentleman was, for many years, a member of Congress from that district—a friend of internal improvement; and he was a man of great literary taste and acquirements.

Dr. CHARLES LEWIS, a younger brother, was at one time a resident of Lynchburg, living in the next house below the Franklin Hotel. He married Miss Irvine, a daughter of General Irvine, of Philadelphia, one of the heroes of the Revolution. Dr. Lewis subsequently, with his family, moved to Philadelphia, where many of their descendants now reside—and amongst them, Mrs. Mary Leiper* and Mrs. Elizabeth Campbell, still well-remembered and beloved by friends known during their residence in Lynchburg.

"William Lewis (the father of Mrs. Agatha Towles) was the third son of John Lewis.† He was an active participator in the border wars, and was an officer of the Revolutionary army, in which one of his sons was killed, and another maimed for life. When the British force, under Tarleton, drove the Legislature from Charlottesville to Staunton, the stillness of the Sabbath eve was bro-

---

* Mrs. Leiper married a near relative of Dr. Kane, and in his "Arctic Explorations" he named a river in honor of her, "The Mary Leiper River."

† For a minute and deeply interesting account of the circumstances, connected with the settlement of Augusta county by the Lewis family, the reader is referred to Howe's History of Virginia, page 181.

ken, in the latter town, by the beat of the drum, and volunteers were called for to prevent the passage of the British through the mountains at Rockfish Gap. The elder sons of William Lewis, who then resided at the old fort, were absent with the Northern army. Three sons, however, were at home, whose ages were seventeen, fifteen and thirteen years. William Lewis was confined to his bed by sickness; but his wife,* with the firmness of a Roman matron, called them to her, and bade them fly to the defence of their native land. 'Go, my children,' said she—'I spare not my youngest, my fair-haired boy—the comfort of my declining years,—I devote you all to my country! Keep back the feet of the invader from the soil of Augusta, or see my face no more!' When this incident was related to General Washington, shortly after its occurrence, he enthusiastically exclaimed, 'Leave me but a banner to plant upon the mountains of Augusta, and I will rally around me the men who will lift our bleeding country from the dust and set her free!'"

Howe's *History of Virginia.*

WILLIAM LEWIS, mentioned in the above extract, owned a princely estate where Staunton now stands; and he, with his brothers, Andrew, Thomas, Charles and Samuel, were in Braddock's defeat. They received their early instruction from the venerable Dr. Waddell, the blind preacher mentioned by Wirt

---

* This lady was a niece of General Montgomery. She was very proud of her sons—whom, when called upon, she would exhort " to do honor to their cause."

in his British Spy. The names of these distinguished men are well known in history, so that only a slight mention of them is here necessary, it being only designed to make a brief record of some of the incidents connected with the family of Mrs. Agatha Towles, some of which we believe have never appeared in print.

William Lewis moved from Staunton to the Sweet Springs, where he died at the age of eighty, revered as a patriarch and honored and beloved by the whole community. Charles Lewis, his brother, was interred on the battle-field of Point Pleasant, like Sir John More,

"With his martial cloak around him."

It was said of General ANDREW LEWIS, by the Governor of New-York, when sent by General Washington to that city in some public capacity, "that his appearance was so grand and imposing that the earth seemed to tremble under his tread."

Colonel THOMAS LEWIS, one of the sons of William Lewis, and also a brother of Mrs. Agatha Towles, was a noble, brave, spirited officer. He was aid to General Wayne, and, on one occasion, when they were hotly pursued by the Indians, the horse of General Wayne fell, and together with the rider being disabled, Colonel Thomas Lewis took his general in his arms, and put him on his own fleet horse, telling General Wayne to feel no uneasiness on his account, as he would seek safety by taking to *his heels*. Colonel Thomas Lewis and his general were much attached to each other, the latter presented the former with a large body of land in Indiana.

William Lewis left three daughters—Margaret Lynn,* who was married to Mr. McFarland, of Pittsburg; Agatha, the wife of Major Towles, and Elizabeth Montgomery, the wife of Mr. Trent, of Cumberland.

The life of Mrs. McFARLAND, Mrs. Towles' oldest sister, was a very eventful one; she having from early childhood been placed in the midst of perilous scenes, from some of which she escaped almost miraculously. Her father built a fort at Staunton, as it was unsafe for families to reside in their own dwellings. On one occasion, Margaret Lynn Lewis had wandered farther than was safe from the fort, and, whilst amusing herself, she saw standing very near to her a large Indian. She was a small child at that time, and, being very agile, she sprang up and ran to the fort, giving the alarm that the Indians were coming. They were in an instant in an attitude of defence, and they gave her the credit of saving the fort.

---

* See Howe's History of Virginia for a most interesting sketch of Margaret Lynn, grand-daughter of the Laird of Loch-Lynn, and the mother of William Lewis.

She married Mr. McFarland, of Pittsburg, and, when she left the paternal roof, she traveled through a wilderness country, infested with hostile Indians, till they reached that place, where they did not consider themselves safe, constantly expecting attacks from Indians. Among the more friendly, she was a great favorite, and, in her house, she had a room which she called her museum, filled with articles of their ingenious manufacture and with all manner of curiosities. She could converse with several of their tribes, and, on some occasions, she interpreted in their councils. Once, when they least apprehended danger, a war whoop was heard, her husband taken prisoner, the tomahawk raised, and she averted her eyes to avoid witnessing the fatal stroke. The river was between them, and she, with her infant and maid servant, of course, endeavored to fly, knowing the inevitable consequences of delay. After starting, the servant reminded Mrs. McFarland of her husband's money and valuable papers, but she desired the girl not to mention any thing of that sort to her at such a moment; but, regardless of the commands of her mistress, the servant returned to the dwelling, bringing all the money and as many of the papers as she could hold in her apron, overtaking, in a short time, her mistress, as the snow was three feet deep. On looking back, they saw the house in flames, and, pursuing their journey, they, with incredible fatigue, reached the house of Colonel Crawford,* a distance of fourteen miles. Mrs. McFarland was very nearly exhausted, having carried her infant child the greater part of the way, but, through the kind attention of her friends at Col. Crawford's, she was soon restored.

She remained under the hospitable roof of Col. Crawford, till her father, hearing of her situation, sent her brother, Col. William Lewis, to bring her home, and they travelled the whole distance on horseback, using pack-horses for their baggage. Throughout the space of three tedious years, the brave heart of this remarkable woman† was buoyed up with the firm hope and belief that she should again behold her beloved husband alive, and at length she received intelligence that he had been carried captive to Quebec, where he had encountered incredible hardships; but the chiefs had agreed, that if a heavy ransom was paid, he might be restored to his friends. Of course, this was done with the greatest alacrity; his brother going on, and returning with Mr. McFarland to Staunton.

In a short time, the husband and wife returned to their desolate home at Pittsburg, where they

---

* Col. C. was afterwards inhumanly burnt at the stake.

† Judge Breckenridge, of Kentucky, who well knew and esteemed this noble-hearted lady, said that "he never saw such a woman, and that she ought to live in history."

literally found nothing left; the Indians having destroyed house, stock and every thing pertaining to their establishment. They re-built their dwelling on the same spot, and for many years they happily and peacefully resided there, leaving a large family all respectably settled about Pittsburg, with the exception of two of her sons, who engaged in the fur trade.

Many years after her return to Pittsburg, Mrs. McFarland came on a visit to her parents at the Sweet Springs, attracting every one by her vivacity and intelligence, and leaving in the hearts of those of her connections, then almost in infancy, a lasting remembrance.

REV. WILLIAM S. REID.

Rev. WILLIAM S. REID was a native of Pennsylvania, and was born about the year 1776. Early in life emigrating to Virginia, he settled at Hampden Sydney College, where he studied for the ministry, which he afterwards adorned by his zeal, piety and eloquence. He married Clementina Venable, a young lady belonging to one of the first families in Virginia, and she was eminently qualified for the wife of a minister. Of excellent disposition, amiable speech, and a heart without guile, she joined to these the most enthusiastic, tender and romantic devotion to her gifted husband, the cords being only strengthened as she became older.

Shortly after his marriage, Mr. Reid came to Lynchburg, where he established the first Presbyterian Church of that place, presenting the ground on which to erect the building, and preaching for some time with little or no salary; and for many years he was the beloved pastor of that Church, walking in all the ordinances of the Lord blameless; but about the year 1828 or '29, a division occurred in his Church, putting to a severe test his Christian character, as some of his oldest and most influential members went over to the new side; but after this time, Mr. Reid continued zealously to advance the cause of Christianity by his faithful ministry for many years. Mrs. Clementina Reid was a lady of great excellence, and she has left in Lynchburg a remembrance of herself that will never be effaced from the hearts of her friends.

Of the ministerial course of this beloved man, it is not here the intention to write; the effects are too well known throughout the State, and they will continue to be felt through time and eternity; but tenderness of emotion impels us to offer a brief tribute of him as a teacher, which station he occupied for many years in Lynchburg, by presiding over one of the best female schools in the State of Virginia. His thorough knowledge of the structure of the English language, his happy talent for imparting instruction, and exciting interest in his pupils; his scientific attainments, his graceful manner of illustrating by experiments, his impartiality, his firmness, tempered by gentleness—all these secured to him eminently the respect and regard of his scholars, who will carry with them through life the most affectionate remembrance of Mr. Reid, mingled with retrospections of the past most pleasing.

How many ladies scattered over the United States has he educated, and how many of the same have beed joined by him in the holy bands of matrimony, and for how large a number of these has he not prayed beside a bed of death, and rendered the last solemn services over their graves! And how many, as they approached the hour of death, have blessed God that they have been instructed by this beloved pastor.

"Oh! blessings on his kindly voice, and on his silver hair,
And blessings on his whole long life, until he meet me there;
Oh! blessing on his kindly heart, and on his silver head,
A thousand times I blessed him, as he knelt beside my bed."

The first coronation of the Queen of May ever known in Virginia took place at Mr. Reid's school. Miss Edgeworth's beautiful story of "Simple Susan"* had just appeared, and its perusal had excited in the pupils the strongest interest, mingled with a desire to have a celebration. It was told to the writer by one of the pupils† who was then at this school, that late in the day on the first of May, they requested of their teacher a holiday, choosing unanimously for their Queen Eliza Clopton, the most beloved of all their school companions. This rustic

---

* Wilson, in the "Noctes Ambrosiane," speaks of Miss Edgeworth as the authoress of "Simple Susan." May not this great and good man be as justly distinguished as the author of "Lights and Shadows of Scottish Life?"

† The late Mrs. Hobson Johns.

fête was conducted with great simplicity, and in the hearts of surviving class-mates will ever be most tenderly remembered. At that time, and for many succeeding years, there were no luxurious armchairs in Lynchburg, and one venerable elbow-chair was every May-day conveyed to Mr. Reid's, and from it the May Queen gently swayed the sceptre over her flowery realm. That chair, from which these lines are penned, sweetly recalls the blithe, happy time when Eliza Daniel was Queen of May. Her smiling blue eyes, her brown hair, surmounted by her wreath of dewy flowers, her graceful form draped in white muslin, are yet present to memory. On her bosom was fastened, by an old-fashioned brooch, a bunch of white rose buds; their stem was broken, and already in their early fragrance and beauty were they fading. What could have been more emblematic of her brief, happy life, than this childish scene.? The flowers of hope and love fading in early womanhood, the stem of her affections broken and crushed, as were those pale flowers, her own life evanescent as her May-day reign, and in the lapse of years, nought left to friends but sweet memories of the past, treasured in their hearts, as pearls of her life's brief story, and by them prized as the most sacred relic of by-gone days.

In the year 1841, Mrs. Clementina Reid departed this life, leaving in the hearts of her family and friends, a void never to be filled. Her death materially affected the health of her devoted husband, and though he submitted to the heavy bereavement with Christian fortitude and resignation, still he was never the same after her departure. Surviving his wife ten years, Mr. Reid was tenderly cherished by a large family, who could not but esteem it a privilege to administer to the comfort and happiness of this, their estimable parent. His death was deeply felt by the whole community in which he lived, and a sketch of his life, by an able divine of Lynchburg, appeared at the time of his death, bearing ample testimony to his worth and of the esteem in which he was held by other denominations. A large family survive him. Miss Reid, and his two sons, William S. Reid, jr., and S. V. Reid, being residents of Lynchburg; and with the exception of Mrs. Martha Calhoun, Mrs. Spencer, and Mrs. Wilson, the rest of the daughters of this family reside in the Western States. This finished scholar and eloquent minister deserves a far better memorial than a passing tribute, and it is to be hoped that some one intimately acquainted with the interesting events of his life, will compile at least a small volume for the purpose of publication, embellished with a portrait of Mr. Reid; a suggestion of this sort will doubtless be warmly responded to by friends, former pupils, and their descendants scattered over the United States.

WATERING PLACES OF LYNCHBURG.

SMITH'S WELL—-RICHARDSON'S SPRING—-THURMAN'S SPRING—TATE'S SPRING.

"Mr. Pickwick began to drink the water with great assiduity. He took them systematically—he drank a quarter of a pint before breakfast, and then walked up a hill, and another quarter of a pint after breakfast, and then walked down a hill; and after every fresh quarter of a pint, Mr. Pickwick declared, in the most solemn and emphatic manner, that he felt a great deal better; whereat his friends were much delighted, though they had not been previously aware that there was anything the matter with him."

PICKWICK PAPERS.—*Mr. Pickwick at Bath.*

"For the use of the water lately discovered by Luther Smith,* we, the subscribers, do agree to pay to the said

---

* From the original paper containing the resolutions, with the list of subscribers annexed. Sent by Dr. Fletcher, of Amherst county.

Luther Smith the respective sums affixed to our names, viz: the sum of $2 for every family during the season, the sum of $1 for every single man during the season. The season to commence from the date hereof, and to expire the first day of October. The money to be paid in advance."

About thirty-eight years since, a man named SMITH purchased a small place on the Richmond Road, about a mile below Lynchburg. Digging a well soon after he settled there, it was found, to the astonishment of all, to be a chalybeate of the strongest character. He then fitted up the place, erecting an arbor, and placing seats around. Then he sent out handbills, distributing some, and carefully wafering the others on the sides of walls and houses. As these publications greatly extolled the waters, and the terms for season tickets were moderate, the good folks of the town rapidly subscribed to his mineral well, and crowds frequented this watering place, twice a day—those unable to walk procuring conveyances—so that hacks, horses and two-wheeled gigs might be seen ever wending their way to this Bethesda of Lynchburg. Most remarkable cures were wrought by these healing waters, several persons professing to have been entirely cured of consumption; and Smith's polite attention to his visitors was so great, that he was fast becoming as popular and important a personage as Barrington's

Dr. Borumborad,* when an unexpected event took place, which forever destroyed Smith's famous well. Whilst at the zenith of his popularity, and at the time of the most wonderful renovation of invalids from the use of the waters, the enterprising proprietor receiving an advantageous offer for the place, sold out, departing speedily for the Western country. For a short time after, the well retained its virtues, but in a few weeks the chalybeate taste became more and more faint, till finally all remains of it had disappeared. The new proprietor, descending to the bottom, found, to his horror, a parcel of old nails, horse shoes, frying pans and ovens, and it was then ascertained that the said Luther Smith had been so fortunate as to have had a chalybeate well at whatever place he had previously located.

After the failure of Smith's well, Richardson's Spring became a favorite resort; the tide of beauty and fashion moving in that direction, on a summer's eve might be seen bevies of young ladies, with their admirers, strolling to that watering place. This chalybeate was undoubtedly genuine; two large bubbling springs continually flowing, showed plainly that there were no old nails, horse shoes, or broken ovens there. Uncle John, as Mr. Richardson was

---

* See Barrington's Sketches, for a sketch of Dr. Borumborad, the Irish Turk of Dublin, with his famous baths.

familiarly called, was in advance of the German doctrine of water cure, and at this place was an immense shower-bath, which must have been a terrible shock to the recipients, as many hundred gallons of water descended from a great height on their devoted heads. The screams of the sufferers could be heard a half a mile, and altogether the shower-bath at Richardson's Springs must have been a trifle more than Clarence's dream.

Mr. Richardson was subject to a few infirmities, the worst of them being a fondness for spiritous liquors; and when under the influence of these demons, he would commit acts of which, in his sober moments, he would have deemed himself incapable. Married to a pretty black-eyed lady,* whom he was frequently heard in his sober moments to compliment for her resemblance to a wax doll, he one day, whilst suffering from mania-potu, actually shot this worthy helpmate; and it was thought that this tragic occurrence would break up the watering place. But not so; the crowds increased, and many who had previously staid away from motives of economy, or from want of inclination, now went to see the man who had shot his wife, and the wife who had been shot by

---

* Mrs. Richardson is still living, and if any one wishes to see all of the almanacs printed during the last half century, it is told them that she has them in her possession.

her husband. For many years this place continued to be a resort for parties of pleasure and for military companies to hold their barbecues on the 4th of July; but those good old times have passed away, and military parades, so suitable on that day, have given way to pic-nic parties and Sunday school processions.

Many years since, Thurman's Spring came into notice : bursting out from a large conical rock, it was considered quite a curiosity; and, in addition to its strong mineral qualities, the water was remarkably cool and grateful. The ground on which it stood was purchased by a man named Williams, who there built a most expensive and inconvenient house—the room designed for a large mercantile establishment, extending over the mineral spring; and a large brick warehouse, built by Williams and standing opposite, gave to this part of the town the name of Williamsburg. The warehouse has long since been destroyed—the spacious dwelling house alone remaining to attest the folly of the builder. Mr. Williams occupied it but a short time, and then the building, like Oliver Twist, was let out to any one whom they could get to take it. At one time, the Rev. Samuel Tompkins rented the apartment containing the spring, there keeping a school for boys; and, whilst they drank in the instructions of Mr. Tompkins in classic lore, as well as of the humbler branches, going up to drink the chalybeate, afforded a pleasant relief to the humdrum of a school-room—and, occasionally too, one of the more daring of the urchins would, to the terror of the more timid, act a pantomime with the water-gourd, making, like Mr. Swiveller, imaginary eights in the air, and then acting as though he intended to discharge its contents on the head of this worthy man. For some years this house was occupied by William Thurmon, a son of the venerable patriarch of our town, and the place takes its name from that circumstance.

Many of the present inhabitants of Lynchburg recollect the violent hail-storm occurring in the month of July, 1835. The storm came on so suddenly that there was no time to shut open windows or to close blinds, in consequence of which nearly all the window-glass in town was broken. The shrubs and trees were much injured, the corn and vegetables destroyed; and, after the storm, enough hail was collected to last several days for ice. A tragico-comico, or serio-comic occurrence* happened at this place then. A young lady residing there was to be married in a few days;—the wedding cake being iced, was placed to dry on a table, near the open window, and the bridal attire,

---

* This is not mentioned on our own authority: it was related by Miss ———, afterwards Mrs. ———, of ———, now deceased.

just brought home, was spread out on a couch, not far distant. The storm coming very unexpectedly, the panic and agitation produced by the noise of the hail was such, that the cake and wedding dress were forgotten; and, after it was over, on going into the room, there was found a complete mass of muslin, lace and hail-stones—and, to use the expression of old Dr. Humphreys, the cake was found "reduced to an impalpable powder."

The inhabitants now moved to the west end of the town in search of health and pleasure, and Tate's Spring became renowned, as, in addition to the chalybeate, this spring contained a solution of sulphur. The place was owned by a fine, old Virginia gentleman, Colonel Tate, who was a great enthusiast on the subject of machinery; and, even at that early date, he clearly prophesied railroads and telegraphs, and those steps proposed by him to advance the cause, though to all others they only seemed vague and imaginary, were clearly to his mental vision a glorious ascent to the very summit of the hill of Science; and it is to be much regretted, that this good man did not live to witness the vast improvements effected in his favorite branch— that of machinery.* During his life, he was en-

---

* Colonel Tate died at least thirty-five years since, and at that time there was probably not a railroad in America. In the Autumn of 1830, a miniature model of a railroad was ex-

gaged in planning splendid improvements at the spring: a ball-room, extending from one hill to another, across a ravine; an elegant dining-hall; and a company of musicians, who were to play as near as possible to perpetual motion; but, before any of his schemes could be accomplished, the solemn messenger called him hence. His venerable widow survived him many years, dying at a great age, during the summer of 1857.

After the death of Col. Tate, a ball-room and a few cottages were erected at the spring, and, during the summer of 1828, balls and cotillion parties were held there occasionally; but the last soiree that took place there was attended with so awful a thunder storm, and the beauties in ball costume looked so panic-stricken, besides being deluged with water from the roof, the elderly ladies, who went as chaperones, concluded that the storm was somewhat a judgment on them for seeking pleasure out of town, especially as there was a great revival of religion at that time going on in all the churches of Lynchburg; so that the sound of music and dancing has never since that time awoke the echoes of the glens and valleys of Tate's Spring.

---

hibited at the Franklin Hotel of Lynchburg, and with its perfect, little cars, it was, of course, viewed with great interest and curiosity.

BAPTIST CHURCH IN LYNCHBURG.

"Our venerable brother professed religion in the twenty ninth year of his age. 'Without conferring with flesh and blood,' he commenced preaching, immediately after his conversion, in the county of Goochland, where he spent the first few years of his ministry. He then removed to Lynchburg, and was instrumental in gathering and organizing the Church of that place. His first sermon was preached in the Courthouse."

Religious Herald—Memoir of Elder J. S. Lee.

The Rev. JOHN LEE was, for a long time, the faithful pastor of the Baptist Church in Lynchburg. The members of that denomination being few and his salary small, it was rendered necessary for him to occupy himself during the week as a carpenter, an employment rendered more sacred and honorable from the circumstance of our Saviour, when on earth, laboring with his reputed father and brethren at that occupation. Mr. Lee did much good by his preaching, but his influence is in a great measure to be traced to his mild, peaceable demeanor, and to the happy, cheerful disposition of his good wife, who was a native of Goochland county and a member of one of the best families in that section of country.

That plain old structure, the Baptist meeting-house, attracted very few worldly or fashionable persons; yet some who worshiped within its walls, were more pure, holy and lovely than could elsewhere be found. Amongst that number was Mrs. SUSAN MASSIE, a native of Goochland county, and a sister of Mrs. John Lee.

Mrs. Massie had been reared by a devoted aunt, and, in her youth, she had enjoyed all the blessings and advantages of an unclouded prosperity. Very lovely in appearance, courteous and refined in manners, it is not strange that she should have been admired, and her hand sought in marriage by many. She became the wife of Gideon Massie, Esq., a member of that family, of whom was General Nathaniel Massie, one of the early pioneers of Kentucky. Some years after their marriage, Mr. and Mrs. Massie settled in Lynchburg, where Mr. Massie employed himself in school-teaching; and, though he exerted himself in that occupation, his health became bad, so that but for the zeal and energy of his wife, his efforts would have been insufficient for the maintenance of his family. It was in this hour of adversity that Mrs. Massie, by her patient, cheerful industry placed her family on a footing with that of the best and highest in

Lynchburg. A few tried friends of her youth, and the counsel of her pious minister were all she had on which to depend; but calmly trusting in God, and cheerfully performing her duties, Mrs. Massie's Christian character was doubtless strengthened by the trials so patiently borne; and, in after years, she blessed God for the sweet uses of adversity, which had been the means of developing in her children such shining qualities. She showed them the love of God; she taught them, next to a holy trust in Him, nothing could so confer happiness here, as a diligent pursuit of their calling, a wholesome relish and love for their employments. Her precepts were blessed, and she lived to see her daughters settled in life, and her sons prosperously succeeding in business. During a visit to her son Richard Massie, Esq., in the summer of 1837, Mrs. Massie died in the city of Richmond, calmly resigning her spirit to God, and giving evidence of the strength afforded to the believer in the solemn hour of death. The sons of Mrs. Massie* survive her, and her youngest daughter is a resident of Clarkesville, North Carolina. Mrs. Samuel Burch, of Lynchburg, well known and beloved there, is a younger sister of Mrs. Massie.

Judging from the intense curiosity and excitement produced whenever the ordinance of Baptism

---

* William O. Massie, Esq., is a merchant of New York.

was administered, we may infer that the Baptist Church at this period made few accessions to their numbers. About the year 1819, the whole town was thrown into a state of enthusiasm and excitement by the intelligence that Miss Maria Gray was to be baptized, at what was called the Little River, and crowds repaired to the spot to witness the ceremony.

On a bright, lovely Sabbath morning, previous to the hour of worship, the solemn ordinance took place, and the sweet rural scenes on the banks of the river, and the rare enjoyment of gathering blue bottles and other wild flowers, is still remembered with pleasure. Though we had been accustomed to seeing this venerable lady almost every week of our then brief lives, at that period, yet, when the carriage was seen in the distance bringing her to the place of baptism, such was the excitement, that a general rush took place to the water side, in unavailing efforts to get the first glimpse of her, as she descended from the conveyance; and those who could not get near, consoled themselves by a minute examination of the hack and driver, which they only saw every day, as it was one of the two best hacks of which Lynchburg boasted, and which were driven by Tom Dyson and Archer Higginbotham.

Fortunately, the crowd was on land; for had they been standing on boats, many persons must necessarily have been precipitated in the water, and possibly drowned. Some years later, during the ministry of the Rev. Robert Ryland, three beautiful young girls* were baptized in the month of November, 1829. The interesting ceremony took place in the evening, and as they stood in the water, their countenances, radiant with holy joy, were farther illuminated by the departing rays of the sun, and so tenderly impressive was the scene, that a bird hovering over them, at this moment, was pronounced a *dove* by one of that excited throng.

Rev. Dr. ROBERT RYLAND commenced his ministry in Lynchburg about the year 1826; and, for a brief period, the old Masonic Hall was occupied by his society as a place of worship. Dr. Ryland was peculiarly adapted to his calling; his gentlemanly, winning ways giving him easy access to the hearts of those he wished to impress: and, during his residence in Lynchburg, numbers were enrolled as members of the Baptist Church, and a bright example was afforded by him of all that constitutes the Christian minister. During the summer of 1828, a great work of God was going on in Lynchburg, in all the churches†—the happiest state of

---

* Maria Richardson, (afterwards Mrs. Ryan, of Baltimore,) Miss Fair and Miss Rhoda Halsey.

† There were three young ministers in Lynchburg, at that time, Rev. Dr. Ryland, Rev. W. A. Smith, of the Methodist Church, and Rev. F. G. Smith, of the Episcopal Church.

feeling existed amongst the ministers of the several denominations; and for a time they all felt no rivalry, each being only anxious to advance the kingdom of the Redeemer. Many young persons were awakened at the Methodist Church by the powerful preaching of the Rev. W. A. Smith; they were gently led on and encouraged by the Rev. Robert Ryland, who, without any feeling other than that of Christian love, witnessed the going over of many of their members to the Episcopal Church; and the sunrise prayer-meetings held by him in that old Hall were the resort of all, and of many who previously had wasted their precious hours in sleep. We cannot but believe that those seasons were blessed, and that the good seed, then sown, fell into many hearts, which, though late in bringing forth fruit, still they now look back to that time, and believe that the Spirit of God was then striving in their hearts.

A new Church was erected a few doors above the Hall, and a singular arrangement was made in the interior. The pulpit stood between the two front doors, which opened upon the street, and the congregation sat facing them; and it was said that the Church was so constructed, to prevent the congregation turning their heads around on the arrival of new comers. So discouraging to the pastor is this want of attention, that it would be well if this plan were more generally adopted.

In the year 1830, Dr. Ryland was united in marriage to Josephine, eldest daughter of the late Thomas Norvelle, Esq., of Richmond, and niece of the late Captain William Norvelle, of Lynchburg. Mrs. Josephine Ryland was a lady of great worth and excellence, admirably calculated to adorn the Christian life, and by her lovely demeanor to aid her husband in winning souls to God. Dr. Ryland was appointed President of the Baptist College of Richmond, and Pastor of the African Church of that city. His able course in this literary institution, and his devoted piety shown in his preaching to the colored population, all these bind him as closely to our warm regard as did his conscientious life in Lynchburg. His excellent wife survived her removal to Richmond only a brief period. The following tribute to her memory appeared at the time of her death in 1846, and we feel thankful for the privilege of inserting it in this place:

"Died, on Wednesday evening, the 28th instant, at the Richmond College, Mrs JOSEPHINE RYLAND, the wife of Elder Robert Ryland, aged thirty-nine years. Mrs. Ryland made a profession of religion about sixteen years since in Lynchburg, where her husband was then pastor. She had, however, from her childhood been the subject of gracious affections, but was constrained from confessing them, by a naturally timid disposition. From the time of her baptism, she was a consistent, devoted and useful Christian. The most prominent trait of her religious character was her love of the Bible—she read it habitually, methodically, reverently. It sustained her midst her trials, and imparted a sweet tranquility to her temper, gave her a strong but noiseless trust in the faithfulness of God. As a daughter, she was devoted; as a sister, affectionate; as a mother judicious; as a friend, unwavering; as a wife, the heart of her husband could safely trust in her. She loved to frequent the courts of the Lord's house, and hear the plainest and most heart-searching exhibitions of truth. From the funds appropriated to her wardrobe, she uniformly reserved a tenth for benevolent objects; but her contributions far exceeded the proportion. When she drew near to her end, she said she preferred living for the sake of her family, but was resigned to the Divine disposal. In her last moments she seemed much engaged in prayer, and she was free from fear, trusted in the Saviour, but experienced no transports. Her death was like her life, calm, thoughtful, submissive. She has left four children on earth, and gone to be united with four who have preceded her. May her meek and quiet spirit, and her self-denying life, be imitated by all her surviving friends."

[Since the above was written, the mournful intelligence of the death of Elder J. S. Lee has been received. The memory of this beloved and excellent man is blended with the days of infancy and childhood. Would that our limits permitted the insertion of the beautiul tribute to him in the *Religious Herald*. His excellent wife survives him, residing in Charlotte county.]

SUPERNATURAL VISITORS.

HAUNTED HOUSE.

We may ridicule the idea of ghosts or of supernatural appearances, but there is in mankind a tendency to listen with interest to these recitals, and even to take pleasure in them, when they make a cold shudder pass over us. It is described as the peculiar delight of Ichabod Crane, on long winter nights, to sit by the fireside, listening to the awful narratives of the old Dutch wives; whilst a row of apples sputtered and roasted at the fire, till his teeth chattered and his hairs stood on end, so that, with fear and trembling, he would again encounter the deep, gloomy valleys of Sleepy Hollow. This fondness for the marvellous and supernatural has, at different times, descended on the good folks of Lynchburg, as will be perceived by the following incidents here recorded:

Many years since, the late Mr. ****, a professional gentleman, was sitting alone in his parlor on Sunday night; his family having retired to rest;

he was so deeply engaged in reading as to heed nought save the volume in his hand. The front door opened noiselessly, and, ere he was aware, a tall, pale stranger stood before him, bareheaded and clothed in white garments. Great as was his surprise, Mr. **** forgot not his usual courtesy, but requested the stranger to be seated. "What is your name, sir?" said Mr. ****; "and may I beg to know if you have business with me?" "Sir," said the apparition, "my name is known only to the Almighty, who has it written in the book of life." "Where are you from, and in what direction are you traveling?" "I have no abiding city," said the spirit. I came from the uttermost part of the earth to-day, and the chariot waits, which will to-night convey me I know not whither. I have heard of your worth and virtues, and, in passing over this place, I determined to tarry with you for a brief period." After a little more conversation, the strange being arose, and saying, "peace be to this house and all within it," he vanished as noiselessly as he had entered. Mr. **** was convinced that his guest was insane, and, on the following morning, the incident was mentioned at the breakfast-table to the family, in the presence of the servants; and going down to Main street, his suspicions were confirmed—learning there that the man was on his way to the Lunatic Hospital at Williamsburg; but, eluding the vigilance of his keepers, he had for a short time escaped, making the visit aforesaid to Mr. ****.

In a few days, the most thrilling story was told all over Lynchburg, and not a doubt was thrown on its authenticity; for it was said and confidently believed, that Mr. **** had seen and conversed with a ghost. Several came in person to this gentleman, hoping to have the truth of this wonderful narrative confirmed, and amongst the number was the late Thomas Wiatt, Sr., who confessed himself much disappointed, when Mr. **** explained away the supernatural, by informing him that his ghostly visitor was no other than an escaped maniac.

This incident was quite forgotten, till about twenty-six years since,* when one night, during a protracted meeting held in Lynchburg, a preacher appeared in the pulpit of ——— church. He bore the name of ———, and as soon as he began to speak, he arrested the attention of the congregation by his striking address, which, as he proceeded, warmed into eloquence, till seeming to lose himself completely, he adored his Maker for his mercy, in thus permitting a sane man to address in *that* place a congregation; for, that many years previous, he had wandered through those streets a fugitive and a lunatic; and it was supposed by many, that even at that time, Mr. ****'s supernatural visitor was

---

* It is, in fact, twenty-seven years.

somewhat deranged, for his language even then was at times wild and incoherent.

In a lone situation, on the left of the old Methodist graveyard, is a large white house.* It may be seen from almost every point of Lynchburg, and when viewed from Courthouse Hill, it seems to stand on the horizon. The location of this dwelling was melancholy, and, consequently, it was hard to get it tenanted; and, in fact, it was somewhat like "Lant street," in the Pickwick: "the rents were seldom collected, and the taxes were dubious."
At this time it was inhabited by several poor families, and the number two, up stairs, was heard to declare that strange and awful noises proceeded from a small, adjoining room. Their respected parent, too, was one day sunning himself in the yard, by way of killing time, when a strange man, in a voluminous, old-fashioned, white great coat, appearing, offered to him the usual salutations with great solemnity; at the same time informing the lodger, that he had been murdered and thrown into

---

* At the time of its erection, this house laid some claim to architectural proportions. It was built at the same time with the house purchased and improved by Mr. William Bailey, but now owned and occupied by Mr. Christian.

the well, which stood in the yard; and that if he would go into the small room adjoining his own, that he would find blood, not upon "a dinted sword," but on the floor of that small room, which had been the scene of his murder. The ghost also assured the number two that he should continue to walk the earth, like the wandering Jew, until he was buried in a Christian manner, and he urged the lodger, for the sake of his own soul, to have his remains removed from the watery grave in which they lay. The story gained ground; crowds going to the house to see the blood-stained floor, and to listen to the horrid recital. Some actually paid to see the room; whilst many, at parting, would offer a gratuity to the worthy lodger for his work of imagination; and, of course, when thus encouraged, the narrative improved, fresh horrors being constantly superadded. But, unhappily for the conclusion of this wonderful romance, the mystery of the bloody chamber was unravelled, by its being proved to have been the packing-room of a large pork dealer; and it was found out, too, that the occupant of number two had, on former occasions, not been at all scrupulous about telling the truth, particularly when any thing could be made by the contrary.

The incident of the self-rocking cradle is of too recent date, and the facts too well known in Lynchburg, to need here any comment. Perhaps, the cradle was slightly in advance of the tables of the spiritual rappers; but the science of steam was not so perfect, and the mysteries of the telegraph undiscovered; therefore, the march of intellect had not then arrived at that point that would permit us to understand the numerous signs given by this most intelligent cradle; in consequence of which, spiritual rapping had there to lay quietly in this, its resting place, till brought out, about twelve years since, by the Fish family.

DANIEL SHEFFEY.

"When we admit the omnipotence, we are bound likewise to admit the omniscience of the Deity; and presumptuous, indeed, must that man be who overlooks the contractedness of his own intellectual vision, or asserts that, because he cannot see a reason for a supernatural interference, none therefore can exist in the eye of the Supreme."

BARRINGTON.

DANIEL SHEFFEY was a native of Frederick, Maryland; but, at an early age, emigrating to Virginia, he settled in the town of Staunton, where entirely by his own exertions, he so arose in his profession as to become one of the most distinguished lawyers in the State of his adoption, and the memory of his active, brilliant, useful career continues to throw a lustre not only on his surviving family, but yet illumines scenes far in the past of long ago, in which he was a participator.

For some years Mr. Sheffey was a visitor of Lynchburg in the months of May and October, at which time Judge Creed Tylor there held his Chancery courts; and it is regarded as one of the privileges of childhood to have seen frequently this remarkable man in social converse with those revered ones who too have since passed away, and who at that time so adorned the bar of upper Virginia.

During the last sitting of the old Chancery Court in Lynchburg, Mr. Sheffey was, as usual, in attendance; his health appeared perfect, and his brother lawyers had never before known his mind more active and discriminating; and knowing that the same band would probably never all again assemble in the good old town, there was amongst them a pecutiarly kind feeling, amounting, in some instances, to a touching, manly demonstration of regret, as the hour approached when they must forever leave a scene endeared by past recollections. Mr. Sheffey had dined at the house of Mr. ———, and towards sunset the party adjourned to the Franklin Hotel to spend the evening; and when the fraternity parted, after

"A heart-warm fond adieu,"

Mr. Sheffey with several other gentlemen retired to his apartment. In the night he awakened the late Peachy Gilmer,* telling him that he had had a most distressing dream. Mr. Gilmer told him that there was no reliance to be placed in dreams, and per-

---

* The impression at the time was, that it was Mr. Gilmer, though it might have been another member of the bar.

suaded him to endeavor to compose himself again to sleep. In less than an hour, Mr. Sheffey again awakened his friend, saying that the same distressing dream had returned to him, and he would now recount it to him. He said: "I dreamed that I was on my way to Staunton, and that I stopped for a time at my farm in Augusta, some miles from my home. I was sitting by the door of the farmhouse, when I saw a very singular appearance in the clouds, which floated on the air, till the apparition was so near as for me distinctly to see and recognize the features of my beloved wife, who, with a mournful countenance and deep, solemn voice, waved to me her hand, saying 'Farewell, we have parted never again to meet on earth.'"

The morning light dissipated the sombre feeling produced by this vision, and it was on the following day spoken of by the friends of Mr. Sheffey, who had taken leave of him on his return to Staunton. In less than three days from this time, the intelligence was received in Lynchburg, that Mr. Sheffey had died very suddenly at his farm near Staunton, never again beholding his happy home and devoted family.

PHILIP DODDRIDGE.

"Philip Doddridge, who died at Washington, in 1832, while a member of Congress, was from Wellsburg. He was scarcely less celebrated in Western Virginia for his eloquence and splendid talents, than was Patrick Henry, in his day, in the oldest portions of the State."

Howe's *History of Virginia.*

This eminent man occasionally visited the city of Lynchburg. He was a member of the Convention, held in Richmond, in the winter of 1830, for the purpose of revising our Constitution; and, on his way to that city, he for a short time remained in Lynchburg, and visited a gentleman there, to whom he related the following incident:*

Governor Poindexter lived to read and reply to

---

* The incident is recorded precisely in the words of the gentleman to whom it was related by Mr. Doddridge, and no doubt has ever been thrown on the story. For a detailed account of Mr. Doddridge's talents and wonderful literary attainments, see *Howe's History of Virginia,* page 197.

his own obituaries, some of them not very complimentary; and the noble Athelstone, in Scott's Ivanhoe, attended his own funeral, and, to use the expression of Cedric, was no doubt highly gratified at the manner in which it was conducted; whilst Mr. Doddridge did not exactly arrive at either of these points; but, after a spell of illness, he was supposed by his friends to be dead, and was put in all the dread array of the grave for more than twelve hours, expecting every moment the arrival of his own coffin; and, whilst listening to the agonized moans of his wife, he was unable to give the slightest intimation that he was still alive. He had, when in health, exacted from her a promise that she would not, for thirty-six hours, permit his body to be interred, and that, during that time, she would use every means for his restoration to life. His only hope was in her, and he could distinctly hear her entreat the persons sitting around to try to revive him; and how he inwardly shuddered to hear them say to her, that efforts would be unavailing, for that the vital spark had certainly fled; but how his heart gave a feeble throb, when she, with the firm resolve of a faithful, loving wife, persisted in using means until he gave signs of life; and when, in the course of an hour or two, he folded her in a rapturous embrace, can our imagination picture any thing more thrilling than this joyful re-union of a wife with one whom all had imagined as having passed through the dark Valley of the Shadow of Death!

Several who had, at times, kept watch by the body of Mr. Doddridge, were quite curious to know if he had heard every thing that had occurred during his trance; and, on his affirming that he had, one of the watchers expressing his disbelief, Mr. Doddridge replied: "Sir, I will convince *you* that I did hear; for whilst you were watching by me with your son, you made him repeat the Fourth of July oration he is soon to deliver." The confusion evinced by the gentleman, satisfied all that Mr. Doddridge was correct.

This incident exhibits the impropriety of secular conversation being carried on whilst keeping vigil over the dead. We know not but that there may still be a mysterious sympathy between the immortal soul and its frail tenement of clay; we are too apt to think that life ceases with the rising and falling of the lungs; but this is not always the case; and even should the spirit have departed, and no longer manifest itself outwardly, we are prone to think that a great immensity of space is between us; whereas, we are told that Heaven is very near us, though the veil of flesh prevents our being sensible of it; and who can say but that "our lost friend is still here mysteriously, even as we are here mysteriously with God?"

BURIAL PLACES OF LYNCHBURG.

PRESBYTERIAN GRAVEYARD—OLD METHODIST BURYING GROUND.

> " The breezy call of incense-breathing morn,
>   The swallows twittering from their straw-built shed;
> The cock's shrill clarion, or the echoing horn,
>   No more shall rouse them from their lowly bed."
>
> For them no more the blazing hearth shall burn,
>   Or busy housewife ply her evening care ;
> Nor children run to lisp their sire's return,
>   Or climb his knees the envied kiss to share."
>   GRAY's *Elegy in a Country Churchyard.*

The most ancient burying ground of Lynchburg, was the lot on which now stands the residence of Henry Dunnington, Esq. Many of the first inhabitants still lie there, though some were removed to the Methodist graveyard, which, for a length of time, was then the only place of sepulture in Lynchburg. A tablet sacred to the memory of John Brown, of Scotland, was removed from the former place, and now stands in the Methodist burying ground.

With the exception of the new Cemetery, recently organized, the Presbyterian graveyard is the most modern place of the sort in Lynchburg. It was first established in 1823 or '24, and it was then a dreary spot, without shade or verdure, but by tender, diligent culture of surviving friends, trees have sprung up, waving their leafy branches over the resting places of the departed; the grass has overspread those sacred enclosures, whilst roses have blossomed, resembling, in their beauty, the sweet, early day-spring of life, and, in their decaying fragrance, meet emblem of those grateful memories of the past, connected with the holy and reverenced dead who there repose.

In this place are many fine monuments, some of a gorgeous and costly style; but there is not one which so impresses the passers-by as that of the late Mrs. Murrel, of Mount Holly, bearing this simple inscription, "To our Mother;" and more touching is this simple record of the devoted affection of her children, than even that most celebrated work of art, the tomb of Madame Langhans.*

---

* The tomb of Madame Langhans, near Berne, in Switzerland, mentioned by Madame de Genlis, and also a subject of one of Mrs. Hemans's small poems. (For description, see Mrs. Hemans's poems; and second volume of "Tales of the Castle," by Madame de Genlis.) At the sound of the trumpet of the angel Gabriel, the figure of Madame Langhans is represented bursting the tomb, her infant children in her arms, and supposed to be saying "Behold me Lord, with the children thou hast given me!"

There is much in this sacred spot that stirs too painfully the past to allow us to linger there, and we will leave its hallowed enclosure, to wander amongst the graves of those loved ones, over whose mournful loss time has gently laid its healing hand.

The place most consecrated to the memories of departed friendship is the old Methodist graveyard of Lynchburg. The lonely seclusion of the spot, the Sabbath-silence of the surrounding hills, unbroken save by the drowsy tinkling wagon-bells, the slow, measured chant of the drivers, and the dirge sung amid the grove by wandering winds—the towering Peaks of Otter, seeming, like the mount of God, to overhang the cemetery, whilst the bright clouds encircling the summit, vividly suggest the gates of Heaven, whose golden portals are ever opened wide to admit the glorified spirits of the departed. All these surround this burial place with holy, cheerful associations, which have served to divest sepulchral rites of the gloomy ideas with which they are connected.

The earliest remembrance of death and burial is linked with this cemetery. ANN ELIZA, the young and blooming bride of John Hampden Pleasants, was thirty-eight years since here interred; and, whilst yet incapable of understanding that one so fair and lovely could die, this solemn scene was witnessed. The tones of the venerable pastor were heard in touching accents, and his voice trembled, as he told that he had educated her, performed for her the marriage ceremony, preached her funeral sermon, and now he stood in silent grief, as the earth was heaped over the pride of her family as well as of her native place; and schoolmates stood around, many giving way to audible grief; and when the hillock was raised over Ann Eliza, they turned away awe-stricken and bewildered that so short a pathway intervened betwixt Time and Eternity.

Not far off may be seen the graves of Mrs. Tucker and Rosalie, Mrs. Daniel and Eliza; and, at a short distance removed, lies the good and beloved Mrs. Elizabeth Morgan, and, by her side, her eldest son Gavin Morgan; and near at hand is the grave of the unfortunate young man, Parham Adams, who was killed by the explosion of his soda fountain; whilst, under the shade of spreading oaks, is to be seen the stranger's grave.* She was a lovely young wife, only resting in Lynchburg to recover strength for a journey to the mountains; but the invalid never reached our healing waters. Sinking rapidly under her disease, she died in our town, whilst ever and anon her fevered lips murmured fond words of home and children, whom she was destined never more to behold. No stone or

---

* Her name was never told, but her grave is not far from that of Mrs. Ann Hancock.

sculptured marble marks the spot, but her agonized husband had her grave enclosed, and, with touching affection, he planted around it the fairest and sweetest flowers, frail monuments! which have continued to blossom and shed around their fragrance, when he that planted and they who nurtured and tended, have long since alike reposed beneath the clods of the valley.

About the centre of the graveyard is a tombstone sacred to the memory of twin-brothers, born in Cork, Ireland. Emigrating to America in all the buoyancy of hope and youth, they trod together the pathway of life, in love and unity, and God in tender mercy permitted them in death to be undivided.

On the outside of this burial ground, in a small enclosure, lie the remains of Marian Fontaine, wife of Dr. Landon Cabell. She died early in the winter of 1834, and it was one of her last requests that she might here be buried, in sight of the beautiful mountains surrounding her native place. Cultivated, accomplished and beloved, Mrs. Marian Cabell passed away just as she had reached the age of twenty-five; and sweet, though mournful, is the recollection of this gifted woman, whose calm death-bed was, doubtless, a precursor of that heavenly rest into which she has long since entered, and where she now delights in joining the angelic choir in ascribing praises to the Most High.

Our meditations, at this sacred spot, must now come to a close, yet we would fain linger awhile, feeling that "it is good to be here," that we may draw more instruction from the graves of the just and good, long since passed away. Let us for a moment, more fully realize that we too shall, ere long, lie in the silent grave, and let us examine ourselves whether our walk and example are such, that, after the lapse of thirty-eight years, they shall be worthy of being brought forward as examples worthy of imitation. Would that the words here written might stimulate all "to press onwards" to the mark of their high calling, making them sensible that no one, ever so obscure, can live in the world, without possessing some influence for good or ill.

May the daughters of Lynchburg endeavor to imitate the diligence, industry and simplicity of those gone before, so that in future years, eighteen hundred and fifty-eight may be remembered as the time when a strong will was put forth to resist the allurements of luxury and fashion, and when the cultivation of mind and heart was considered paramount; and when, mingled with countless blessings, trials and adversities, incident to mortal existence, were patiently and cheerfully borne, and with the eye of faith even welcomed by believers as so many phases of human life, designed by an all-wise, Heavenly Father for the promotion of our spiritual progress; and should the preceding chapters have made the smallest impression, they will not have been written in vain.

"Lo! what a cloud of witnesses
Encompass us around!
Those once like us by suffering tried,
But now by virtue crowned.

Let us, with zeal like theirs inspired,
Strive in the Christian race;
And, freed from every weight of sin,
Their holy footsteps trace.

FINIS.

A, Mr 44
ADAMS, 117 Parham 360
ALFORD, 232
ALLEN, Elizabeth 165 Miss 263 264 Mrs 262-264 Susan 262 263
ALLIBONE, Susan 53
ALLISON, Dr 171
ANDERSON, Mrs 161
ANDREWS, 278 Mrs 278
ANNIS, Mary 31 32
ANTHONY, Anna 49 Anna W 48 Anna Woolston 48 C 117 Christoper 34 Christopher 94 260 302 Christopher 13 34 38 40 46 49 52 58 Christopher Sr 198 Joseph 40 Mary 85-87 Mr 38 39 41-47 51 52 54 199 260 Mrs 50-54 87 Samuel 85
ANTOINETTE, Marie 223
ARMISTEAD, A 210 Anderson 166 Elizabeth 166
ATKINSON, Rev 182
BALDWIN, 201 Dr 73 Margaret 73 74
BARBAULD, Mrs 112
BARCLAY, 30
BARNES, 258-263 265 Mr 258 Mrs 258-260
BARRINGTON, 58 330 351
BARTON, Bernard 48
BATES, 43
BELL, Lieutenant 110 Margaret Cabell 110
BIGGERS, Mildred 162 Mr 161
BILL, 203 Blind 205
BILLY, Blind 204
BIRDSALL, Master 115
BLACKSTONE, William 56
BLAENNERHASSET, 43
BLAMIRE, 189
BOB, 300

BOGGS, Ann Eliza 89 F J 89
BOGUS, Tandy 200
BOHANNAN, Dr Mrs 219
BORUMBORAD, Dr 331
BOTETOURT, 207
BOUDAR, Constance 273 Madame 273 Mercie Hyacinth 273
BRADFUTE, 291 Davidson 291 Evelyn Carter 292 Mary 292 Mr 291 292 Mrs 291 292
BRANSFORD, Alfred 68 John William 68 Mr 66-68 Mrs 68 Samuel 66 68 298 Samuel Jr 69
BRECKENRIDGE, General 217 John C 217 Mrs 217
BRENT, 303 Mary 303 Mrs 303
BRIDGES, David 294 M Miss 295 Martha 294 Mrs 294 Roy Mrs 295 William 295
BROWN, 119 Edwin 171 Eveline 171 Henry 158 Howell 171 James 196 John 196 357 Mary 19 134 135 228 297 Matthew 171 228 Miss 171 Mrs 196 197 Polly 158 S 228 Thomas 196
BRYANT, W P 158 W P Mrs 158
BUCKETT, Inspector 70
BULLOCK, Isabella 299 James 265 299 James Mrs 265 John 265 Martha 265
BUMBLE, Mr 260
BURCH, Samuel Mrs 339
BURD, Amanda 288 Evelina 287 Mr 286 William 286
BURNEY, Miss 148
BURNS, 31 Robert 40
BURNS', Highland Mary 300
BURR, 42
BURTON, 118 Sarah 95
BUTLER, Fanny Kemble 314

BUXTON, Thomas Fowell 96
BYRD, 172 291 Ann Ursula 107
   291 Colonel 291 Mary 292 Mr
   291 Mrs 107 William 291
   William Otway 107
CABANISS, Mr 161
CABELL, 216 220 Alice 220 Dr
   116 208-210 214 215 Eliza 79
   288 Eliza B 81 Emeline
   219 Frederick Sr 220 221
   George 174 207 210 211 218
   220 221 George Kuhn 210
   Harrianne 214 J 214 215 J
   Breckenridge 210 John 115 207
   212 213 220 John J 212 John
   Jordan 212 John Mrs 226
   Joseph 206 216 217 Joseph C
   221 Landon 211 217 361
   Landon Mrs Sr 163 Marian 361
   Marian Fontaine 211 Mayo 81
   Miss 316 Mr 218 Mrs 210
   Nicholas 207 P H 218 R H 218
   Samuel 218 Samuel J 219
   Sarah 174 175 210 220 221
   William 206 217 William H
   18 William Lewis 79-81 165
   211 288 William Mrs 226
CADWALLANDERS, 26
CALHOUN, Martha 328
CALLAWAY, 156 157
CAMM, Elizabeth 161 Mr 161
   Mrs 161 Robert 161
CAMPBELL, 28 Elizabeth 317
   Mr 225 Mrs 224 Victoire 224
CAPERTON, Allen T Mrs 159
CARGILL, 120 Mary 121 Mr 121
   Mrs 121
CARLYLE, Mr 69 Thomas 69 70
   99
CARRINGTON, Alice 211 Walter
   211
CARTER, 172 Charles 305 Maria
   305
CARY, John 152 154 Mr 154 155
CASKIE, J Kerr 167 Mary 166 167
CATO, 204
CECILIA, Miss 202
CHANCELLOR, 58
CHARLES, Mr 116
CHARLTON, George W 126 Mr
   126

CLARENCE, 332
CLARK, 45 Christopher 44 Miss
   11 Mr 44 45
CLARKE, General Mrs 65
CLAY, Ann 195 196 William 195
   196
CLAYTOR, Mrs 268
CLOPTON, Miss 282 Queen
   Eliza 326
COBBS, Mr 173 Nicholas 173 178
COHEN, Joseph 71
COLE, Margaret 285
COLEMAN, Miss 197
COLLINS, 311
COLMAN, 119
COLQUHOUN, Anne 279 Mr 279
   Thomas 279
COOPER, Archie 70 158 Milly
   158
COPELAND, Mrs 163
COUCH, Anna 42 48 49 Mr 48
   Mrs 49 Samuel 48
CRABBE, G 114
CRALLE, Richard 277 Richard
   Mrs 216
CRAWFORD, 117 Colonel 322
   Marie Antoinette 92 Mr 178
CRUMMELES, Mr 121
CULLENSWORTH, Mr 160
CUMBERLAND, 119
CURRAN, 58
CUVIER, Baron 308 Clementina
   308
D'ORSAY, A 234
DABNEY, C 245 Chiswell 192
   233 245 John Blair 316 John
   Blair Mrs 315 316 Judge 316
   Martha 233 Martha Ann 233
   Mrs 246 N Mrs 245 Nancy 245
DANIEL, Eliza 79 288 327 360
   Judge 75 79 171 218 Margaret
   73 77 Mrs 75-78 87 360 Pauli-
   na 218 William 73 74 William
   Sr 58
DAVIES, Harrianne 214 Howell
   113 204 299
DAVIS, Henry 34 180 273 Henry
   Mrs 34 John 30 Miss 158 273
   Mrs 35-37 Sally 34 Samuel 37
   Sarah 30 180 William 31 273
   Wm Jr 29 30 Wm Sr 26 159

DAVIS (continued)
  Zalinda 30
DAVISES, 26
DEARING, M A 16
DEGENLIS, Madame
DICK, Mr 272 Uncle 276
DICKENS, 228 271 John 139
DIDLAKE, H M 265
DIGGES, William 119
DIGGS, William 175
DIUGUID, Sampson 270 271
DOANLD, Mrs 161
DODDRIDGE, Mr 355 356 Philip 354
DOUGLAS, Miss 27
DOUGLASS, Mr 164 Mrs 164
DOUGLASSES, 26
DUDLEY, Mrs 159 Peter 158 Peter Mrs 273
DUFFEL, 158
DUFFY, Mr 161
DUNNIHEW, Mr 116
DUNNINGTON, H 237 Henry 50 90 233 279 357
DUPUY, Miss 294 Mrs 293
DUVAL, Frances 93 William 93
DWIGHT, Dr 159
DYSON, Tom 154 340
EARLY, Bishop 89 124 Dr 265 Elizabeth 124 Henrianne 215 John 123 Mary 215 216 222 Mrs 125 Paulina 216 Robert 239 242 Samuel Henry 215
ECHOLS, Edward 159 Eliza 159 John 159 Joseph 159 Mrs 159 Robert J 160
EDGEWORTH, Miss 148 326
ELLWOOD, 30
ENFIELD, Dr 298
EPPES, Elizabeth 194 Francis 194 Harriet 194
ESSEX, Eliza 134 Mr 134 Mrs 133
FEAZLE, Mr 171
FISHER, Charles 27 28 Friend 28
FITZHUGH, Miss 303 Nancy 304
FLETCHER, 91 Elijah 91 Grace 91 Marie Antoinette 92 Mr 91 92
FONTAINE, Marian 361
FOOTE, 119

FOSTER, Mr 115
FOWEL, Thomas 31
FOX, 24
FRIEND, Thomas Mrs 216
FRY, Mrs 94
GARLAND, Anna 163 David S 163 Maurice 186 197
GEORGE, 277
GIFFORD, 190
GILDEROY, 71
GILLIAM, James 159
GILMER, Dr 59 158-162 Mary 59 Mr 59-61 352 Peachy 58 59 352
GLADMAN, Claborn 90
GOGGIN, 112
GORDON, Misses 65
GRANDISON, Charles 57
GRATTAN, 58
GRAY, 357 Maria 340
GRETTEL, 263
GRIGSBY, Hugh Blair 207 216
GRILLET, Stephen 29
GURNEY, Priscilla 31
HACKETT, 118
HAMILTON, 71
HANCOCK, Ammon 134 Mary 134
HARDY, Chesley 278
HARE, Jesse 242
HARRISON, Burton J 98 Gessner Mrs 310 Isaac 204 Jesse B 111 Jesse Burton 97 100 Mary 303 Mary E 97 Mr 94 95 99 Mrs 96 310 Samuel 94 97 98 296 Sarah 95 96 Tipton 303
HARTSHORNE, Miss 195
HEMANS, Mrs 130
HENDERSON, Walter Mrs 252
HENRY, Elvira 211 Patrick 222 288 354 Spottswood 211
HERBERT, 120
HERSEY, Father 130
HIGGINBOTHAM, Archer 340
HILTON, Miss 127
HINDERSHOT, Ann 259-264
HOFFMAN, D 243 Martha 243 Mary 243
HOGAN, Enoch 44 45
HOHENLINDEN, 28
HOLCOMBE, Arthur 204 Captain 248-252 Dr 282 283

HOLCOMBE (continued)
James P 100 284 Lucy Anne
253 Mary 248 Mrs 252 283
Philemon 247 282 Royall 252
Thomas 282 Thomas A 247
251 252 Thomas A Mrs 254
Thomas Philemon 253 William 252 William J 282
HOLMES, Colonel 184
HOPKINSON, Judge 41
HOUSE, Mary 59
HOWARD, 76
HOWE, 318 354
HOWITT, William 99
HOYLE, George 297 Mr 296 297 Mrs 296
HUDSON, Charles Mrs 68
HUGHES, Mr 150 Mrs 149-151
HUMPHREYS, Dr 21 298-300 335
Isabella 299 Jane 20 299 Mrs 298 299
HUNT, Mr 115
HUTTER, Mrs 65
INCHBALD, Mrs 119
IRVINE, A Mrs 89 Ann 89 129
Ann Eliza 87 88 Anne 84
Charles 84 Charles Mrs 163
Frances 88 89 General 317
Mary 84 85 Matilda 85 Miss
317 Mrs 87 88 90 Samuel 89
IRVING, Washington 87
ISABEL, 73
ISABELLA, 202
IVANHOE, Scott 355
JARLEY, 277
JARRAT, Rev 178
JEFFERSON, 107 Thomas 98 194
JENNINGS, 201 Brother 210 Dr
209 Rev 281 Samuel K 209 281 283
JOHN, Uncle 331
JOHNS, John 222 Mary 222
JOHNSON, John F 171 Lucy 153
JOHNSONS, 26
JOHNSTON, Mrs 64 Virginia 177
JONES, John M 71 Lucy 302 Mr 261
JORAM, 271
JORDAN, 94 Cornelia M 112 Mrs 112 Wilhelmina 226
JUDGE, Margaret 29

KENNEDY, Miss 65
KIDD, 200 Ballad 200 Mr 200 201
KINCKLE, William 182
KING, Mary 278
LABBY, Captain 260 Mrs 259 260
Pleasants 258
LAFAYETTE, 112 131 207
LAMB, Charles 34 61 72
LAMBETH, Meredith 302
LANDON, Letitia 68
LANGHANS, Madame 269 358
LANGHORNE, 38 Elizabeth 165
166 Frances 168 169 Henry
168 170 John S Mrs 246 M 167
170 Maurice 19 165 168 170
197 Mr 170 Mrs 170 Sally Cary
165
LAPORTE, Madame 223 224
Victoire 224
LATHAM, Henry Mrs 148 Jane 149
LATIMER, Rev 282
LEE, Elder J S 337 John 337
John Mrs 338 Mr 337 Mr Rev 63
LEFTWICH, Thomas Mrs 236
LEGARE, 101
LEIGH, William 58
LEIPER, Mary 317
LEWELLEN, Charles 277 Green B 161 Miss 276
LEWIS, 216 Agatha 314 Andrew
313 318 319 Ann 194 195
Charles 317-319 Clown 115 Dr
317 Elizabeth Montgomery 320
John 206 Margaret Lynn 320
Monk 148 Mrs 195 316 317
Samuel 318 Thomas 318-320
William 216 316-318 320 322
William Mrs 216
LIGGAT, Alexander Mrs 20
LIGGATT, Alexander 13
LIPMAN, Master 115
LOYD, Mrs 152
LYMAN, Eliza 134 M 134
LYNCH, 11 15 22 Anne 265
Anselm 15 20 Capt 17 Charles
9 10 15 Charles Henry 16 Col
10 Edward 18-20 Edward Mrs
27 Hannah 20 Jane 20 21 161
299 John 9 12 13 15-18 20 30

LYNCH (continued)
John Sr 13 Mary 18-20 Micajah 265 Micjah 20 Miss 161 Mr 10-13 Mrs 11 15 16 Staunton John 171 Susan 16 William 20 21 78 161 Wm 299 Zalinda 19 30
LYNCHES, 26
M'CHEYNE, 84
MALLORY, Mr 171
MARTIN, 129 E 144 Elizabeth 129 136 Mr 128 129 Mrs 129 130 160 William 128 129 William P 136
MASON, Mr 70 202
MASONS, 254
MASSIE, Gideon 338 Martha 244 Mr 338 Mrs 338 339 Nathaniel 338 Richard 339 Susan 338 William 244
MATHEWS, Mrs 171
MAVOURNEEN, Kathleen 187
MAY, Sarah 186
MCCORKLE, Samuel 52
MCFARLAND, Margaret Lynn 320 Mr 320-322 Mrs 320-323
MCKANE, Rev 281
MCKINNEY, Martha 294 Martha L 294 Martha Louisa 294 Mr 294 Mrs 293 294 Peter D 294 Thomas 293 William 294
MEEN, John G 271
MEREDY, 50 173 Mrs 50
METCALFE, James 97
MICAWBER, Wilkins 199 204
MILLER, Ellice M 128 Miss 15 127 Mr 242 Sarah 242
MILTON, 168
MINNISS, Callowhill 58
MITCHELL, Harvey 103 104 Harvey Stephen 103 Mr 104 Stephen 104-106
MITFORD, Miss vi
MONTGOMERIE, Anne 279 Hugh 279 Mr 279
MOORMAN, Anne 265
MORGAN, Elizabeth 171 360 Gavin 360 Lady 148 Wm 171
MORRISS, John Mrs 219 Mr 239 240 Mrs 240 Robert 192 196 239 297 Robert Mrs 185

MOSBY, Charles L 254 Charles L Mrs 254
MOSELEY, James 199 Mary 225 Mr 198 199 222
MOSELY, James 198
MUNFORD, Ann Ursula 107 291 William 107
MURREL, 267 Hardin 175 267 270 John 267 268 270 Mr 267 269 Mrs 267-269 358
MURRELL, Hardin 119
NELL, 277
NELSON, George W 61 Mr 61-63 Robert 285
NEWHALL, Antoinette 266 Mortimer 266 Mr 265 266
NORVELL, 230 Emeline 232 Fayette 232 John E 234 Lorenzo 97 Martha 178 Martha Ann 233 Mr 62 Mrs 231 Samuel G 232 William 178 232-234 William Mrs 97 William Sr 230
NORVELLE, Edmund 177 John E 176 Josephine 343 Saluda Mrs 177 Thomas 343 William 343
NOVELL, Anne 230
OGILBIE, 117
ORAM, 271
OTEY, John M 230 John M Mrs 232 Lucy 246
OWENS, 148 Benjamin Franklin 149 Dr 148 Jane 145 149 Mr 146 Mrs 146 147 150 153 Owen 145 147 149 Sarah 149 Septimus D 149 William 146 148 149 152 162
PARDIGGLE, Mrs 200
PARKHILL, Lucy 194
PASTIER, Plesant 164
PATTERSON, Alexander 162 Amanda 288 Ann Eliza 89 David 162 David Mrs 161 Frances 88 John 88 89 160 Mr 288 William M 89
PAYNE, D 165 210
PECKERWOOD, Molly 198
PEGRAM, James 64 James W 63 177 Mrs 63 Virginia 177
PENDLETON, Edmund 313 Eliz 136 John 136 Micajah 249

PENN, 24 Alfred 292 Evelyn
  Carter 292 293 Gabriel 207
PERRY, Jesse 115
PETE, 203
PHILIPS, B A 199 Benjamin A
  199 James 64 65
PHYSICK, Philip Syng 207
PICKWICK, Mr 113 329
PLEASANTS, 43 91 Ann Eliza 88
  359 360 Hampden 88 James
  246 James Mrs 163 John H 89
  John Hampden 13 46 88 89 92
  162 359 Marcella 89
POINDEXER, Governor 354
POLLARD, Margaret Cabell 110
  Richard 110
POPE, Wm 43
POPE'S, Man of Ross 240
PORTER, General Mrs 217
POWELLS, 26
PRESTON, E 218
PRICE, Miss 302
PRIDE, Armistead 204
RADCLIFFE, Mrs 184
RANDOLPH, 195 Arthur 194
  Elizabeth 194 James 194 Jane
  190 191 John 9 Mary Page 194
  Mr 190 192 193 Mrs 193
  Thomas 190 Thomas Eston
  190
RAWSON, Mr 153
REBECCA, the Jewess 278
REID, Clementina 324 325 327
  John 152 Miss 328 Mr 324-328
  S V 328 W S 152 218 William
  S 178 306 309 324 328
RICHARDSON, 300 George P 119
  Mr 255 331 332
RISQUE, Ferdinand 65 James B
  64 261 Major 65 Mrs 65
RIVES, Dr 316 Elizabeth 124 125
  George Mrs 310 Landon 315 P
  Miss 316 Robert 110
ROBBINS, Mary Jane 288 Mrs
  288 Z C 288
ROBERT, Mrs 161
ROBERTS, Mr 161
ROBERTSON, Archer Mrs 196
  John 183 186 271
ROBINSON, Martha Harrison 111
  Robert Mrs 97

ROHR, Charles 28 William 28
ROLAND, Madame 223
ROSE, Anna 163 Anne 84 Dr 163
  Gustavus 163 Hugh 84
ROYALL, Anna Keith 256 John
  255 Judith 254 255 Lizzie 289
  Mary 248 Miss 254 Mr 254 256
  257 Mrs 254 William Jr 254
  William 255 William Sr 254
  255
RUSH, Dr 41
RYLAND, Dr 341 343 Elder
  Robert 343 Josephine 343 Mrs
  343 Robert 341 342
SAM, 203
SAUNDERS, Dr 163 James 77
  Mrs 236 William Mrs 161 Wm
  265
SCHOOLFIELD, Mr 156
SCHOOLFIELDS, 157
SCOTT, Dr 253 Lucy Anne 253
SCRUGG, B E 219
SCRUGGS, Emeline 219
SELKIRK, Alexander 258
SHEFFEY, Daniel 58 351 Mr
  351-353
SHELTON, 288 Ann 288 Mr 288
  Mrs 288
SHERIDAN, 119
SIDDONS, Mrs 314
SIMMS, Caroline 315
SIMPSON, James 133 Jane 133
  Mr 133 134 Mrs 133 134
SMITH, 330 331 Ellice M 128 F
  G 87 154 174 175 179 211
  Franklin Genet 181 Horace 114
  John 265 Judge 181 Louisa 89
  Luther 329-331 Marcella 89
  Marcellus 89 Martha 265 Mr
  89 128 174 176 180-182 Mrs
  180 181 Sarah 180 Sidney 104
  W A 342 William A 127
SOPHY, 204
SOUTHEY, Mrs 77
SPAIN, Captain 202 203 Epps 202
SPENCER, Mrs 328
SPOTTSWOOD, Mrs 163
STABLER, Edward 24 32 Mary 32
  Robinson 32 293
STAEL, Madame De 112
STEPTOE, Frances 168 J 168

STEWART, Dugald 196
STOWE, Beecher 261
STROTHER, 273
STUART, James 160 Mrs 237
SUBLETT, Antoinette 266 Mr 266
SUMPTERS, 157
SWIVELLER, Mr 334
SYDNOR, Fortunatus 289 Lizzie 289 Mr 289 290 Mrs 290 Royal 289
TAIT, Nancy 160
TALIAFERRO, Judge 302 303 Lucy 302 Mrs 302 Norborne 302 Roderick 302
TARDY, Captain 184
TATE, Colonel 335 336
TAYLOR, Anna Keith 256 Chancellor 56 Charcellor 90 Creed 56 George Keith 256
TERREL, Mary 18 Miss 16
THACKERAY, 228
THURMAN, John 265
THURMON, 157 John 126 132 133 John Mrs 133 Mr 131 132 158 Mrs 276 277 Richard 276 Sally 276 Samuel 277 Uncle 131 William 334
TILDEN, Cornelia M 284 Dr 284 285 Evelina 287 Mary 285 Mrs 287 Richard Swift 287
TODD, 272 Mr 272 Mrs 272
TOLER, 91 Frances 93 Mr 93 Richard H 92
TOMPKIN, Mr 333 Samuel 333
TOMPKINS, Alexander 292 Alexander Mrs 291 Rev 158 Susan 158
TOWLES, 311 Agatha 314 316 317 319 320 Alfred 315 Bessie 316 Colonel 311-314 Henry 312 Major 315 320 Maria 315 Mrs 314 320 Oliver 311 314 William 315
TOWNLEY, K B 28 29
TREADWAY, 173 Mr 173
TRENT, Dr 232 Elizabeth Montgomery 320 Emeline 232 Mr 320 Mrs 233
TRIMMER, Mrs 112
TRUSLOWS, 272

TUCKER, 172 305 George 106 158 305 Lelia 310 Maria 305 Mr 106 309 310 Mrs 306 309 360 Rosalie 305-309 360
TURNER, G W Mrs 268 Mrs 269
TYLOR, Creed 351
TYREE, John H Mrs 68 Mildred 158 Richard 27 158 Richard Mr 27
VALENTINE, Dr 113
VALENTINES, 272
VAWTER, Bransford 108-110 Mr 156 171
VAWTER, Silas 156
VENABLE, Clementina 324
VICTOR, 285 Edward William 285 John 285 Margaret 285 286 Maria 153 Mr 285 Mrs 153
WADDELL, Dr 318
WALKER, Mrs 246
WALLACE, 158
WALLER, Maria 232
WALTON, Miss 68
WARD, Giles 175 Henry Mrs 216 Martha 178 Mr 178 Mrs 65 Seth 173 178 Seth Mrs 178 William Norvelle 179
WARWICK, Abram 236 Corbin 236 Daniel 236 Daniel Mrs 232 Ellen 244 James 237 John M 236 John Mrs 232 Major 235-237 Mary 284 William 160 235 236 284
WASHINGTON, 131 General 128 131 217 277 312 313 318 319 Mr 312
WATSON, 155 157 Mr 155
WAYNE, General 313 319
WEBSTER, Daniel 91 Grace 91
WELLS, Mr 164
WESLEY, 122 123 281 Charles 122 John 122 123
WHITE, Bishop 35
WHITEHEAD, 273
WHITELOCKE, George 160 177 306 George Mrs 218 Mr 218
WIATT, Anne 230 Captain 228 Caroline 222 Colonel 226 227 John 222 226 228 230 237 242 Mary 228 243 Mina 226 230 Mr

WIATT (continued)
  242 Mrs 227 228 242 Nancy
  245 S 228 Samuel 228 Samuel
  Mrs 171 Sarah 242 Thomas
  242 245 Thomas Sr 242 347
WICKHAM, Mr 65
WILHELMS, Miss 279
WILLIAM, Edward 286
WILLIAMS, 285 333 Jehu 157 Mr
  333 Susan 158 W P 158
WILLIS, Dr 194 Harriet 194
WILSON, 161 196 Mrs 328
WINFREE, 285 Christopher 279
  284 Cornelia 284 Mary 284 Mr
  284 Mrs 284
WINSTON, 220 225 Alice 220 221
  Caroline 222 228 Edmond 11
  Edmund 169 210 220 222 228
  George 222 Judge 222-225
  Miss 223 Mr 222 Nathaniel 19
  Sarah 210 220 Zalinda 19
WOODROW, Henrietta 303 Mr
  303 Mrs 303 304
WOODSON, Mrs 112
WORD, Giles 119
WORKS, Eagle Marble 278
WRIGHT, Ann O 291
WYATT, Thomas 174

www.ingramcontent.com/pod-product-compliance
Lightning Source LLC
Chambersburg PA
CBHW071951220426
43662CB00009B/1090